Henrietta Antonia Clive, Countess of Powis (1758-1830), was a British mineral collector and botanist. She married Lord Robert Clive's eldest son and heir, Edward Clive, in 1784, who went on to become the Governor of Madras in 1798. Her time in India with her husband forms the basis of *Birds of Passage*. The marriage was beneficial to both families; the bride's family had a prestigious name but considerable debts, while the groom accrued wealth built during Clive's military campaigns in India. The couple finally settled in Walcot Hall, Shropshire.

~

Nancy Shields, a former professor of English specialising in contemporary British and American literature, has done fieldwork in a variety of cultures, including a study of participatory theatre in South Kanara, India, and has published a book on the Japanese novelist and playwright Kobo Abe's years of intense theatrical experimentation. Her other works includes the novel *Looking at Air in Tuluva*, set along the South Indian coast of the Arabian Sea, the narrative of which revolves around fragments of tales told by past and present travellers. She now lives in Texas.

Birds of Passage

TRAVELS IN SOUTH INDIA, 1798-1801

HENRIETTA CLIVE

Edited by Nancy K. Shields

SPEAKING TIGER

SPEAKING TIGER PUBLISHING PVT. LTD
4381/4 Ansari Road, Daryaganj,
New Delhi–110002, India

First published by Eland Publishing Limited 2009
First published in India in paperback by Speaking Tiger 2018

Letters & Journals of Lady Henrietta Clive are
reproduced by kind permission of
the Earl of Powis and the National Library of Wales.
The journal of Charlotte Clive, and the paintings
therein, are reproduced by kind permission
of Peter Rosselli and the British Library

ISBN: 978-93-87164-68-0
eISBN: 978-93-87164-69-7

10 9 8 7 6 5 4 3 2 1

Printed at Thomson Press, Noida

Contents

Acknowledgements 7

Glossary 11

Dramatis Personae 15

Map 20–21

Introduction 23

Prelude: A Bird of Passage 41

1798

Aboard the *Dover Castle* 45

- The Cape of Good Hope, South Africa 52
- Fort St George, Madras, India 57

1799

War with Tipu Sultan, 'Tiger of Mysore' 72

- Miserable in Madras 81

1800

Travelling the Great Horn 100

- Arcot: March 12th–14th 111
- Vellore: March 15th–17th 113
- Crossing the Ghauts: March 17th–30th 119
- Ryacottah: March 31st to May 15th 123
- Bangalore: May 18th to July 13th 138

Seringapatam: August 6th–10th 179

Mysore: August 11th–14th 188

Travelling through the Guzelhutty Pass into Coimbatoor Country: August 14th to September 8th 193

Trichinopoly: September 9th–16th 222

Tanjore: September 20th–22nd 231

Tranquebar: September 29th to October 1st 244

Coromandel Coast to Madras: October 2nd–14th 247

1801

Aboard the *Castle Eden* 260

Vizagapatam, India 265

Simon's Bay: The Cape of Good Hope, South Africa 279

St Helena, British Colony 293

England 298

Coming Home 299

A Brief Bibliography 311

Index 315

Acknowledgements

Birds of Passage is not a long book, but it has been a long time en route. Easily tempted, as I've been wont to be, I've meandered down other roads in other countries (Tibet, the Gobi Desert, Bolivia) pursuing other projects, travelling elsewhere as the opportunity has arisen. Henrietta might well have wished for a speedier resolution to our journey. Be that as it may, we have arrived and here she is. Along our way, I have benefited from the help and advice of many people.

In particular, I am grateful to the Seventh Earl of Powis [George William Herbert, 1925–1993] who gave me access to Henrietta's India papers while they were still at home at Marrington Hall, Chirbury.

My profound thanks go to Pat Kattenhorn, Prints Room Librarian in the old India Office Library, for surprising me with Lady Charlotte Florentia Clive's journal, an extraordinary document with watercolours, presumably copies after those of Anna Tonelli.

I want to acknowledge my gratitude to Mr Peter Rosselli who so generously responded to my request to publish passages, pen and ink sketches and watercolours from Lady Charlotte Florentia Clive's journal.

I am indebted to R. Guy Powell for his gracious help in answering my questions about the descent of Lady Charlotte Florentia Clive's journal as well as providing information about the family background of Signora Anna Tonelli.

To Anne Buddle, Registrar, Victoria & Albert Museum, I offer my grateful thanks for the exhibit *Tigers Round the Throne: the Court of Tipu Sultan (1750–1799)*, Zamana Gallery London, 1990, an experience that enriched my interest in Henrietta while expanding my knowledge about Tipu Sultan's world.

I want to express my appreciation to the British Library whose librarians have assisted me in many ways over the years. In particular, I thank Jean Wooler and Chris Lee.

At the National Library of Wales, where Henrietta's papers now reside, I wish to thank Glyn Parry, Head of Archival Data Section, for his kind help.

Many thanks to the National Trust Powis Castle curators, Emma Marshall and Margaret Gray, who gave me the opportunity to see the original watercolours painted by Signora Anna Tonelli during her 1800 journey in India. And thanks to Rafela Fitzhugh for information concerning the descent of the Tonelli watercolours to her family.

Thanks go as well to Professor Kathy Holcomb, who helped me learn how to decipher Henrietta's sometimes difficult-to-read eighteenth-century handwriting.

I want to thank my brother, John, at whose suggestion I went to Welshpool to see the Clive exhibition at Powis Castle in the first place, and my niece, Nancy, who at age seven, accompanied me to Aberystwyth from West Texas. Deemed too young to sit in the National Library of Wales reading room, she sat and read her books in the hallway while I got on with my endeavours. I am, as well, gratified by my nephew Will Tom's continuous support of whatever I might be involved with.

Special thanks go to Dr Ravi Kapur of the National Institute of Advanced Studies, Bangalore, and Dr Mala Kapur of the National Institute of Mental Health, Bangalore, for their kind hospitality and friendship.

My particular thanks to Doris Lessing, with whom I have shared many conversations on many topics, including Henrietta, and who generously let me use her downstairs flat on numerous occasions over the years.

I am grateful to Jane Slattery, stage designer, who has provided me with a London couch to sleep on as the need arose, and who continually enquired about Henrietta.

Mention must be made of two free spirits who have figured prominently in my life: Richard Cahill (1924–1998), seafaring captain, and Dr Milton Miller (1927–2005). Each truly believed that one day I would publish Henrietta's journey as part of my own travels.

Acknowledgements

I am beholden to Jacqueline Bowker, friend of many years, who urged me on, saying, 'Try Eland for a publisher.'

I am much obliged to Calvin McGowan, rancher, who, concerned at how long Henrietta has been collecting dust, enthusiastically encouraged me to apply a cowboy axiom and, 'Move her out'.

My deepest gratitude goes to another long-time friend, Charles Stewart Robertson, 'gentleman scholar', eighteenth-century specialist and retired Professor of Philosophy at the University of New Brunswick, Saint John, who has affectionately challenged me with his continuing and generous enthusiasm for Henrietta.

And finally, special thanks go to Barnaby Rogerson, whose free spirit was willing to accept this rather curious travel book at Eland, and Rose Baring, whose meticulous concern with the manuscript has polished it.

And now, I give you, Henrietta, alone but strong on her own feet.

NANCY K SHIELDS
2009

Glossary

All the words in the glossary are italicised in the text:

bandy	a small cart
begum	a lady
betel	the leaf of the *piper betel* that is chewed with areca-nut and *chunam* staining the lips and teeth red
Brahmin	a member of the Hindu priestly caste
bubris	stylised tiger stripe pattern that decorated many of Tipu Sultan's possessions
caffers	black tribes of south Africa
chintz	printed, painted and dyed cotton
chita	a cheetah used for hunting
choultry	halls used for public business or by travellers as a resting place
chunam	a polished lime plaster made from seashells
darbish muslin	thin semi-transparent fabric
diwan (*dewan*)	prime minister or the vizier in charge of administrative finances
doolies (*dhoolies*)	covered litter
dragoon	armed cavalryman
droog	fort
dubash (*dobashe*)	interpreter
durbar	audience hall
dussera	a nine-night or ten-day festival in October at the close of the wet season
fakeer (*faker, fakir*)	Muslim ascetic
ghauts	the mountain ranges parallel to the Eastern and Western coasts that lead from the table lands above to the coasts below

havildar	a Sepoy non-commissioned officer, corresponding to a sergeant
howdah	a framed seat usually with no canopy carried by an elephant; sometimes made of silver
'imam (*i'man*)	the prayer leader of a mosque
jamadar	native footman, head of the running footmen
kincob	gold brocade
knaut	an enclosure used by a prince to surround an encampment of wives
lascar	a sailor
looties	plunderers
lunghi	a type of sarong worn by men
Maharajah (*Rajah*)	King
Mahratta	a famous Hindu warrior class
masoollah	the surf boat of capacious size, formed of planks lashed together with coir-twine and used on the Coromandel Coast
munshi	private secretary or language teacher
musnud (*masnad*)	the cushions and bolsters that make up the throne of an Indian ruler
Musulman	Muslim
nabob	English corruption of the Hindustani *nawab*, in England a term of derision
nautch	a traditional Indian dance performed by women
nawab	Muslim title of rank
nayres (*nahir*)	a military caste of the Malabar coast
nullah (*nalla*)	a water-course, not necessarily dry though this is frequently indicated
ottah (*otter*)	usually 'attar of roses', a perfume made from the oil in rose petals
padshaw	an emperor, the king
pagoda	temple
palanquin	a box litter for travelling in, with a pole projecting before and behind, which is borne on the shoulders of four or six men

pandal	a shed
pettah	a town adjacent to a fortress
pilow (*pilau*)	a Muslim dish of meat or fowl boiled along with rice and spices
polygar (*polygaress*)	feudal chiefs (male and female) with predatory habits, who considered themselves independent, occupying more or less wild tracts in the Madras Presidency
Ranee (*Maharannie*)	a Hindu queen
sayres	local and arbitrary charges levied by *zemindars* with a show of authority on all goods passing through their estates
sepoy	a native soldier disciplined and dressed in European style
shroff	bankers, money-changers
soubadar	the chief native officer of a company of sepoys, a captain
tappal	express mail carried by camel
tonjon	a sort of sedan or portable chair carried like a palanquin by a single pole and four bearers
zemindar (*jemidar*)	landholder or local ruler who pays revenues to the government directly
zenana	the apartments of a palace in which the women are secluded

Honourable Miss Harriet Clive

Honourable Miss Charlotte Clive

Dramatis Personae

The Players

HENRIETTA, LADY HENRIETTA ANTONIA CLIVE (1758–1830)

Henrietta, a feisty, independent and spirited traveller, was a Herbert of the 'princely Powys', daughter of Lord Henry Arthur Herbert of Chirbury, first Earl of Powis (second creation) and wife of Lord Edward Clive, the eldest son of Lord Robert Clive (Clive of India). From 1798–1801, she lived and travelled in South India. In 1804, she and her husband were created Earl and Countess of Powis by royal decree, the Earldom having become extinct on the death of Henrietta's brother in 1801.

LORD EDWARD CLIVE (1754–1839)

Whereas his father, 'Clive of India', had great charisma, Lord Edward Clive, although a good man, had little. When appointed Governor of Madras by the East India Company in 1797, he had no previous government experience but grew into the job during his India tenure (1798–1803). He was much appreciated for establishing higher pay for the Indians serving in the British military.

HARRY, HARRIET ANTONIA CLIVE (1786–1835)

Harry, the elder and more conventional Clive daughter was twelve years old when she travelled with her parents to South India. Less is known of her as her journal, if she kept one, is not available. From her letters I think she was also rather lively. She became an accomplished harpist and later married Sir Watkins Williams Wyn.

CHARLY, CHARLOTTE FLORENTIA CLIVE (1787–1866)

Charly, who at the beginning of her travels to India was eleven years old, was a lively, sparkly personality, who was curious about everything –

whether counting the steps of Mount St Thomas in Madras, mastering the flag codes at sea or attending a Hussein Hassan festival. Throughout her travels to, within and from India, she kept a journal. She excelled in languages and learned 'Hindustani', 'Moors' and Italian during her India sojourn. After marrying the Duke of Northumberland and becoming mistress of the castles, she published *Castles of Alnwich and Warkworth*, illustrated with her own watercolours and dedicated to her mother. She went on to become governess (1830–9) to Princess, later Queen, Victoria, the future Empress of India. She must have been a tactful woman to get on with her Highness's overbearing mother.

SIGNORA ANNA TONELLI (1763–1846)

Artist and governess to the Clive daughters

Anna Tonelli was the daughter of Florentine miniaturist, Nistri. She married a violinist whose family name, Tonelli, is associated with musicians in and around Florence and in Parma, Modena and Carpi to the north. In 1794–7 she exhibited her paintings (portraits, watercolours and pastels) in London's Royal Academy of Arts, a rare distinction for a woman artist and a foreigner. While in India she recorded her travels by watercolour sketches of scenes and people. Among her India paintings was a rendition of Tipu Sultan on his golden throne, for which she received advice from his *munshi* after the fall of Seringapatam. She also painted portraits of other dignitaries, such as the Maharajah of Tanjore, Sarabhoji, and the Maharajah of Mysore, Krishna Wodeyar. A number of her India paintings illustrate Charly's journal. After accompanying Henrietta and the girls back to England in 1801, she returned home to Florence to join her children in 1802.

The Madras Players

COLONEL ARTHUR WELLESLEY (1769–1852)

Colonel Wellesley was one of three Wellesley brothers in India during the final campaign (1799) against Tipu Sultan. His elder brother, Lord Mornington, was Governor General of India; his younger brother, Henry, was secretary to the Governor General. Colonel Wellesley, of

His Majesty's 33rd Regiment of Foot, assumed command and restored order at Seringapatam after the defeat of Tipu Sultan. He was appointed Governor of Mysore and Chief Political and Military Officer in the Deccan and Southern Maratha Country. Colonel Wellesley would use the techniques learned in India in his victory against Napoleon Bonaparte at Waterloo in 1815, which led to his being made Duke of Wellington.

LORD RICHARD COLLEY MORNINGTON (1760–1842)

Lord Mornington, Eton and Oxford educated, and Governor General of India, left no stone unturned to succeed in the execution of the defeat of Tipu Sultan. He moved from his Calcutta headquarters to Madras, judging it to be a better command position for the war. As a precaution, for the duration of the war, he assumed the power and authority of the Governor of Madras in Council.

LIEUTENANT-GENERAL GEORGE HARRIS (1746–1829)

British Commander-in-Chief of the Armed Forces of South India

General Harris led the battle of Seringapatam. Almost immediately following the victory he was replaced by his junior officer, Colonel Arthur Wellesley. He organised Tipu Sultan's funeral with all honours. General Harris later received the Barony of Seringapatam and Mysore, E. Indies and of Belmont, Kent.

Off stage, but significant

TIPU SAHIB (1750–1799) *Sultan of the South Indian State of Mysore*

Tipu Sultan, the 'Tiger of Mysore', was an irascible, cultivated and brave South Indian potentate. His animosity to the British invaders was as ferocious and unpredictable as that of a tiger. Indeed, his possessions were marked with emblems of the tiger, in particular, *bubris,* tiger stripes. He was an intellectual whose library contained over 2,000 volumes dealing with many topics including Sufism, cosmology, jurisprudence, mathematics and astronomy. In a painting depicting him as he led his troops to victory in 1780 at the Battle of Pollilur, he is dressed in splendid *bubris*, a large emerald dangling from his turban, riding in a silver *howdah* on the back of an elephant and holding a rose in his hand. He was killed by the British on May 4th 1799 at the battle of his island kingdom, Seringapatam. For Henrietta, in many ways, he seemed the very personification of the East.

GENERAL NAPOLEON BONAPARTE (1769–1821)

Bonaparte's ambitions were to advance through Egypt and to conquer the land route to India in order to assist Tipu Sultan against the English in India. The brilliant, mercurial Bonaparte was defeated by Lord Horatio Nelson at Aboukir Bay, Egypt, August 1st 1798, putting paid to these plans. In 1804 he became Napoleon I, Emperor of France.

LORD ROBERT 'CLIVE OF INDIA' (1725–1774), *Baron of Plassey*

As a result of his wild and daring escapades, Lord Robert Clive secured India for the British. He acquired great wealth from his India adventures and triumphs. For Henrietta, he remained a living presence. She and his granddaughters sought out places where he had been: the church in Madras where he married Margaret Maskelyn, daughter of the Astronomer Royal, and the scenes of his victories at Vellore, Arcot and Trichinopoly.

GEORGE EDWARD HENRY ARTHUR HERBERT (1755–1801), *2nd Earl of Powis*

'My dearest brother' was Henrietta's confidant and the recipient of her most private musings in her letters from India. The Earl of Powis, educated at Eton, was left in charge of the schooling of her sons, his nephews, Edward (aged thirteen) and Robert (aged nine), while the Clives were in India. The Earl of Powis had extravagant tastes and indulged in high living. He died in January 1801 while Henrietta was still in India, leaving his estate saddled with huge debts, partly because of the monetary problems of his parents. Henrietta's first son, Edward, became heir to his uncle and received by royal licence the name and arms of Herbert in lieu of Clive in 1806.

LADY FRANCES DOUGLAS (1750–1817)

Lady Douglas was Henrietta's trusted friend and correspondent. The letters that Henrietta wrote to her were fashioned to emphasise the Eastern aspects of her journey, as well as to give an account of her India experiences.

KRISHNA WODEYAR, *Maharajah of Mysore*

At the fall of Seringapatam, the British put this young boy in place as ruler of Mysore.

DHOONDHIA WAUGH

This able Muslim brigand commander had many disgruntled men fighting under him in the early summer of 1800. In theory, he hoped for French aid to restore the government and country of Tipu to his sons. In reality, he planned to build a kingdom of his own in an area larger and more populous than the British Isles. He was defeated by Colonel Arthur Wellesley on August 20th 1800.

SARABHOJI, *Maharajah of Tanjore* (*ruled* 1798–1832)

The Maharajah Sarabhoji, an orphan, was raised by the Danish Missionary C. F. Schwartz, who founded a mission in Tanjore, educated the Maharajah Sarabhoji and helped him regain his throne. Henrietta was lavishly entertained in Tanjore; on her return to England, she took with her some of 'the gentleman cows and their ladies' which Sarabhoji had given her as a gift.

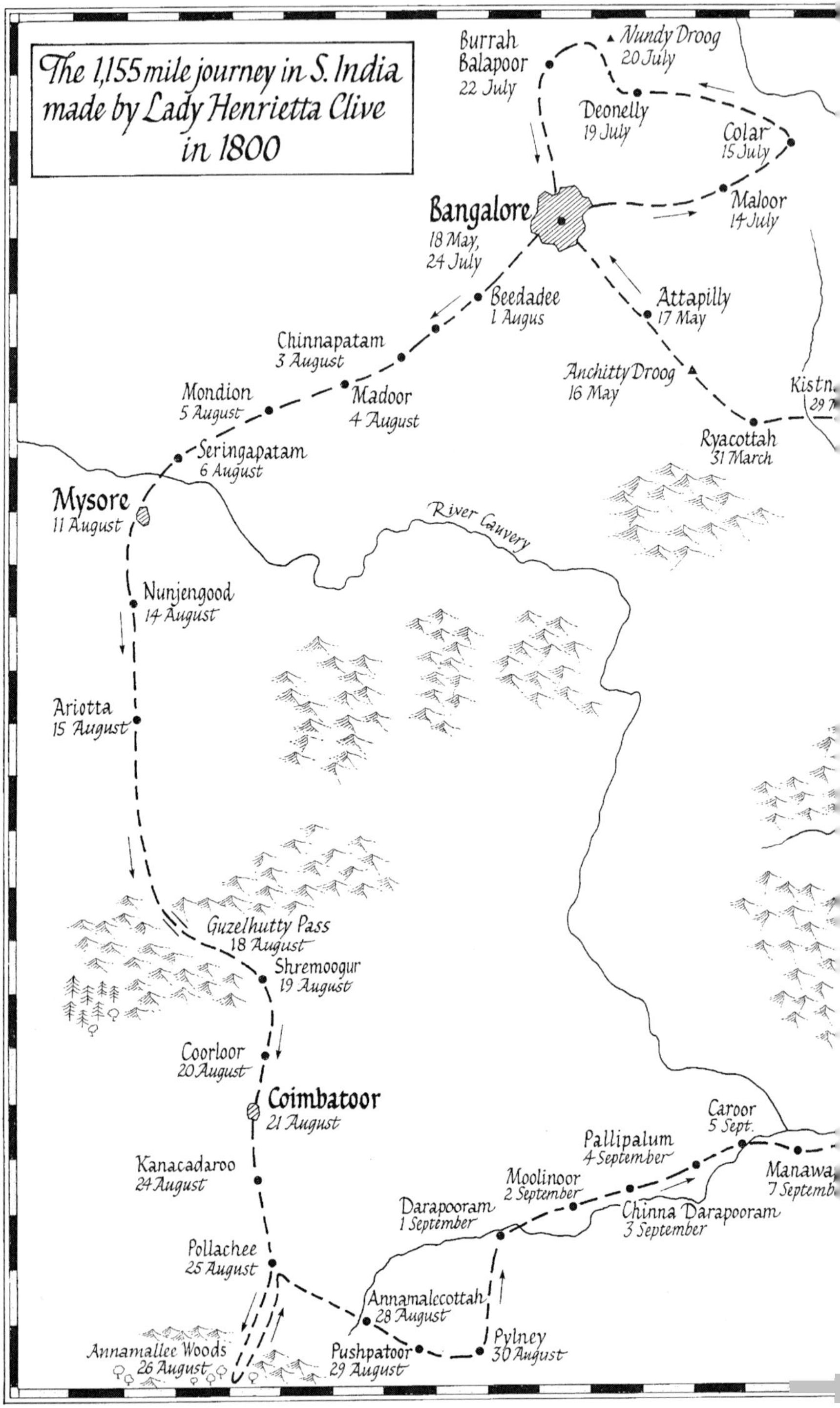

The 1,155 mile journey in S. India made by Lady Henrietta Clive in 1800
Burrah Balapoor
22 July
Nundy Droog
20 July
Deonelly
19 July
Colar
15 July
Maloor
14 July
Bangalore
18 May, 24 July
Beedadee
1 Augus
Attapilly
17 May
Chinnapatam
3 August
Anchitty Droog
16 May
Kistn.
29
Mondion
5 August
Madoor
4 August
Ryacottah
31 March
Seringapatam
6 August
Mysore
11 August
River Cauvery
Nunjengood
14 August
Ariotta
15 August
Guzelhutty Pass
18 August
Shremoogur
19 August
Coorloor
20 August
Coimbatoor
21 August
Kanacadaroo
24 August
Caroor
5 Sept.
Pallipalum
4 September
Moolinoor
2 September
Manawa
7 Septemb
Darapooram
1 September
Chinna Darapooram
3 September
Pollachee
25 August
Annamalecottah
28 August
Annamallee Woods
26 August
Pushpatoor
29 August
Pylney
30 August

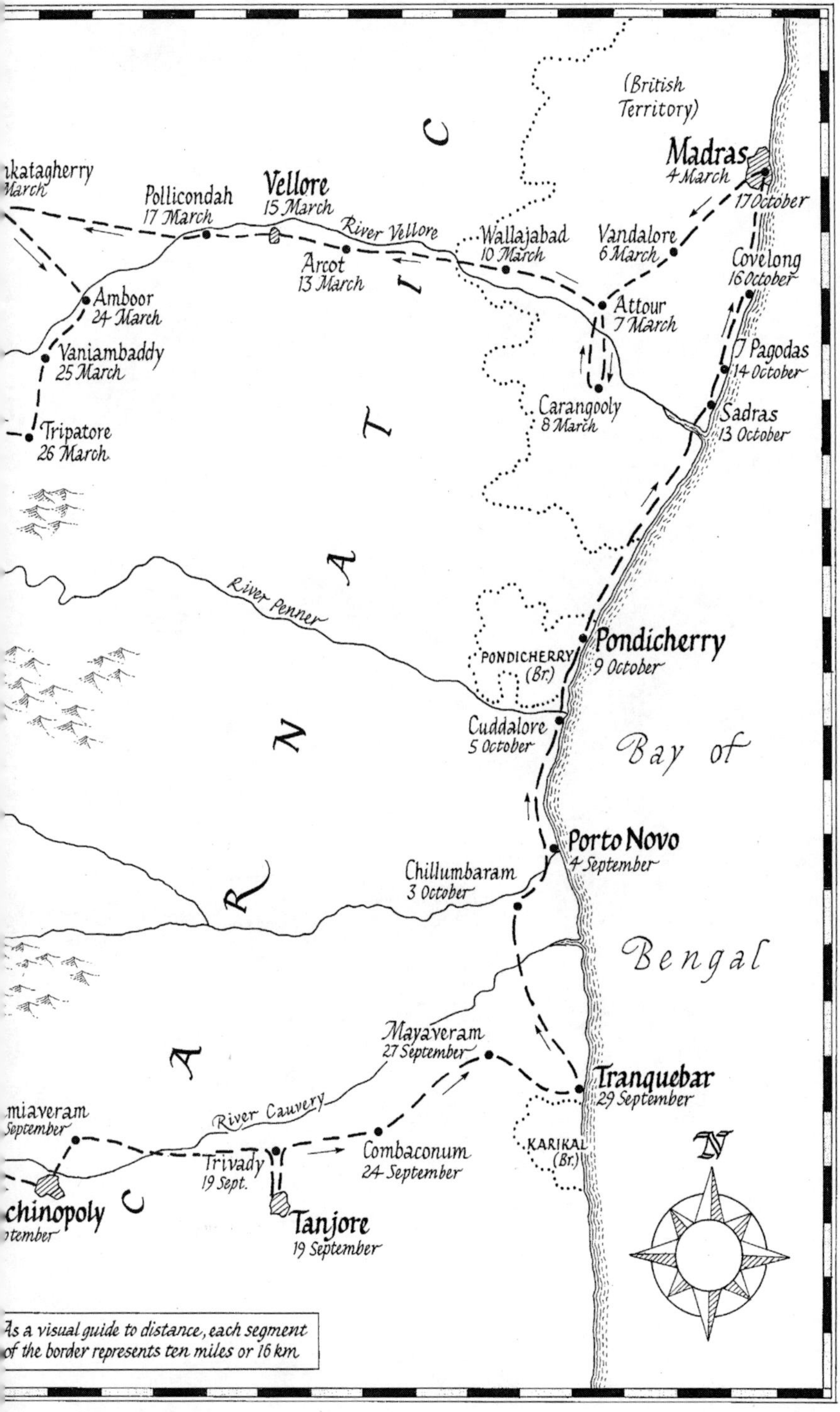

(British Territory)
Madras
4 March
17 October
Vandalore
6 March
Covelong
16 October
Wallajabad
10 March
Attour
7 March
7 Pagodas
14 October
Carangooly
8 March
Sadras
13 October
Vellore
15 March
River Vellore
Arcot
13 March
Pollicondah
17 March
katagherry
March
Amboor
24 March
Vaniambaddy
25 March
Tripatore
26 March
River Penner
Pondicherry
9 October
PONDICHERRY (Br.)
Cuddalore
5 October
Bay of Bengal
Porto Novo
4 September
Chillumbaram
3 October
Mayaveram
27 September
Tranquebar
29 September
KARIKAL (Br.)
River Cauvery
Combaconum
24 September
Trivady
19 Sept.
Tanjore
19 September
miaveram
September
chinopoly
tember
C A R N A T I C
N
As a visual guide to distance, each segment of the border represents ten miles or 16 km

Introduction

'A ship came in yesterday that left England the beginning of March, but had no news, having left England without having gone to Portsmouth and having left all the passengers and brought their baggage, besides a poor woman who took her passage from Deal to Portsmouth. Think of anybody coming to the East Indies by mistake!'

Lady Henrietta Clive, Madras, 1799

On March 4th 1800, Lady Henrietta Clive took the first steps in the realisation of a dream. In fulfilment, as she put it, of 'a most indescribable wish to go and see' Seringapatam and whatever remained of Tipu Sultan's world, she set forth on a seven-month excursion into South India that would cover over one thousand miles. Accompanying her were her daughters, Harriet (Harry aged thirteen), Charlotte Florentia (Charly aged twelve) and an Italian artist, Signora Anna Tonelli. A Captain Brown commanded her bodyguard and baggage train. Fourteen elephants carried tents, as well as a harp, a pianoforte, and Henrietta's one horse *bandy*. One hundred bullocks hauled provision carts; camels delivered express messages. Escorted by an enormous retinue of over seven hundred and fifty people, including sixty-six infantry, cooks, *palanquin* bearers, maids, hangers-on and her Persian teacher, Henrietta made her way over mountains and through 'tygerish' jungles and crocodile-infested rivers, camping for the most part along the route, studying her Persian verbs, searching for local flora and fauna, reviewing troops, visiting with East India Company officials and British military representatives, meeting *polygars* and *fakeers*, calling on the wives and older sons of Tipu Sultan, *Ranees*, *Maharajahs*, and even the Danish Commandant of Tranquebar. Henrietta did indeed visit Seringapatam, and 'all the great horn, besides', travelling the while, as she wrote to her friend Lady Frances Douglas, 'not with seven leagued boots, but with elephants and camels like an Eastern Damsel with all possible dignity'.

* * *

My personal introduction to Lady Henrietta Clive came some years ago. Like my subject, I had recently been in South India. A strange curiosity led me to Powis Castle, Wales to have a look at the collection 'Treasures from India: the Clive Collection', acquired primarily by Lord Robert 'Clive of India', and later added to by his son, Lord Edward Clive, Governor of Madras, and daughter-in-law, Lady Henrietta. Although I found the artifacts to be interesting enough, it was Henrietta herself, a Welsh woman traveller, journeying to and within the interior of South India at the turn of a now-distant eighteenth and nineteenth century, who rather gripped my attention.

By virtue of my own Indian journeys and projects I had acquired a certain eclectic familiarity with South India. My experiences were certainly varied and sometimes even happenstance. In Mysore, for example, I had the great good fortune to meet and converse with R. K. Narayan on several occasions. Sitting on his upstairs verandah, watching the changing colours of the sunset, listening to cicadas and the occasional chirp of a gecko and drinking milky sweet, South Indian coffee, we gossiped about his characters dwelling out there in the fictional world of Malgudi. Narayan conceived of the lives of his characters, all lives for that matter, as part of a continuous flow of coming together and parting. I had myself spent countless sultry, full-moon nights in isolated temples or under ancient trees observing the ritual healing dances of masked spirit dancers in South Kanara (once the Kingdom of Tuluva), a narrow strip of land along the Arabian coast of South India. The narratives recited by the dancers were odd and compelling tales of left-over-life-still-to-live. After having seen the Powis Castle exhibit, I found myself musing about how Lady Henrietta Clive's historical adventure in the East might contain its own inherently fascinating tales. Anxious to know more about her and her journey to, within and back home from the South India of that period, I took my first steps.

A few weeks later while at home in West Texas, I rang the 7th Earl of Powis [George William Herbert, 1925–93] at Chirbury, introduced myself and asked where Lady Henrietta Clive's India papers were held.

'Her letters and a journal are at home in the castle,' said the Earl of Powis, seemingly unperturbed by this unexpected call from West Texas. 'Please speak more loudly, as I have difficulty hearing.'

'Would it be possible for me to see them?' I shouted obligingly.

'Yes . . . but not today,' he responded.

We set a date when I would return to Powis Castle and left it at that.

A light snow had fallen when I appeared once again in Wales.

'It is too cold for you to work in the castle,' said the Earl of Powis, a kind, scholarly man, as he looked me up and down. 'You are so "wee" you might freeze to death.' He then added decisively, 'You must use my study at Marrington Hall.'

So it was that I drove the narrow lanes to Marrington Hall in Chirbury from Shrewsbury each morning to examine, in the comfort of the Earl of Powis's state-of-the-art, centrally heated study, several boxes of documents. At eleven o'clock he would bring me a cup of coffee and chat briefly about the Herbert family history and, in particular, its strong women. Around three o'clock, after a cup of tea, he would send me on my way before dark settled in on those short January days. In those moments in snowy Wales, indirectly, through the 7th Earl of Powis, I was welcomed aboard and accepted as a fellow traveller with Henrietta. Henrietta and I joined hands, as it were, both in her Welsh setting and her journey through South India. She led me into her story, rekindling in me the Indian sights and smells and sounds which so fascinated, and for a time, intoxicated her. In a different period, I, too, had breathed and looked at that air.

Henrietta's words, written in an eighteenth-century script of now faded ink, were often difficult to decipher. The Earl of Powis encouraged me to use his Xerox machine to copy whatever documents I wished. When my schedule did not permit me time enough to finish going through the papers, he allowed me to come for another visit before he relinquished the boxes to the National Library of Wales at Aberystwyth.

Certainly Henrietta's journalistic narrative is not wholly unlikely for the times. For example, Mrs Eliza Fay, thought to have been the daughter of a sailor, sailed to India on three separate journeys and wrote letters about her experiences. Her first voyage was in 1779 with her East India Company lawyer-husband, who was going out to practise as an Advocate at the Supreme Court of Calcutta. Of Mrs Fay's letters the liveliest and most interesting one was written on her initial trip out when she was held captive by Haidar Ali on the West coast of India in Calicut. After divorcing her husband, who had run off with another woman, Mrs Fay sailed again to Calcutta on her own in 1784 and a final time in 1815. She died in 1816 in Calcutta; her letters were published in 1817. Two years after Henrietta had returned to England, in 1803, Mrs Maria Graham, daughter of Rear Admiral George Dundas, sailed with her husband, a Captain in the Navy, to India. Her collected Indian letters, *Journal of a Residence in India* (published in 1813) offer a more refined and educated voice than Mrs Fay. However, Mrs Graham did not seem particularly to enjoy India. Her knowledge of it was fairly circumscribed, dealing for the most part with port calls to Bombay, Ceylon and Madras.

Henrietta's narrative is unique, precisely because it bears the voice of Henrietta's letters and journal from the interior of South India. Prior to her adventurous trek, western travellers in this little-travelled region had been, for the most part, the British military, various foreign missionaries and East India Company representatives, although two British artists, Thomas Daniell (1749–1840) and his nephew, William (1769–1837), had toured South India in 1792, recording hill forts, temples and antiquities. Henrietta's perspective allowed her to illuminate the turbulent historical backdrop following the fall of Tipu Sultan from the point of view of a woman traveller. In a manner unlike that found in the writings of a professional soldier such as Colonel Arthur Wellesley and/or an East India Company envoy for British commerce such as Lord Richard Mornington, Henrietta offers a down-to-earth account of whatever situation she found herself in. In a narrative style that is conversational, captivating and, indeed, reflecting her own vitality, her writings provide a sense of permanence to the fleeting moments, people, places and events which ebbed and flowed about her. Likewise Anna Tonelli, Henrietta's travelling companion, recorded the first watercolour sketches of scenes and people painted by a Western woman artist in the South Indian interior.

Each day throughout her journey, Henrietta opened her writing box, took her pen in hand, dipped it into ink and inscribed her impressions, if only for the length of a page, in her multicoloured Indian paperback notebook. Letters to her husband began with a formal 'My dear Lord Clive', and gave an account of the sights and events experienced, along with a commentary about her health and that of their daughters. Although letters addressed to Lady Douglas and the Dowager Lady Clive occasionally contained personal references, for the most part they were more general and meant to be passed around for the entertainment of a select audience of friends and acquaintances. Letters to 'My dearest brother' were more intimate and provided Henrietta with a much needed outlet 'to seem to talk to you'.

I was to see only a few pages written by Henrietta's brother, George Edward Herbert, whose early reluctance as a letter writer was noted in an undated letter written by his mother, Lady Barbara, to his father, the Earl of Powis, relaying a message to her young son from his little sister, Henrietta Herbert: 'Henrietta and I agree George has neither pen, ink or paper for her and therefore we send him a sheet of paper and desire that he will borrow a pen from Will Thomas, ink from John Davies, and sense from the ass whose milk you drink. This is H. H.'s message.' Throughout her life, any letter from 'my dearest brother' was greeted with Henrietta's joy. On August 6th 1786, just before she and her husband set out for Naples on an extended stay in Europe, Henrietta responded to an unexpected letter from her brother saying, 'At last to my great surprise I beheld the most beauteous scrawl of your lordship and tho' I confess it was a letter yet it was not too long nor did it contain too much news and therefore you cannot expect a very long one from me.'

Her brother was of immense importance to Henrietta. Presumably her personal vitality, her fearless passion for living life to the full and her *joie de vivre* were shared with him. Quite possibly Henrietta, or someone in the family, discreetly destroyed his letters to her, as well as many of hers to him. Jane Austen's letters were edited by her sister, who cut out parts and burnt others for privacy's sake. Lord Byron's missives to his beloved sister Augusta were obtained by an indignant Lady Byron, who vindictively publicised their contents. Byron probably did not much care about privacy, but Henrietta, even as Jane Austen, was a careful and private person.

Letters from other periods of Henrietta's life were also in the boxes, but it was her depiction of life in India that propelled her compelling narrative forward with her accounts of sailing to India, residing in Madras, experiencing a beyond-the-ordinary seven-month adventure while travelling in South India and then sailing home. India is never easy, but the difficulties Henrietta encountered were heightened by her living in an age much less appreciative of such courage and tenacity in a woman. For the most part, wives were left at home. But then Henrietta was more than a wife: she was her own person of note. She did not fit with the prevailing attitudes of her time or with that of the *memsahibs* to follow in later years. Colonising and proselytising did not interest her in the least; a hands-on coming to know the world of India, however, emphatically did. Henrietta endeavoured to understand and to appreciate.

* * *

Henrietta's avid desire to experience 'the magnificence of the East' was put in place when, as a girl, she had thrilled to first-hand accounts of the India adventures of her neighbour and mentor, Clive of India. On his return from India with vast wealth, Lord Clive had purchased Oakly Park from Henrietta's father, Henry Arthur Herbert, the Earl of Powis. This transaction was to provoke discussions between the two men about the desirability of a marriage between Clive's son Edward and the Earl's daughter, an alliance that would offer prestige to the Clives and the possibility of reviving the fortunes of the titled and landed, but financially strapped, Herberts.

When Henrietta was fourteen, her father died, having made no financial provision for his daughter or wife, yet all too typically, leaving his son, George Edward, heir to the Powis estate. Henrietta went to live in London with her brother, a foppishly fashionable and extravagant young man, who was three years older than she. He was to become part of the London social scene and a great favourite with the 'Majesties', King George III (1732–1820) and Queen Charlotte (1744–1818), driving elegant phaetons with spirited horses and hosting lavish and expensive festivities. For Henrietta he was always 'my dearest brother', her confidant. Brother and sister became deeply estranged from their mother, who as an habitué of the gaming tables with an addiction to the card game '*loo*', vied with her son in spending the remaining Powis wealth. George Edward spurned his mother's pleas to have him pay her gambling debts. In return Lady Barbara refused to sanction her son and daughter living together. In a letter to Probert, who looked after the family's financial affairs, Lady Barbara noted her concerns: 'It is not to be expressed what I feel. Henrietta would be undone if anything happens wrong.'

The portrait that Sir Joshua Reynolds painted of Henrietta when she was nineteen depicts a good-looking, small, compact and shapely young woman. She stands against a backdrop of dark feathery tree branches without any of the psychological or social props such as a book, or a bust or needlework frequently employed by portrait painters of the time. Her gaze is contemplative. It is as if she has just turned to speak and one guesses her movements to be nimble, graceful and strong. She is dressed in a stylish but modest pale silk eighteenth-century costume that covers her arms and neck. The distinctive large hat that tilts at a precarious angle over the piled-up tresses of her wig and her stole, were added sometime later by a different hand. There is something oddly affectionate in the way Reynolds has offered the viewer a sense of Henrietta's independent Welsh spirit, capturing her in an open-ended moment that seems to depict her inner potential as much as her lovely exterior. She gives every indication of being able to handle whatever might come her way.

Clive of India died in 1774 leaving his son Edward a wealthy man. The marriage of Henrietta and Edward which the fathers had hoped for did not take place until ten years later, in May 1784. Not long before the wedding, Edward (aged thirty) wrote to his mother the Dowager Lady Clive to announce his decision to marry Henrietta (aged twenty-six): 'I have ventured to declare my attachment to a Lady every way calculated to make me happy as a wife and I have been so fortunate as to meet with the most full and unreserved consent on her part. On yours, my Dear Madam, I have ventured to assure Lady H. Herbert there would be the most cordial concurrence and this I have presumed to do from knowledge of the sentiments you and my father entertained of the amiable person on whom depend all my prospects of comfort and felicity. To know that in following my own inclinations I run along with your wishes and what were those of his whose opinions to me are sacred is an important satisfaction.' They were married in London at the Portland Place address of Henrietta's brother, the Earl of Powis. Lady Barbara, with whom neither daughter nor son had resolved their conflicts, was not invited to the wedding. In a note to the aforementioned Probert, she commented that 'my situation as a mother is I believe rather uncommon as neither the day or any other circumstance has been signified to me either by the bride or Lord Powis'. Lord Clive called on her afterwards to inform her of the event.

Over the next five years Henrietta had four children: a son, Edward, was born on March 22nd 1785 and a daughter, Harriet Antonia (Harry) on September 5th 1786. On September 12th 1787, while she and her husband were still on their Grand Tour, Henrietta gave birth in Florence, Italy to their third child, Charlotte Florentia (Charly). To her brother left at home in England with the older children ('the brats' as she affectionately called them) Henrietta, a committed traveller, sent a steady flow of lively, lightly humorous letters. There was no doubt that she found Italy invigorating: 'I draw a great deal now and shall soon equal Raphael.' She easily handled the less desirable aspects of being in strange locales: 'Fleas and bugs are in a very flourishing state in Italy and feed most comfortably upon poor me.' Moreover Henrietta seemed pleased with Lord Clive's commitment to looking after her health, noting: 'Lord Clive makes me walk *miles* everyday . . . I live upon vegetable – neither Irish beer or wine or anything but milk and water.'

In March 1788 Henrietta and her husband saw that Charly was inoculated with smallpox vaccine in Rome. Henrietta wrote to her brother that 'this event makes a great noise in Rome as inoculation is looked upon with great horror and the old friars settled in the English coffee house that she would certainly die the third day, but now people are growing more reconciled to it and if she succeeds the Surgeon who attends (but only looks on) is to inoculate ten or twelve directly . . . therefore your niece's name will be early *famous*, at Rome and she will occasion the safety of many children.' For this first trip abroad, the ever industrious Henrietta had learned to read and speak Italian. Not long after the family reunited in England, the Clives' fourth and last child, Robert, was born on January 15th 1789.

* * *

In November 1797 the East India Company offered Lord Edward Clive the Governorship of Madras. An elated Henrietta felt herself to be on the threshold of 'all sorts of things – like the *Arabian Nights*'. On April 2nd 1798, Lord Clive, Henrietta, their daughters, Harry and Charly, along with the girls' governess, the Italian artist Signora Anna Tonelli, embarked on the East Indiaman, the *Dover Castle*. The Clive sons, Edward and Robert, remained behind in England at school and under the supervision of Henrietta's brother. An arduous journey to India was made doubly difficult by the fact that England was at war with France. Foul weather and an attempted mutiny on one of the ships in the convoy added to the hardships. In June 1798 the *Dover Castle* sprang a leak and called in at the Cape of Good Hope for repairs.

Henrietta delighted in being once again on land and took enormous pleasure in the proliferation of flora and fauna in South Africa. Lady Anne Barnard, an old acquaintance of Henrietta, offers a glimpse of the Clives during this stop-over to India. 'She [Henrietta] had a mind open to receive pleasure from everything, to please as far as she can, is incapable of offending and will not tire, I am sure, of any situation she is placed in.' Of Lord Clive, Lady Anne raised a question: '. . . how comes it that they are going at all? People so wealthy – a man apparently so little ambitious! By implication though not by direct words, I had a reason to think the matter was offered to him, and I did not think Administration – any Administration I mean – was so rich in great appointments as to give without the boon being solicited. Perhaps his *name* is held to be a lucky one to go to India. He seems in good spirits, but says little . . . we talked of everything *but* Madras.'

On reaching Madras on August 21st 1798, the travellers found to their surprise that nothing was as they had expected. Preparations for war were underway against the legendary Tipu Sultan. The engaging, physically fit and strong-willed Colonel Arthur Wellesley of the King's 33rd Regiment was soon to make his presence known on stage in Madras. Though newly arrived in India, he understood that the Mysore campaign would be extremely risky and that a division of counsel (political as well as military) would impede it. Despite their differences in age and social status, Colonel Wellesley wasted little time in assessing the capabilities of the son of the famous Clive senior. He wrote to his brother, Lord Mornington, the newly appointed Governor General of India in Calcutta, that he found Lord Edward Clive to be 'a mild moderate man, remarkably reserved, having a bad delivery, and apparently a heavy understanding'. He then amended his description by adding, 'I doubt whether he is as dull as he appears, or as people think he is.' A month later in September, Colonel Wellesley followed up his earlier observations in another letter to Lord Mornington saying, 'Lord Clive opens his mind to me freely upon all subjects. I give him my opinion and talk as I would to Mornington. The truth is he does not want talents, but he is very diffident of himself. Now that he has begun to find out that he has no difficulty in transacting the business of Government, he improves daily, takes more upon himself, and will very shortly have less need for the opinions and abilities of those who have long done the business of the country. A violent or harsh letter from Fort William [Calcutta] would spoil all.'

With Lord Mornington's entrance on to the Madras scene on December 31st 1798, Lord Clive was relegated to the role of being Governor in name only for the duration of the war. Pragmatically, he summed up his initial relationship with the Governor General as 'a Awkward but a right one'. Henrietta was considerably harsher in her assessment of Lord Mornington's usurpation of centre stage. She described him to her brother as 'extremely pompous . . . and bringing *his* authority to bear on me, and everybody in conversation. Lord Clive likes him very well, but you know he does not mind many things, which I confess, disturb my *Welsh Spirit.*' She found it 'entirely an awkward thing to have a *Supremo* to come over us'. Likewise, she considered Lord Clive's loss of authority to be unjust, 'a great mortification', even though her status in society was not affected, since Lady Mornington had not accompanied her husband to India. Regarding the people of the Madras social scene as 'not much enlightened', she declared herself to be 'most *outrageously* civil' in letters to her brother and Lady Douglas.

Indeed, to Henrietta's disappointment, everything about Madras soon became military: 'There is nothing but business and solitude,' she noted. She was not alone, however, in her eagerness for things Oriental. Colonel Wellesley's own scholarly bent caused him to pursue his continuing studies of India and the Persian language. He had even gone into further debt on his voyage out to add to his library of books on the East. Napoleon Bonaparte's fervour for the glory of the Orient caused him to include scholars and artists in his expedition to Egypt in June 1798. It was there, en route to aid Tipu Sultan in overthrowing 'the iron yoke of England', that he lost his entire fleet to Admiral Horatio Nelson at Aboukir Bay on August 1st 1798. News of Bonaparte's defeat did not reach Madras until October. If aid had arrived from France, Tipu Sultan would have been an even more dangerous adversary. Fears that the French might have captured the overland trading route, much used by the British for supplies and mail, prompted Henrietta to quip: 'perhaps Bonaparte has got some of *my manuscripts.*'

Not willing to be upstaged by 'the fidgety', Oxford-educated Lord Mornington, Henrietta asserted her own scholarly identity by immediately 'building a room in the garden and a *laboratory* for all sorts of odd rocks and works'. Her pursuit of Persian, the language of Indian courts, was well underway, as she had begun her studies shortly after learning that she would travel to India. In Madras she wasted no time in acquiring two tutors: one for Persian and the other for spoken Hindustani. She also carried on a correspondence with young Captain Malcolm assigned to the British diplomatic service in Persia.

Having early shouldered the responsibility for her eclectic education, Henrietta was deeply committed to overseeing the instruction of her daughters. In Henrietta's world, women were not allowed many legal rights; nor could they be educated at universities. Perhaps Henrietta gave her girls boys' names because on one level she wanted to treat them as such. More likely, she simply thought it fun to do so. In India she encouraged Harry and Charly to be open towards the astonishing world unfolding around them and saw to it that they experienced as many levels of Indian culture as possible: meeting Armenian merchants, Muslim *Nawabs* and Hindu *Maharajahs*; attending a variety of religious festivals, as well as *nautchs*; visiting markets, mosques, temples, forts, palaces and *zenanas*. In their daily lessons they studied Indian plants, rocks and shells, as well as animals, birds and butterflies. Hindustani and Persian became part of their curriculum. The girls were also tutored in conversational Italian and read Dante. They played harp and pianoforte and were skilful at drawing. Even in such tasks as writing letters or keeping a journal, Henrietta did not have written examples set for them to follow. Indeed, her own independent attitude must have served continuously as a lesson to them. Above all else, Henrietta emboldened Harry and Charly to make decisions. Lord Clive wrote to his brother-in-law, expressing his satisfaction with their education, 'The girls will not, I believe, suffer any loss of accomplishment from residing in India except in their dancing.'

As a woman of her time, Henrietta was all too aware of the discrepancies in what was allowed for English men but unacceptable for English women. It was her wont to point out such inequalities. In a letter written to Lord Clive after he had assumed in full his assignment as

Governor of Madras and she was on her magnificent trek, she noted: 'If you want collectors or *collectoresses* I think I should like to *extremely* . . . and grab over strange countries, particularly near Hyderabad. I should delight in it above all things. It is hard that we poor females are not to get anything in this Asiatic world.'

Henrietta's dedication in seeking to know India was that of a highly motivated and disciplined amateur. From England she brought with her Robert Orme's *A History of the Military Transactions of the British Nation in Indostan from the year MDCCXLV*, whose detailed accounts of Lord Robert Clive's courageous acts in India underscored Henrietta's visits to the scenes of his triumphs. Thomas Macaulay characterised Orme's accounts as 'minute even to tediousness', but nonetheless had a high regard for his writings. The more charmingly readable Madame de Sévigné's *Lettres* also went with Henrietta to India. In her will, Henrietta would later bequeath her copy of *Lettres* to Charly. For her Persian studies, Henrietta acquired in India some of the lines of the *Diwan* written by one of the greatest Sufi poets, Khaja Shamsuddin Hafiz, hoping 'in all due time to be able to read Hafiz and all the learned books'.

* * *

On May 4th 1799 at 1:30 in the oppressive South Indian afternoon heat, the English Army attacked Seringapatam, the island capital of Tipu Sultan. The rains had not yet come and the waters of the River Cauvery (Kaveri) were low, allowing relatively easy access to the walls of the city. Some two hundred and fifty miles away from Seringapatam on the Coromandel Coast at Fort St George, Madras, Henrietta learned of the 'Tyger of Mysore's' death and the end of what she termed 'this abominable war'. With a keen interest, she followed the descriptions of the treasures found within Tipu's Daria Daulat palace which included: sumptuous Persian carpets, extraordinary jewels, a golden throne, a book in which Tipu recorded his imaginative dreams of white elephants and emeralds, his gigantic collection of Persian books on diverse topics and engraved swords and guns. Decorative patterns of tiger stripes and jewelled tiger heads were on everything. There was as well a wooden mechanical tiger which with a turn of a handle made sounds of roaring, as a screaming Englishman feebly lifted an arm to protect himself.

Having been confined to Madras for the duration of the final Mysore Campaign, Henrietta believed that now she would be able to realise her passion to wander amidst South India's exotic landscapes, religions and peoples. Immediately following the battle, plans had been made for Lord Mornington and Lord Clive to travel to Seringapatam, with Henrietta to follow somewhat later. Even though their luggage had been sent ahead, Lord Mornington, ever fearful for his health, decided at the last minute that the party would remain in Madras for the victory celebration and forego the trip to Seringapatam altogether.

Refusing to relinquish her schemes to travel, Henrietta simply bided her time, waiting for a more favourable opportunity. Undaunted by the difficulties of journeying in the interior of South India, Henrietta perused the maps and descriptions used by the military. Travel conditions were demanding; roads (when available) were primitive; bridges were non-existent. *Polygars* and unfriendly rogue military bands, such as that of Dhoondiah, threatened. There was, as well, a significant risk of contracting diseases such as dysentery, elephantiasis, cholera, smallpox, malaria, or other indigenous fevers.

After spending eight months in Madras, the overbearing Lord Mornington left for Calcutta in September 1799. He was to say that he and Lord Clive had lived at Madras as brothers. Lord Clive now assumed his responsibilities in full as Governor of Madras, an area roughly the size of Great Britain. He had weathered the initial pitfalls related to his lack of experience in government affairs and had gained in self-confidence. Indeed, Lord Clive found that India afforded him the opportunity to develop his own capabilities.

Although chafing at her confinement, Henrietta continuously offered her advice and support to her husband. She described hers and her husband's relationship to her brother as being 'perfectly comfortable in our selves'. Yet there remained an undercurrent of sadness as she noted that in Madras 'our lives are so very dark and so really *triste*'. Exacerbated by her profound sense of 'the terrible distance from one another', in what she termed 'the first year of our banishment' she confided to her brother that 'I sit alone and think like this and I make myself quite uncomfortable'. A miniature painted on ivory during his Madras sojourn (1798–1803) depicted Lord Edward Clive as a sturdy middle-aged man with a pleasant face wearing a uniform associated with his job. He appears to be something of a late bloomer and at no time a character of such dynamic depth and radiance as Henrietta. He did not join Henrietta in her South India travels, but remained in Madras to take care of his duties there.

* * *

With a host of furious fancies
Whereof I am commander,
With a burning spear and a horse of air
To the wilderness I wander.

'Tom O'Bedlam', *Popular Ballads*, *c.*1620

In December 1799, shortly before her departure on her South India journey, ominous news of her brother's illness arrived with the East Indiaman, the *Eastern Magnificence.* In spite of this, however, Henrietta got off to a good start on March 4th 1800. She was an adaptive traveller who appeared to thrive on the unpredictability of India. To avoid the heat Henrietta's party was on its way each morning by four or four-thirty. Experiencing the before-sunrise freshness, the heat of midday and the after-sunset drop in temperature, she came to know the smells and tastes of India as never before. Depending on the terrain and the weather, she covered up to twenty-one miles a day. Most nights Henrietta camped in a tent; sometimes she stayed in an East India Company Collector's house or in a bungalow belonging to a military officer. She visited the forts made famous by Clive of India – Arcot, Vellore and Trichinopoly; she crossed the *ghauts* and the Guzelhutty Pass. On the road, Henrietta was an active participant: controlling her pet lion with a whip; driving her *bandy* over rough surfaces; being jostled in a *palanquin*; 'scrambling' to the top of a 'rock'; admiring the cattle of the *Rajah* of Tanjore; or lurching about on an elephant. Elephants were to figure prominently as she not only kept on the lookout for wild elephants in forests, but she had to contend with the deaths of several of her baggage-train elephants, whose rations had been purloined by their handlers. During her Bangalore stay Henrietta had followed avidly the Madras newspaper accounts of the Madras Lottery, whereby objects were raffled off to make funds for the native poor of Madras for such projects as hospitals and dispensaries. She wished, though seemingly without success, that she might get lucky and win.

Certainly Henrietta's wanderings in South India were diverse. At austere Ryacottah, she spent a month living up a mountain, dealing with monkeys and seven discontented sister goddesses. Later when Henrietta resided in Tipu's abandoned Bangalore palace, Colonel Wellesley and Lieutenant-Colonel Barry Close arranged for Tipu's *munshi* to become her Persian tutor. The *munshi* praised Henrietta's accomplishment and suggested that the translation of Hafiz would be a worthy project for 'an illustrious female oriental traveller'. Walking in Tipu's still-beautiful classical gardens, now grown wild and filled with fragrant white rose trees, listening to the sounds of birdsong and flowing water, Henrietta applied herself to her studies of Persian. While in Bangalore, she translated a number of Hafiz's ambiguous, multi-level lines that spoke to her of the inconstancy of fortune, of the transitory nature of the present moment.

Throughout her journey, Henrietta pursued not only languages and poetic philosophy, but also continued to acquire plants, animals, birds, butterflies, shells and rocks. Unhesitatingly she queried any and every degree-holding naturalist she found along her way with all the *chutzpah* of one naturalist to another. During this period of the expansion of naturalistic knowledge all over the world, naturalists were fairly numerous in India. At Cape Town on her voyage out Henrietta had met Dr William Roxburgh, superintendent of a botanical garden established by the East India Company at Sibpu, near Calcutta, who reinforced her interest. At Tranquebar she met Danish naturalists with whom she discussed their acquisitions. Dr Benjamin Heyne, the superintendent of the company's botanical garden in Madras, helped her to form 'a complete collection of the Mysore, as well of the plants of the Carnatic, already described by Dr Roxburgh and of any Birds, likewise, Stones or Minerals'. In another age Henrietta might have become a botanist as her interests were particularly keen as a collector of botanical specimens. Lord Clive shared her interests in botany and she sent plants and trees to him as she travelled.

In her letters and journal, Henrietta offered her readers a view of the ongoing drama of her life in India, enlivening her descriptions of place with her tales of 'tygerish jungles', alligator-infested rivers and nights spent in the dust and noise of Muslim and Hindu festivities. With perceptive and telling comments she depicted the variety of people she encountered: *Ranees*, Danish missionaries, Hindu priests, naturalists, *Maharajahs*, military officers and their wives, Pashas, East India Company Collectors, *polygars* and *fakeers*. Simultaneously she confronted a persistent undercurrent in her own bouts of sadness engendered by being, as she wrote to her brother, 'at such a frightful distance from one another'. She worried, too, when she did not hear from Lord Clive, writing, at one point when there had been a long period in which she did not have a letter from him, that she waited 'as much in vain I am afraid as for the rain. Perhaps both may come together'. In a letter to her husband she used the phrase, 'the unpleasantness of absence', a rather extraordinary understatement for her growing anxiety at his not having written during the last stages of her trek. On another occasion she scolded him by saying 'I know as little of Madras as Japan'. Missing him she wrote on October 3rd that 'I think when I see you again it will be one of my most happy days'. Much of her anxiety she invested in worrying about the health of her travelling party, and particularly of her girls.

Henrietta's journal ended at the seaside village of Allamparva on October 11th 1800. While still on the road, she penned one last letter to Lord Clive in which she confided alarm in the physical alteration of both daughters and expressed her concern that remaining any longer in India might permanently injure their health. Recalling Lord Robert Clive's epileptic seizures, she reminded her husband of 'fatal instances, weak nerves, and constitution' in the Clive family. Increasingly, she had become fearful about the state of her brother's health. In 1788 when she and Lord Clive had been travelling in Italy, Henrietta had yielded to a similar compelling need that she described as a 'most amazing' longing to see her brother, noting that, 'We have been a long time wanderers upon the face of the earth'. In the autumn of 1800, near the final stages of her South India trek, Henrietta abruptly decided that it was time for her and her daughters to turn towards home.

PRELUDE

'A Bird of Passage'

'Neither you nor myself believed it *prophetic* when you called me a *bird of passage** which I really am in preparing to take a very long flight,' Lady Henrietta Antonia Clive wrote on November 1st 1797 to her friend, Lady Frances Douglas in Scotland, announcing the East India Company's appointment of her husband as Governor of Madras. 'You will easily believe in what a fidget I have been these ten days when I tell you we are going to the *East Indies*.'

On December 20th 1797 Henrietta sent a progress report to Lady Douglas saying:

> My girls are not at all *averse* to going in a *ship* upon the sea with their Mother and she is not a little delighted that there does not seem a doubt that the climate is wholesome and cannot do them injury. On the contrary, it is said to be remarkably otherwise at their age. Signora Tonelli has consented to go and I have great pleasure in the idea of having her with them. She has sent me a miniature of them so very like that I wish I could show it to you just to look at for a moment that you may know what they are *like* as I think their dispositions are visible in their countenances . . . As myself, I look forward to all sorts of things – like the *Arabian Nights* – and put away every idea of all other places as much as possible.
>
> The behaviour of the Shropshire Regiment I must say is flattering to my *Welsh pride*. Several of the officers have desired to go and this

* A bird that migrates at the changes of season in spring and autumn; hence, anyone who roams about.

> morning a body of thirty or forty men came to desire to go with their Colonel . . . The band have decided the same and I am sure you will believe how sensibly we both feel it and that I really can hardly keep it in I am so much moved by their behaviour.

On January 27th 1798 once again she wrote to her friend saying,

> I have been on the point of answering your long and pleasant letter twenty times, but a pen and ink and I have not met so much as we ought to have done, except to assist in ordering apparel. I am exactly in the situation of Moussellina, *la serieuse*,* in great want of the same part of dress people in London will not comprehend [a thin cotton chemise] and I am in despair, not having had, like her, eleven thousand to try on. I am now in the very act of going to London and at Oakly Park taking leave of all there with a complete persuasion I shall see nothing so beautiful as my own oaks in the East.
>
> I have seen the Captain of my future Bodyguard (which title makes me laugh). He has told me all sorts of things and hints that it will not be thought dignified and proper for me to march upon my hind legs at Madras in mud, if I am lucky enough to find it, as I have been used to do in much better countries . . . I leave my boys in the care of my brother and the Bishop of Bristol, a very old friend of his and mine, who will exactly attend to everything about them with my brother's advice therefore as to health and education. I am at ease they will go to Eton, at least the eldest next summer . . . I have met with a learned man who has given me my alphabet in Persian. He says it is not difficult. How you will envy me if I can ever speak to a *Brahmin* in his own language.

With departure close at hand, Henrietta sent Lady Douglas a final message on March 2nd 1798 that touched on her anxiety at being so far from home and her brother.

* Count Anthony Hamilton's (1645–1719) *Tales*, which ridicule infatuation with the *Arabian Nights*, includes a story about Moussellina the Serious who is attacked by a monster crocodile, and removes her shift so that she can swim faster.

> We are told that on the 10th everything must be ready and the East India Company will rejoice when we are gone. But I trust the convoy will not be ready and that we may stay till the end of the month. One principal reason is that when I came to town I found my brother so unwell and so altered that it made me quite miserable. He is now infinitely better and thinks himself so, and I am especially easy about him; yet I should like to see him nearer to perfect health. I did not want this additional anxiety and it really made me uncomfortable. So many things *pulling*, each a different way. He is *alone* which he has not been for some years and I go to him every evening unless he happens to come here. Therefore I know little of the world except what I hear and see in a morning and indeed I do not much like going out as people are so civil sometimes and think it right to be sorry and to say things that I do not like by way of being civil.
>
> I hear I'm supposed to be delighted with the thoughts of going to the East, which is certainly not true. Yet, I have so made up my mind, and it will keep itself up I hope till I get into the ship when the hurry I am worked up to is over. I am afraid my spirits will not be very good joined to seasickness and confinement. I am afraid it will be necessary to fortify myself with all possible *philosophy*.

Officially England had been at war with France since November 27th 1797. But Henrietta did not dwell on this unpleasant reality, passing lightly over the troubled situation of the world, sharing instead a few bits of gossip with her friend:

> People seem to think the French will make some attempt, but they do not fear which is saying a great deal. They must attempt to satisfy their own people if it costs the lives of their whole army, but I believe there is not the least fear or danger in this country. And Ireland I hear, is in a better state than it has been and much subdued. The rafts, as they are described, are to be worked by pullies and will depend much more on the winds than common vulgar ships, by which happy invention the whole army may be carried into the Atlantic Ocean to feed the fishes. People say the Bonaparte is much

worse to the attempt and wishes much for peace but does not dare show it. Mrs Bonaparte goes to the theatre with a sort of *dame d'honneur* standing behind her and travels with much more state than even queens used to do. At Bologna she went to the opera with a picture of the Queen of Naples on her neck, which she had sent to Bonaparte. I think that was shabby don't you to bribe the chief of those executioners who has murdered her sister . . .

The ship is the *Dover Castle* and the Captain says if we set out by the end of this month, he will insure our being there in less than four months, which is comfortable though we are not to land anywhere. There is an end of the *hedges of Cape Jasmine* which I expected to see. The only chance of a blade of grass is at the Brasils . . . *

* Although the boat was due to sail round Africa, the trade winds which were used to travel meant that the *Dover Castle* would have neared South America before turning east to skirt Africa for India.

1798

Aboard the *Dover Castle*

'Going to the East.'

From the fair copy of Charly's journal made by W. H. Ramsey in 1857

On April 2nd 1798 Henrietta's journey East got underway when she, Lord Clive, their daughters Harry and Charly, along with the girls' governess, Italian artist Anna Tonelli, boarded an Indiaman, the *Dover Castle*, at Portsmouth. An Indiaman usually was outward bound in January or March and returned by June or July of the following year. As most East India Company ships, the *Dover Castle* weighed four hundred and ninety-nine tons, a weight deliberately chosen, as a vessel of five hundred tons and over was compelled to carry a chaplain. The Clives, who were not particularly religious, made do with Mr Thomas, their surgeon, who held church on deck and officiated as necessary.

Other passengers on board the *Dover Castle* included, Mrs Wodehouse, Major Grant, Captain Brown, Mr Thomas, Mr Cartwright (Secretary), Mr Richard Strachey, Messrs Smith, Keen and Malton (cadets), three ladies maids, five men-servants, two cows, four goats, Friskey, a terrier, the Ship's Officers – Captain Sampson, Mr Champion, Mr Rymer, Mr Cowls, Mr Trimmer and the Mates. Their fleet consisted of – the *Leopard*, Captain Surridge; a frigate, the *Good Hope*, Captain Hilton; the *Walpole*, Captain Butler; the *London*, Captain Looking; the *Princess Charlotte*, Captain Butler; the *Dover Castle*, Captain Sampson; the *Henrietta*, a Danish ship; and two little whalers.

In the ship's cramped space, the Clives stowed themselves and their gear as best they could. Henrietta had her own cabin carved out of the dining room. Lord Clive had the roundhouse to dress and sleep in. In the stern gallery, pots of geraniums hung before the windows. Lord Clive, Charly, Harry and Henrietta had most of the great cabin. The rest of it was for their maids.

Henrietta began, soon after departure from Portsmouth, to chronicle her voyage in letters. Indeed the sending, receiving and waiting for letters would be of great importance throughout the journey. Charly, too, wrote the occasional letter but she also depicted the fabric of their daily lives throughout their travels in a journal which she began on board the *Dover Castle*. Henrietta would later record her 1800 travels in South India in two small paper-backed, Indian notebooks (one multicoloured, the other a brick-red) which she acquired after her arrival in Madras.

April 2nd, Henrietta to her brother, George Herbert, 2nd Earl of Powis

At four o'clock in the evening we weighed anchor, set sail, and proceeded as far as Cowes, but afterwards laid to for fear of shoals.

Undated, Henrietta to George Herbert, 2nd Earl of Powis, continued

I have a great wish to see dry land again. The waves are so great and so various that I confess I do long for a little quietness. I shall finish this tomorrow when I hope to be better as I have not attempted to dine since I parted with my 'Dear Boys' and 'My Good Uncle' till yesterday. Your little box sits on the bed beside me and I assure you its motto is not necessary to remind me for I am not a little subject to *penses a vous.*

God bless and give you health my dearest brother and everything you wish is the wish of your sincerely affectionate

H. A .C.

Undated, Henrietta to George Herbert, 2nd Earl of Powis, continued

My dearest brother – We have taken the pianoforte out of its green cover and placed it between the doors opposite to the windows with the harp, which remains in its leather cover having not yet been uncrated. The girls will be able to practise most days and their other affairs will go on as usual. I am not yet able to work, but we read all together and are as comfortable as our circumstances will allow. The heat at present is very troublesome to us.

April 7th, Charly's journal

In the evening, as we were sailing very fast, a sailor, who was on the yardarm, unfortunately fell into the sea. We were sometime before we could stop the ship and as soon as he fell overboard he wished his friends farewell, and said he was sure he could not be saved; some of the sailors in the anxiety to save him jumped into the boat that was hanging at the stern, and instead of allowing the people above to lower them down, they cut the ropes, and fell headlong into the sea; the boat was consequently overturned and it was with difficulty they saved themselves by catching hold of the rudder. They came in at the windows of our cabin, and came through the round house to go upon the deck. We had some plants in the boat, and one of the sailors had taken a few of them, and put them in the stern-gallery and as he passed through the room, he pointed to them and looking at us said, 'It was I that saved these plants.' The Whalers took up the boat, and sent it to us the next morning. The first poor man was not to be found though the boat of another vessel was sent out likewise in search of him. You may imagine how unpleasant we felt that evening and the confusion in the ship during the time of the accident.

April 21st, Henrietta to her brother, George Herbert, 2nd Earl of Powis

My dearest brother – Yesterday we had a grand chase of another sort, which Lord Clive says is better even than a fox chase and bid me tell you so. A strange sail was seen. The *Walpole* pursued it and brought it in. The people have every appearance of being pirateers. They had sixteen guns and only four visible with musquetry and blunderbusses *charged* so highly that the Captain said they would not venture to fire them off. They have besides other merchandise, twenty chests of sabres. You may suppose this was a great *Event*. The men, two of them, were brought here in the morning and ten more in the evening. I must say their countenances are not the most favourable to them. I never saw such a set of Banditi like visages.

We continue to be well satisfied with our Captain, but I do not know how I shall have the joy of finding myself near land. I am so entirely tired of my situation from never feeling quite well.

May 7th, Henrietta to her brother, George Herbert, 2nd Earl of Powis

My dearest brother – I shall conclude the history of our prize by telling you that Mr Petrie translated the list of things. He believed they had *sabres*, but from the little Spanish I know, I discovered that they were chests of *nails*, so they were released and with great joy proceeded on their voyage. Some of the sailors from the *Walpole* that was sent to remain in the ships pillaged it extremely. There is something in the name of Walpole, I think, but it was all returned and the principal offender punished on the spot. The chief mate, who was here and whose picture Anna Tonelli has painted, was satisfied with his treatment.

Charly's journal entry about the ship that was 'almost a prize' added the final details: 'The sailors were so happy at having had their liberty restored; that they did not wait for ropes to help them up the ship's side, but climbed up as they could. In the morning Papa bought a cask of wine and Captain Sampson sent one of the sailors with a guinea to buy anything from them. The chief mate sent a roll of ribbons as a present to Captain Sampson and would not receive the guinea. Captain Sampson gave the ribbon to be divided between my sister, Harry and me. We wore it last Sunday. They were out of sight on the 23rd.'

May 7th, Henrietta to her brother, George Herbert, continued

We have suffered a good deal from heat lately. The cabins are close in spite of all the doors, windows, and portholes being open, but we are all well and no sickness in the whole ship.

I am much better lately. I believe from a hope of landing at Rio Janeiro. It seems we have a small leak which, though of little consequence, it is not thought safe to pass the Cape in that state. The Captains are to meet this morning, if the Wind will allow them to come on board. Captain Sampson is in hopes they will go on and leave us to go into Rio Janeiro and they will go straight on. They sail much slower than we do and are a great hindrance to us as we are obliged to take down sails and wait once or twice in the twenty-four hours with the fast winds. Lord Clive has a great longing to go into the Cape which will I hope not be done. We have orders not to stop anywhere unless for absolute necessity. All that can be wanted we may get at Rio much better than at the Cape. As to provisions though, in reality, Captain Sampson told me last night he had water and provisions for sixteen weeks more.

I am quite delighted with the thoughts of landing anywhere and particularly in such a beautiful place as Brazil. I hope, too, we shall meet with some ships going to Europe that you may know we are alive. We are now busy in finding out what plants or animals we can get there, which is something to do. Lord Clive is quite well except now and then a bilious day or two. I believe much from not having exercise except in boxes in the boat. The girls are quite well and as anxious as myself for land. I hope it will be decided today.

May 8th, Henrietta to the Dowager Lady Clive

My dear Lady Clive – No vessel has appeared consequently no letters are gone. We have had a most prosperous voyage with only a few squalls and are all in good health. I am much improved lately and can now work and read. We are all a good deal tired of our confinement and are most anxiously wishing for a little dry land.

When there is a calm evening Richard Strachey insists on dancing upon deck. Our band comes forth and the girls dance with our damsels and gentlemen dancing together make seven or eight couples. It is exercise for them and amuses them much.

We have lately seen some albatross and pintada birds, which are a great delight as they are seen as objects not a little scarce. At one time we had some sharks taken and I *fished* for dolphins, but I must say without success. I cannot help thinking of England with much anxiety and wishing most ardently for letters from you and everybody else there. I do not know when we shall have the sight of a letter.

May 30th, Henrietta to the Dowager Lady Clive

My dear Lady Clive – We have had uncertain weather: sometimes going quick with hardly any motion; sometimes calm and yesterday a great deal of wind. Today it is better. Yesterday evening we had an eclipse of the moon. We were sitting after dinner and Captain Sampson did not know it was to be till he went out. He came directly to tell us and we went upon deck. It began at six o'clock we were to learn. When we saw the moon it was more than half hid and was not entirely clear again till seven minutes before eight. We looked at it through telescopes. We wished much for Grandmama who would have explained all about it to us. I do not think I ever saw one so complete before. By Captain Sampson's observation the timekeepers are within a minute or two right.

We are now within two hundred miles of the Cape and it is not quite certain if we shall land. We are preparing letters. The girls are preparing theirs for Grandmama. You will excuse them if they are not just like Madame Anna because I let them write them without letting letters be made for them, which I hope you approve. I hope to hear news from the Cape or something to tell you. Therefore I will not waste my paper with the vacancy of sea news. I am almost ashamed to send you such a sheet of *nothing*.

June 1st, Henrietta to her brother, George Herbert, 2nd Earl of Powis

My Dearest Brother – It is all settled that we go into the Cape if the wind and weather will permit as the reasons are the leaks which may increase and we have only eight weeks water which they say is the least we ought to have. It is a very rough day and I cannot write.

June 2nd, Henrietta to her brother, George Herbert, 2nd Earl of Powis

The *Good Hope*, after refusing to go in to the Cape, and detaining us in consultations without, has determined to go in as we are within seventy miles with a great swell but a gentle favourable breeze, which this vile ship will make us lose. I hope to be there either tomorrow or to land on Monday morning.

Just after I had finished the above, a report was spread of land being seen. We put out our eyes all day and evening without being quite convinced. Before daybreak Captain Sampson came and told us it was quite visible. I never saw anything so beautiful. It was quite clear and the outline perfect. In a short time the sun was just beyond Table Mountain in the most majestic manner I ever saw in my life and I was even more pleased from our having been detained the 2nd time by the Ship *Good Hope*. We lost time and the wind changed. Since yesterday morning we have been tacking aft and are all in hopes of being at anchor sometime before night. Imagine how we have watched since yesterday morning. Tomorrow I hope to say that we are on dry land once more . . . The night was perfect but this morning we are just where we were yesterday at the same time in distance but in a better situation. I hope to land tomorrow morning.

June 4th, Henrietta to her brother, George Herbert, 2nd Earl of Powis

We lost sight of the ships in the morning, but we saw them again in the evening. We tacked twice for fear of breakers. We had a beautiful moonlight night to enter False Bay.

The Cape of Good Hope, South Africa

'A country beautiful and very wild.'

June 7th, Henrietta to Lady Douglas

My dear Lady Douglas – I must just say a word that you who are so good on my behalf may know that I am in the land of the living and in Africa. We have had a voyage without the smallest storm or even a gale of wind, which I am told, is quite a marvellous thing and the weather so fine that if I did not hate a ship it really might be called pleasant. The greatest inconveniences were calms and on the line when we were really worried as there were small leaks (which does not sound well) in several parts of the ship. It was thought right to come here, particularly as we might meet with some French vessels from the Isle de France. It was proper to enquire about them that my history might not be improved by being taken prisoner and my valour, I confess, would not have been great upon such occasion. I have thought with some little horror of a retreat into the hold when I heard of a strange sail being in sight.

I have been in Africa ten days. It seems like a dream. We came in on the finest of days I ever saw. Sir Hugh Christian* sent his boys and once again I landed on a sand bank. Think of my extreme delight and ecstasy in finding many of the most beautiful plants which are poor creatures in England in our hot houses and which are now, perhaps blooming behind the bench in the green house at Bothwell, all under my feet. My girls and myself were like fools. In short I am sure that nothing is like Africa.

There are not any inns, therefore we live with some very good people in a large house and I ramble about all day hunting for plants. There happens to be a most learned botanist from Bengal who is such a boor that it is more than I can bear. He will collect for me and I think I shall be able to send plants in from all parts of the world. Would you believe that there is not a

* Admiral of the Cape Station

soul that collects or will collect such plants, roots or seeds. They seem to think of more substantial ways of getting money. This disappointed me as I had a great mind to send you something from the land of the Hottentots.

We had an order last night to be at Simmons Bay, twenty miles from hence as soon as possible. Lord Clive is gone. I am in the midst of plants and black slaves, but I would not omit telling you something about myself and my infants. They suffered very little from the sea. I was a wretch for five weeks and am a little afraid I shall have it to begin again. I set out tomorrow morning at daybreak and shall travel this country covered with the most beautiful flowers and heath, not such a thing as an *oak* or a beech to be seen, all with flowers and yet they say there are *more*, as it is winter. In six weeks I hope to be in Madras. I cannot help thinking a great deal of England and Scotland. Perhaps my brother may be there now.

Adieu, my dear Lady Douglas.
Pray let me hear from you . . .
Ever yours, affectionately,
H. A. C.

June 17th, Henrietta to her brother, George Herbert, 2nd Earl of Powis

My dearest brother – We have been here since the 7th and it is quite fairyland. I rejoice much that we are here, but it is too pleasant to last. We are ordered to go tomorrow. Lord Macartney has been very civil to us and talked much of you to me, which did not *displease* me. We are to have a convoy or rather if the truth is known, which is now a *secret*, that we are to go with a small *fleet* going to take the Isle de France. It seems the greater part of the people wishes to have the English in possession of the Island and this secret expedition is to go with us.

There has been much mutiny about. From Admiral Sir Hugh Christian we learned that the *Princess Charlotte*'s crew had mutinied just after we parted company. In the fleet of three ships each had on board one of Parker's delegates,* who had been pardoned after the Mutiny of the *Nore*. In each vessel the delegates tried to persuade their shipmates to mutiny. In the *Dover Castle*, the plot was soon made known and Peter

* Mutineers, whose eight articles included the right to dismiss the ship's officers

Allen had been immediately examined by the officers and Lord Clive and found guilty. He was kept in chains on the poop until the fleet arrived at the Cape and then made over to the King's ships. He had been flogged more than once before we left the port. The *Prince William* was equally fortunate in discovering its delinquent, but the *Princess Charlotte*, had a regular outbreak. One day when the officer and passengers were at dinner, the mutiny broke out. Happily they were able in some measure to subdue it, but were obliged to be much on their guard, and gave out false observations that the sailors might not find out they were going into the Cape. The plan of the mutineers was to take possession of the ship, murder the captain and some of the officers, and take the ship into the Mauritius and sell her to the French. It was discovered, but the Captain did not pretend to know it and brought the ship into Cape Town. Three are tried today. Since the *Good Hope* came in with us there was a mutiny on board and the Captain put up the signal. The boats from the Admiralty came just as the *dragoon* in the ship were going to fire on the sailors. In the *Walpole*, there was something, too. In short, I am persuaded there are ill disposed people spread in all the ships.

This place is beautiful with all sorts of the most beautiful flowers growing wild though it is winter. I believe in summer it would be too charming. We find everybody civil and I am going with a great quantity of plants . . . Lord Clive desires many things to you, as each of your nieces, who are fat and sleek. All our household desire many respects to you. I think I shall hear from you when I get to Madras for really when I think of it, it is terrible to me not to know something of you and my boys.

God bless you my dearest Brother.
May you be as well and as happy as I wish you to be.
Ever your most sincerely and affectionately
H. A. C.

June 23rd, False Bay, Henrietta to George Herbert, 2nd Earl of Powis

My dearest brother – as we have been detained here since Monday by contrary winds I write a few words while our effects are taken on board. Admiral Christian has lent us his home where we have been since

Tuesday. The wind is fair and the signal made; therefore we expect to sail in the course of the day. This colony is very flourishing. The number of whites are 20,000 and of all others 40,000.

We have found delightful plants and have scrambled till I can scarcely move, but we are all well and I believe quite as comfortable in a thatched house with two rooms and a barrack as we shall be at Madras. Four days ago the *Britannia* came in here, having suffered much from weather. The ship had lost her foremast by lightning and one of her quarter galleys . . . We were fortunate in being in harbour on that day, 16th June. The storm extended to a great distance and we should have been exposed to its greatest force.

Sir Hugh Christian gives us a convoy to man the Line. We are going along with four King's ships whose object is to destroy everything French on that coast. This you are not to mention till you hear it otherwise, it being a private communication from the Admiral to Lord Clive and as a marked favour to him. He sends the *Brave*, a 40 gun ship, considerably to the North East of Madagascar with us.

The Captain of the *Indiaman* just arrived from Ceylon brings unpleasant intelligence regarding Madras. General Harris, delirious from a fever, is incapable of holding the government. A want of money exists, not from real scarcity but on account of the state of Europe, which staggers the money holders in Madras, but as this came from the Captain of a ship, Lord Clive says he hopes to find it exaggerated.

You will hear how far the spirit of insubordination has shown itself on the coast. Admiral Rainier* had sent eighteen men to be tried for mutiny, and three artillerymen, long in a disorderly state, have been blown from the mouths of cannon. All this information I have taken from Lord Clive's knowledge so it is true.

God bless you.
H. A. C.

* East India Station Command from 1793–1804

On June 25th 1798 the travellers boarded a seaworthy *Dover Castle*, joined a convoy – the *Stately*, the *Brave*, the *Garland* and the *Starbrig* – and departed the Cape of Good Hope. For several days until July 5th the ships battled gales. On the *Dover Castle* the main yard broke and a small one was put in its place. Henrietta's brother's birthday was celebrated and all the ship's company had grog. A shark was caught: five minutes after its head was cut off it bit a piece off a sailor's finger. The *Garland* chased an American frigate, boarded her and ordered her to keep in sight, but she escaped in the night. From her crew they learned that a ship had left Mauritius with a regiment on board. They saw some boobies.* Tiresome calms set in followed by 'squally thunder, lightning and rain'. On August 16th a strange sail hove into sight and they prepared for action. It turned out to be the *Victorious* 74 guns. Three officers came on board to press twenty of the crew for the King's service, but seeing Lord Clive, the Governor of Madras, on board refrained from doing so. On August 18th four strange sails appeared to be chasing the *Dover Castle*, but by the 19th they had lost sight of them. On August 21st at a little past 5 o'clock in the morning, land about Madras was visible. A strange sail was observed about the same time. At noon there was calm, but at 2 o'clock it was possible to make the anchorage.

* Booby gannet, a large tropical sea bird with eyes near the base of the bill

Fort St George, Madras, India

'Distracted with expectation and disappointment and joy.'

And finally they were anchored in the roads off Madras. Charly verbally sketched the highlights: 'Some lascars scrambled into the ship through the port-holes. Dobashes dressed in fine muslin dresses brought fruit on board; other blacks were nearly naked. We ladies were to go on shore first and therefore embarked in a *Masoollah* boat; the boat-men sung the whole way through the surf, which was really nothing. The sea came in a little at the sides of the boat. It wet me a little, but I did not mind it at all.'

August 21st, Henrietta to her brother, George Herbert, 2nd Earl of Powis

My dearest brother – About 5 o'clock in the afternoon, boats came directly to take us on shore and I confess I was not much delighted with their appearance, or with the thoughts of the formidable surf; but we were lucky to a great degree. There had not been known a day so calm for a long time and we did not suffer in the least. I left the ship a little before Lord Clive that I might see him come in and go through all the necessary ceremonies. I landed with the girls and went, in a *palanquin* to the East room on the top of the Admiralty house, to see him go to the council room and from thence to a veranda in the square, to hear the commission read, which was done within a square of *sepoys*, who fired three simultaneous volleys afterwards.

The concourse of people was immense and the strange variety of dress very amusing. The girls couldn't be persuaded that the people dressed in *long* muslin *dresses* were not women, though some had *long grey beards.* General Harris, who has had the command of everything until Lord Clive's arrival, came with Lord Clive to General Sydenham's veranda where we were sitting.

Afterwards Henrietta and the girls went with General Harris to the Garden

House where the Clives were to live. Everything pleased Henrietta. Charly pronounced 'both house and garden, beautiful. We took a delightful walk before and after supper, and were very tired.' Everybody's baggage had arrived except for Henrietta's, Charly's and Harry's which did not appear until the next day around 10 o'clock along with Friskey, the terrier.

General Harris breakfasted with the Clives. The *Nawab* sent a present of oranges to Henrietta and of figs to Charly and Harry. The girls took a walk after dinner near the seaside, and met a sand snake that was killed, brought home, and preserved in vinegar.

On August 23rd Lord Clive and Charly visited the *Nawab*, who put a string of flowers round his [Lord Clive's] neck, and perfume on his pocket handkerchief and told him that Lord Mornington had made him sick, but that he, Lord Clive, was his doctor. The *Nawab* enquired after Henrietta and said that as soon as his health permitted, he would call upon her. As they were in the verandah a cassowary paid them a visit, which pleased Charly.

August 24th, Henrietta to Lady Clive

My dear Lady Clive – the country and the appearance of the people are so different from anything we have ever seen, that it is amusing. We got up at 5 o'clock in the morning to take a walk. The house is very pleasant, but there is little room. I cannot say we admire the *fruits*. I am told it is a bad time of the year. It may be so; but certainly there is not anything so good as a peach, or a strawberry. I wrote to you a few days ago by a ship that was to sail from Tranquebar* . . .

August 24th, Henrietta to Lady Douglas

My dear Lady Douglas – I sat in form last Tuesday, Wednesday, and Thursday to receive the ladies and gentlemen, which were pretty numerous. I am terribly inclined to believe the fair sexes in this country are not too agreeable. Many women have come out to Madras to marry. If I dared, I would tell what my Ladies and Gentlemen are like. It will be

* Tranquebar, a Danish settlement along with Pondicherry which had been French, was a reminder of the European presences located along the Coromandel Coast.

difficult and I hope my evil genius is not now looking over me and going to publish my observations on them. I really think I never saw so many females that had quite forgot what beauty *might* be. I have no idea of so many peoples assembled without one that would be thought tolerable in London. I sat perched upon a chair at the end of a large room during three hours for three successive nights – when they all came and curtsied – till every bone ached. I have given two assemblies that, if you could have seen, would have made you laugh. I looked, I hope, sufficiently *civil.* As for society it seems quite out of the question even amongst themselves and really except three or four that I have met with don't much wish to be admitted to enjoy it. There are just a few with good manners and sensible, but for the greatest part are as much otherwise as any body can invent. As you see, I am none too happy with the level of entertainment in Madras, equating Madras society with that of Ludlow in Shropshire.

In a day or two I shall start to return my visits, which will be a troublesome ceremony from their houses being so dispersed.

There is a *town* or rather the *capital* near my gate that leads to the *Nawab*'s palace where the murmur and noise is beyond all belief. The *city* is rather *irregularly* built all composed of huts made of cocoanut leaves and the inhabitants are more irregular than their houses, which I understand, are not of the first fame and that it is a compound of all the worst of both sexes. The people have fêtes and all sorts of ceremonies. A marriage keeps us awake for a week. All their amusements are during the night.

I live on a dead flat, which is not proper for one's imagination. I have no thick covert and woods but a cocoanut tope with straggling trees and not even a ditch in my garden. I am building a room in the garden and a *laboratory* for all sorts of odd rocks and works and shall endeavour to fancy myself in England. I mean to learn Persian in the Moorish language. I must do something to make me understand and be understood. Besides I hope that, as I must do *something*, I shall grow *prosperous* and hold forth in all the eloquence of the East and in that style I may pour forth my soul at your feet when I return. I cannot help already thinking what I shall do when *I go back again.*

Henrietta did not condone being idle, but believed in staying occupied. By August 25th the settling-in had taken place. Charly observed in her journal that the harps were 'all quite safe, but Mamma's, which was a little the worse'. Henrietta and the girls began to investigate their surroundings and drove out to see the Mount Road, one of their perimeters. Inside Fort St George they visited St Mary's Church, a personal landmark for them as Lord Robert Clive and Margaret Maskelyn had married there in 1753. They began to acclimatise to the temperature which was, they all agreed, 'extremely hot'. Henrietta occupied her days in receiving visits from the ladies of the settlement and the girls took rides in the morning with Captain Brown. Mr Petrie was obliged to leave his house on account of snakes: a cobra was found in his house and another pursuing the gardener about the garden. Anna Tonelli painted watercolour sketches of local scenes; one was of their Madras neighbourhood.

Entertainment was scarce and included the seasonal arrival of ships. On September 3rd, Henrietta used her fortieth birthday to return visits of the ladies who called on her. The visits were paid in the evening on account of the heat. Ten or more boys ran before the carriage, each carrying a lantern. Jugglers and snake charmers arrived to entertain them. The *Nawab* called, accompanied by his son and his nephew in a beautiful *palanquin* ornamented with gold and with glass doors, preceded by a conveyance in the shape of a peacock. His attendants were numerous and there were elephants, horses and camels in his procession. His dress was made of a shawl; he wore an enamelled dagger, a present from the King of England. His son and nephew wore muslin dresses, trimmed with gold. On September 8th the family breakfasted with Admiral Rainier, Captain Brown and Captain Grant. Charly rode for her first time upon an elephant.

September 8th, Henrietta to George Herbert, 2nd Earl of Powis

My dearest brother – There is a packet going overland, but it is reckoned an uncertain conveyance at present; therefore I shall not tell you all my news as in all probability this letter may never reach you. We are all well.

Lord Clive bears his business, though it is continual, without suffering much from it. At first I was afraid for him but it is now gone off and I am persuaded he will be able to go through with it with as much care as can be expected. The girls are quite well neither losing health nor spirits. I have a long letter preparing for you which I should be sorry it was lost therefore shall keep it till an English fleet sails and in all probability the *Dover Castle* may give you the first notice of our arrival here, though I wrote by a Danish ship and am now writing again. We are in the greatest anxiety about English news and everyday in hopes of the signal of an East Indiaman.

September 24th, Henrietta to George Herbert, 2nd Earl of Powis

My dearest brother – I have already written a very long letter to you which will go by the common post but this is so much *between us* that I thought it better it should be separate and I shall contrive it shall go with the dispatches and be thrown overboard in case anything happens. I particularly wish that you should know all that has happened since we came here as to *politics* and *state affairs.*

You know that Mr Petrie came in the same fleet with us and that Lord Clive knew little of him before we set out. He professed a wish only to come if Lord C had nobody he preferred and that it was *quite agreeable* to him. Lady Campbell gave *me* the *message* from him to Lord Clive. She said, I am pretty sure, and have heard the same since, that whenever he has a seat in council, which is to be on a vacancy, that he was determined never to oppose Lord Clive in Council. Let him do as he would and that if he differed in opinion with him he would be silent and wished to be considered as his *decided* friend. I recollect Strachey wrote to Walcot* saying he was sorry to say that Petrie was moving heaven and earth to come. He afterwards said little about him. Petrie came to us occasionally on the voyage. The first thing that struck me was about our going into Rio de Janeiro on which he gave a decided opinion without waiting to hear Lord Clive's against *our going in*. On Lord Clive's going out of the cabin

* Clive family estate

he asked me what we thought of it and to my great surprise on his return gave directly the *opposite* opinion. I thought no more of it at the time. He was a good deal with us at the Cape and was pleasant, but I thought sometimes *too civil.*

When we came here, Petrie met us, as all the principal people did in the ship (as he had come in a week before us). For the next two days he never left Lord Clive *a moment* from morning to night. It surprised me that none of those that came on the ship came here again, though he had visited all day long. Lord Clive was worried with the business and a little heated. Neither of us could sleep well as there was to be a council on the Thursday morning. Mr Petrie said to me at breakfast that Lord Clive must take care and not make himself ill, that he must put off the council.

I confess I did not see that Lord Clive was unwell enough for that. Soon afterwards Petrie sent up Mr Thomas to tell me that he desired I would by all possible means prevail on him not to have a council. This appeared extraordinary to me. I went down to Captain Grant and Brown and told them the message I had had. Grant said he must have a council. It never was otherwise. There never was ever an instance of a Governor not having one the second day after his arrival. No orders can be given but in Council. He said he understood Mr Petrie came for it and with considerable warmth told me that it was his object to appear to govern Lord Clive or be entirely in his confidence for his own views and that it was so much thought to be so from his having been here constantly that General Sydenham, General Harris, Mr Webbe* who are most respectable people and, in short, the chiefs of each department were determined not to act with Petrie and that Lord Clive appeared so much in his hands they could not come to him.

I desired Grant to tell Lord Clive directly. He said he had examples that indicated Lord Clive had talked a great deal to Petrie in the ship, yet it might be though impertinent and that he meant to govern him, but that I might say what I pleased to Lord Clive and make what ever I chose

* Josiah Webbe, Secretary of the Madras Council and one of Lord Mornington's bright young men.

of his name. It was an awkward thing for me to interfere in politics or business and I was afraid Lord Clive would not take it right of me.

Brown who had left us in the beginning of this conversation came to me soon and told me that he had heard the same thing. I told him I thought it his duty to tell Lord Clive directly which he did and referred Lord Clive to me for farther explanation which I gave him. He was much surprised and said he thought Petrie stood very high here. It made so much noise that Ashton, who was ill, came out of bed to tell me of it and that Lord Clive was undone if he did not shake off Petrie who is a very distrusted man and had bills protested and returned from this country last winter and added to that it is known by papers, beyond all doubt, and which I believe came into or through Ashton's hand, and at Tanjore, that in Lord A: Campbell's time he and Montgomery Campbell, and I am afraid Lady Campbell herself, received very large sums of money which Lord A Campbell never knew till just before he left this country and that Petrie was a person to sell or betray any person for his own interest. Besides that he is intimately connected with people in very bad repute: Roebuck and Abbott Merchants here. All this distressed me extremely.

Lord Clive immediately spoke to Grant, who most fully and properly told him everything and indeed has conducted himself most honourable to Lord Clive. He was recommended very strongly by Lord Cornwallis and Lord C: Oakly and really I believe most deservedly. Lord Cornwallis told Grant that if Lord Clive fell into Petrie's hands it would be *ruinous.* The moment Lord Clive had had this conversation, for Petrie had prevailed about the council being put off till the Friday next, he desired to see all the heads of the departments. I had the pleasure to know that while they were closeted with Lord Clive, Petrie was waiting below. Lord Clive still sees him a good deal but not as he did. He endeavours to make it appear he is a good deal here by coming at times when people are coming to dinner and going away without showing himself which as he is the only person going about in a chaise makes him remarkable and sometimes he stays 2 or 3 hours.

I hope and believe Lord Clive sees Petrie's self-interested motives and that all will go on well. As stories are so very much exaggerated from hence I thought it right you should know the exact truth. Petrie appears to me too civil with a degree of *servility* that I confess struck me before I knew any of these stories. Many of the principal people will scarcely speak to him.

Lord Mornington [at Calcutta] torments Lord Clive a good deal. He is precipitate and rash and wishes to do too much at once. The treasury is *empty* and in debt and there are great fears that Lord Mornington will get into a war with Tipu without men or money. The offensive army here, when Ceylon is deducted, consists of but 2,000 men.

Lord Clive seems now getting the better of his first fatigue, my friends Grant and Brown tell me, with great satisfaction to everybody here. They tell me news, which I tell Lord Clive which he likes and I must say that he has said *many civil things* to me on my being, as he says a great comfort to him so much so that notwithstanding all I have *felt in body* and *mind* on coming here, I am glad I have done it and I really do believe I have been of some use to him relieving his mind by occasionally talking of less interesting or more pleasant things.

Our expenses here will probably be much less than the income. We have no servants but those paid by the Company, except for my *palanquin* and the carriages. Horses are extravagantly dear. A saddle horse for Lord Clive costs *150 guineas*. He has four of them for him and Captain Brown. He had been obliged to subscribe pounds 3,000 to the voluntary subscription and as he has not received any money from England has been obliged to borrow. All except the military are paid in paper at the loss of seven percent. My other letters are full of common news but this is only for your own eye and I do not wish Probert nor anybody to know of it.

September 27th, Henrietta to George Herbert, continued

All is going on as well as possible. The report of Petrie's influence has travelled all over the country, but it is wearing out here. Lord Clive asked me yesterday what I had heard about it and I was glad to give him good news. I forgot to tell you that Lord Mornington has *quarrelled* with his council and has consulted lawyers if he could not dismiss them. They decided he could not. You may guess the confusion that must occasion. His brother Colonel Wellesley is here with the 33rd Regiment. He came ten days ago. Lord Clive sees him often and I believe he knows a good deal of Lord Mornington's mind on peace or war. Colonel Wellesley told me that Lord Mornington is so miserable without Lady Mornington and their children that the name of Europe is sufficient to make him quite wretched. This does not look as if he would stay long.

October 1st, Henrietta to George Herbert, continued

The *Thetis* came in about 4 o'clock, but the letters are not yet delivered out. The *Osterley* is come, too; therefore we shall have all the news we are to expect for an age. The *Thetis* has been nearly lost from a leak, which was sudden and so bad that sailors, soldiers and passengers were constantly employed in passing and lading out the water with buckets. The lady passengers were sent to the *Osterley* as they expected not to be able to save the ship. What a dreadful idea. Though our leak on the *Dover Castle* was not of such consequence, how right it was to go into the Cape and service ourselves from all risk.

October 2nd, Henrietta to George Herbert, 2nd Earl of Powis

My dearest Brother – I have had a great heap of letters most of them mentioning you and that you were quite well, which gives me the greatest satisfaction. Your letter to Lord Clive about the Regiment is not yet arrived. We are in hopes it is with another Fleet that sailed 14th May and is not yet come in.

October 3rd, Henrietta to George Herbert, 2nd Earl of Powis

My dearest Brother – the letters are all come, I take it for granted now, as they have been dropping in all day yesterday. And this morning came George Strachey, who had seen you two days before he left England. There is something very charming in finding one that had actually seen you well. Everybody agrees in your perfect health which is a great blessing for me and those that know it say that though you have a great deal of business on your hands you do it with *wonderful dispatch.*

October 6th, Henrietta to Lady Douglas

My dear Lady Douglas – I have been so nearly distracted with expectation, disappointment and joy that I am not quite certain I am now really and truly *compos mentis*. I have seen his *Highness* the *Nawab*, who is a hideous little old man much more like an old woman. He disappointed me by not bringing in with him any of his *grandees*. They waited in the sun while he made his visit. He had neither pearls as large as pigeons' eggs nor diamonds, but an old shawl, *bed gown*, and an enameled dagger, that was anything *but handsome*, a present from our most gracious sovereign. In short people may talk of the magnificence of the East, but it is certainly not to be met with here with this ruler. The *Nawab* goes about in a shabby coach when he goes for an airing with the worst looking guards in white calico. In short there is nothing like Haroun Alraschid or the Viccer Giafor* to my great disappointment.

I wish much to see his wives. He says he had *seventy-four daughters* born in *one year* and that was last year, which *I doubt*. He asked Lord Clive how many wives he had and told me he hoped I should have some *Madras children*. He made some confusion by way of saying how he should like them, which sounded as if he intended they should be *his own*. It was such a strange visit, as you cannot imagine. Part was said in English and part was to be translated and as it is usual in translations I believe there was great discrepancy from what he said by the faces of most that understood or interpreted who were English. He admired my girls and asked if they were married! He thought them quite old enough at 11 and 13 for marriage in this country.

It's like being *Queen of stark naked black people* amongst whom I walk about as unconcerned as if they were dressed like human creatures. They

* Harun ar-Rashid, the caliph of Baghdad and his vizier, Jaffar, who accompanied the caliph (disguised as a merchant) in his nightly wanderings about the streets of Baghdad are recurrent figures in the *Arabian Nights*. Quite possibly Henrietta read the original French translation of Antoine Galland which appeared in 1704 and 1717 (based on an earlier collection of Indian-Persian fairy-tales entitled *Hazar Afsanah*, '*A Thousand Tales*').

really are so near *stark* that it is wonderful seeing how well *we look* in clothes. They do not imitate us.

I have been established since the first three days and comfortably though the house is like a cage. It is impossible to be invisible a moment without going round and shutting fifty Venetian blinds in every direction, there being neither glass in the windows or doors. All is perfectly open which annoyed me terribly at first. At every moment the first night I saw a black face and a turban through the blinds. It was sometime before I could express that I did not want such *faithful* attendants. I am now left more at my ease and only find six or seven upon every staircase. Women with parasols appear the moment I go outdoors that no entreaty can get rid of them despite all my acts and ingenuities. I have tried everything but getting out of a window to escape. They certainly are the most attentive servants I ever met with and I am growing to like them extremely.

October 8th, Henrietta to George Herbert, 2nd Earl of Powis

My dearest brother – last night Lord Clive had a letter from Lord Mornington who says he is going to send for *Lady Mornington** and *his children*. I trust we shall not *outstay him.*

Upon the most exact calculation we shall not exceed £3,000, taking in everything of establishment except salaries, governesses, and secretaries. The calculation is about £200 a month without wine which is uncertain. This takes in all but the European servants who I hope to get rid of. Butler is of scarcely any use. Indeed none. He was at first troublesome and expecting to be *maitre d'hôtel* and pay everything. He has been ill since and I believe wishes to return . . . The rest go on well and the old coachman braves all weathers.

I am really quite ashamed to send such packets but what can I do? It is such a relief and a comfort to tell you everything and to *seem* to talk to you that I cannot help it and I wish you to know how we go on.

* Lady Mornington (née Hyacinthe-Gabrielle Roland), an actress at the Palais Royal, had three sons and two daughters by Mornington before they were married in 1794. She was shunned by high society. In a fine portrait by Élisabeth Vigée-Lebrun in 1791, Hyacinthe is stunningly beautiful.

Richard Strachey is going to Bengal. He came to me the other day full of surprise at the things he had heard amongst people and young men here of Petrie. He says that they say he *will do anything for money.* He says he knows his father was very sorry when first he was talked of as coming out here but said no more latterly. I believe Strachey senior always thinks that it is right to be civil to those who may *have* power. Richard Strachey says that people express great horror at Petrie's ever succeeding to the government. God Bless you, my dearest Brother.

October 11th, Henrietta to George Herbert, 2nd Earl of Powis

My dearest brother – A packet came last night overland with letters of great importance. Lord Clive says that Bonaparte has succeeded in Egypt. I am very sorry and am afraid he will come here, as well as Tipu. It is very unlucky if there is a War on all accounts. This packet left London the 19th June. Strachey is gone to Bengal to his brothers and it is doubtful when he returns. Lord Clive has written a very handsome and kind letter in his favour to Lord Mornington. I shall be glad when the dispatches are ended and these letters gone. Lord Clive has a great deal to do and to think of and it will be a great relief to his mind.

October 14th, Henrietta to George Herbert, continued

Tomorrow the dispatches are to be sealed up so there will be an end of writing for sometime to come. We are all well except Harry who has had continually, almost ever since we came here, a disorder in her bowels and a disposition to being nervous and hysterical which is unpleasant to me, but I have not mentioned it in any of my other letters. I cannot help being afraid that the violent perspiration night and day will weaken us all and not agree with her. The cool weather is coming on, but I must say I am afraid it will not do. I have not said so to Lord Clive because it is a great pleasure to him having them and we must try every thing as he would not like to part with either them or myself and yet I cannot help being a little afraid. Thomas says if we will rely upon him he will do all he can and thinks all will be well, but she is too young to be nervous like me. I shall write by every opportunity. If Egypt is really taken, there is an end of the overland dispatches.

I have had a very unpleasant affair happen to my maid who has been in a most abominable and cruel manner seduced by an officer in the ship. The story is so bad against him that Lord Clive has taken it up and, he will, I hope, be made to provide for her as she is unfortunately in a way to produce. Lord Clive has behaved in the kindest manner to her and me upon the subject and her behaviour is so proper that when she is visible again she is to be established in some business here and we have got her a proper place where she will be concealed for some months. This has hurt me much and is a great inconvenience to me besides. She has been with us several years and is sister to one of your Damsels at Powis Castle and really a most excellent person. We endeavour if possible that nobody should know it in England, as it is in all ways a very distressing affair. *Adieu* my Dearest Brother I am quite ashamed of the quantity of nonsense I have been writing these two months to you but, as I said before, I cannot help it at this distance. God bless you and keep you in good health, as well as my boys.

Just before the ships sailed in the evening, Henrietta added a last-minute note to inform her brother about gifts on board for him and her sons: 'two buffalo horns which Captain Grant gave us. They are in a box of things sent to the boys.' This bit of family trivia was followed by momentous news. 'We heard yesterday of the French fleet being burnt at Alexandria by Lord Nelson and are in great hopes it is true.'

On October 15th, Anna Tonelli painted a watercolour of St Thomas's Mount in Madras. Charly's journal kept a running account of daily events:

October 16th Colonel Cotton, Major de Grey, and a few other gentlemen dined here; the two colonels and the major of the 25th regiment made 66 between them. The 25th Regiment was one of the experiment, all of the men being under 25 years of age. Colonel Cotton, Colonel de Blaquiere, Major de Grey being at their head. It was thought their youth, might make them more fit to endure the heat of the Indian climate.

October 19th Mamma gave an assembly.

October 20th We went to see Colonel Wellesley's regiment, the 33rd.

October 21st In our morning drive we met the *Nawab,* his sons, nephews and ministers, going to attend a religious ceremony four miles beyond the Mount.

October 23rd A large dinner party.

October 24th Mamma and my sister began to learn Hindustani.

October 25th Mamma went to the Asylum in state, taking Mrs Harris with her.

October 26th In our morning drive we stopped to look at a beautiful leopard. We met also a royal tiger, and some bears that some men were leading for show. We saw the tiger kill a sheep. The royal tiger was a beautiful beast; I cannot say the bears were.

Abruptly the certain menace of war appeared amidst the drives, dinner parties and the quotidian affairs of their lives. Charly's commentary continued: '*October 27th*: We went to see the guns that had started before daylight to go to Vellore, each drawn in carriages by sixty bullocks. After we met them, Papa joined us and took us on to St Thomas's Mount, where we breakfasted.' '*November 19th*: Mamma, Signora Anna, my sister and myself went in *palanquins* in the evening to Triplicane to see a Malabar feast round the Hindoo Tank.' '*November 24th*: Col Wellesley dined here.' '*November 30th*: A young cobra was found in the garden near our sitting-room . . . Papa gave a grand dinner.'

For the most part December was given over to dinners, assemblies, a ball and the novelty of seeing a Sepoy corps. On December 7th the Clives allowed themselves an outing to the Red Hills for a day and Anna Tonelli painted a watercolour of a large house by the edge of a lake. On December 9th Charly noted a surprise: 'We returned to the Garden House, and found Friskey with seven puppies.' On December 27th the family attended an amateur theatrical production, *The Absent Man: the Mogul Tale.*

December, Fort St George, Henrietta to George Herbert

My dearest brother – as there is a ship going to the Cape, I shall write by it and take my chance of your receiving this whenever it may happen. I have the pleasure to tell you that we are all well. I think Lord Clive at times much occupied by the continual business and with the additional anxiety from the approaching war with Tipu Sultan. As for myself I never was better in my life and your nieces are so, too.

I must tell you that we have had much concern from the death of poor Ashton* who was killed in a duel, at last died in five days afterwards in consequence of a ball that went into his stomach, perhaps through the liver and lodged in the hip after popping the backbone and in a degree injuring the spine. He was in great hopes of his life, as the situation of the ball was not ascertained till after his death (till he expired, he not having had on that morning any bad appearance, though he had been in the utmost danger for the first twenty-four hours after it happened). You may imagine how much it has shocked us and it is a sad thing for the service. He fought twice. The first with Major Picton ended well, but the second was with Major Allen, both of his own Regiment. The dispute was about regimental affairs in which I understand poor Ashton was perfectly in the right. I will endeavour to get an account to send you.

Charly's brief and understated final entry for 1798 spoke volumes about the man who appeared to have come for dinner, but who would stay until September 1799: '*December 31*: Lord Mornington arrived from Bengal, and dined here. Richard Strachey was in attendance upon him.'

* Col Henry Harvey Ashton, in command of the King's 12th Foot, was killed in a duel with a Major Allen. His friend Col Arthur Wellesley was sent to take over Ashton's command at Ameer, Arcot and Vellore. Before he died, Ashton gave his Arab horse, Diomed, to Wellesley.

1799

War with Tipu Sultan, 'Tiger of Mysore'

'This abominable War.'

The year 1799 began slowly and ominously in Madras. Lord Clive had no choice but to accommodate to what he described in a letter to Lord Powis as 'a temporary suppression of my authority, but that feeling is so tempered by the circumstances . . . I have had no difficulty in giving a cordial and willing cooperation and concurrence to the measure of Lord Mornington's government.' Despite the fact that Bonaparte, after his defeat by Nelson at Aboukir Bay, was not able to transport troops to assist Tipu Sultan, war remained imminent. Henrietta chafed under the travel restrictions imposed on her. For entertainment the household kept a menagerie of animals, including for a short time a tiger, said to be tame, who immediately tore Henrietta's umbrella which she had held out to him. Lord Clive refused to let it stay. They acquired two little bulls and a little cow no larger than calves; a hog deer; an antelope; a cockatoo that talked and whistled; a canary; a mina; and some avadavats.*

January 2nd, Henrietta to George Herbert, 2nd Earl of Powis

My dearest brother – on the December 31st 1798, Lord Mornington, the Governor-General, arrived in Madras from Calcutta with a great many attendants to stay here this campaign. I am *sorry and glad*. He will take a great deal of responsibility from Lord C, but I suspect will plague him

* Very small weaverbirds native to Southeast Asia but often kept as caged birds

very much as he is a fidgety man. He has been with us these three days and it went off better than one could expect from the presence of two governors and it is certainly an awkward thing to have a *surprise*, though Lord Clive does not think so. Lord Mornington is pompous, ridiculously so at Calcutta, though it is, I find, surprising to have some form and state there, as he told me from the very vulgar familiarity of the people, which is really not the case here.

In all respects, we go on well. Lord Clive speaks *very wishfully* of Walcot and I believe will be *sincerely glad* when he sees it again. There is no such word as *comfort* in this country. There is nothing but business and solitude. There is not a possibility of *society*; at least I cannot produce anything like it as yet, though there are several pleasant women and men. When the war begins these women will certainly be more with me and I have some little occasion, but at present it is very dull and when I pass six or seven hours *alone*, except visiting your nieces at their lessons, England does attack my mind most powerfully.

I find Lord Mornington has sent a gentleman to fetch Lady Mornington here. It is an awkward thing for me to receive her, which I must do, and then she goes *safely to be received* at Calcutta. The Directors refused her coming with him and I wish may prevent her again. It is impossible for me to refuse, and yet I know I shall be criticised in England for it, as his family does not receive her. It looks like condoning him, which my *Welsh dignity* does not like. You will find out from Mr Bensly or Strachey if she comes. I wish she was not I confess – he talks to me of her constantly and what she is to do on the voyage as if it were quite settled and certain – I do not see if it was refused at first how she can now be *so much more proper now.*

There is an alarm of famine in this country. We have not had the usual rains and the crops will almost universally fail, which is terrible. But by great cautions, rice is brought in constantly and most happily the upper part of India is overflowing so much so that they had left rice in the fields not giving themselves the trouble to gather it. Lord Clive has managed so well that I find he is much praised by the Blacks. I really believe nothing can go on better than he does in all respects. He is really quite indefatigable and attends to nothing but business which sometimes fatigues him extremely. The ships sail in an hour.

Your affectionate.
H. A. C.

February 3rd, Henrietta to George Herbert, 2nd Earl of Powis

My dearest brother – we are all tolerably well with but little to complain of, *yet not so perfect*. Lord C has never, I think, been entirely well since we came – partly from anxiety – and partly the climate. I bore it better than anybody till within these three weeks and though I have not had much the matter with me, I am not quite comfortable. The girls and I all feel equally the climate, which from the want of the usual rains is uncommonly hot and oppressive, adding to that, in most of our minds, *thoughts of England*. You may suppose how we are . . . there not being much to interest or amuse me here. Out of this house there is no society and Lord Clive has been so very much occupied with Lord Mornington's arrival that it is endless.

The army is now encamped at Vellore and I trust Lord Clive will now have a little more quietness. We were in hopes to have gone to Vellore to have seen it, but after much consultation it is not thought safe for fear of Tipu's *looties* coming down and attacking us on our return. Lord Clive is not to go alone which would be more easily done than with women, but he is advised to stay which is a great mortification and a pity as I think it would have been of service to him.

Everything is military. There is a militia established of Europeans, Portuguese and Armenians and they have the same uniform as the *Shropshire*. I must say my old regiment has the *advantage* no small degree. But the generality of the people have come forward in a very handsome way. Some of the young men are a little troublesome. It is understood that those that will not enrol themselves are to (after all due admonition) *return to England*. All descriptions of people are enrolled in the fort division. The writers and gentlemen are privates. Brown is the Regulating Captain and I believe likes anything like a drill. He is as anxious as possible.

We are much disappointed by the loss of all the private letters and the directors' dispatches by the overland packet about the 6th October. Having been sent in some fine box, which the Arabs suspected to contain jewels, they seized it. Probably there were letters from you. It is so long since I heard and the probability of the boat not sailing at the usual time, from the distractions of the troops, will make it a terrible long interval. There are more ships going soon direct to England by which I shall write all I have to say.

God bless you my dearest brother.
How happy I shall be to see you again.
Ever yours, affectionately
H. A. C.

February 8th, Henrietta to George Herbert, 2nd Earl of Powis

My dearest brother – we have had Lord Mornington here near *6 weeks* and I shall be glad when he is gone. He is extremely pompous, which you know he always was: never having even an airing without *more* guards than *the* King usually has and bringing *his authority* to bear on me, and everybody in conversation. He is certainly overbearing. Lord Clive likes him very well, but you know he does not mind many things, which I confess, disturb my *Welsh Spirit.*

In regard to our health we are pretty well in general, but between you and I, I have much anxiety about the girls, particularly Harry who has very often complaints in her bowels, which she never had before and is reduced to nervous and hysterical disposition with the least fatigue. I dread the hot winds, which I expect to be very unpleasant, and unwholesome. I am trying to persuade Lord Clive to let us go into the country occasionally for a change of air. We left this place for two nights two months ago and were all astonishingly improved by seeing a very pretty place nine miles off and having a little variety. I find from everybody that change of air is really necessary here.

This abominable War has prevented our making a journey up the country, which I was in hopes to have done. There is so much conversation about Tipu's *looties* . . . who sometimes come suddenly down that people do not like to leave Madras, but I believe with our Body Guard we are quite safe anywhere.

Charlotte is well but they both are very thin as they grow so fast. I held out a long time but within this last month have been unwell with what is bilious, and I believe a little to do with the liver, of which Lord Clive doubts, but I have some. It is now gone and, except not feeling in great spirits, I am well.

But to tell you my whole mind, which I like to do as it relieves me much, I doubt our being able to stay long here. I am perfectly determined to fight as long as I can as I am here, but we must not sacrifice my own life and health or my girls. The next six months will decide. If the hot winds do not affect us materially, we are safe, but if they do, there is but one thing to be done. I have not breathed a thought to Lord Clive on this subject nor shall I, because his situation would be very sad, alone in this country. The event must speak for itself. He has never been quite well since he came here and will not soon be so I am *persuaded*. And that the hot winds will affect him very much as he feels everything, but I know he will not give it up and particularly during this War. I hope in any case that this time – it is really a most miserable life and he is tired of it and . . . has said that there is much more than he expected. The War adds to that and altogether it is really hard though I do not say so to anybody.

February 8th, Henrietta to Lady Clive

My dear Lady Clive – I was in hopes to have heard from you among a very few letters I had the happiness of receiving the day before yesterday, but as there were not any from William Strachey, I suppose they are in a ship that is coming in the next fleet as these came by a Danish vessel which is uncommon for private or any letters. I had a letter from my brother in great spirits and that the boys are well. I hope and believe you are so too, but shall be very glad to see it in your handwriting. I shall endeavour to tell you all I can, but events have been scarce that could amuse you though we live in great deal of business.

The War with Tipu has given great occupation to Lord Clive. The preparations – which, you know, in this country, are endless – are all that is. There are 18,000 men with all their followers and bullocks encamped near Vellore ready to march towards Seringapatam. It is supposed that Tipu was disappointed at the defeat of Bonaparte and that all will end in this campaign. I hope it is true, as it seems the general opinion is our force is much superior to what it ever was, and the battering train is in great order. This has swept away all our military society, which are indeed the most pleasant, but I trust it will be soon over. I was in hopes to have been able to have gone to Vellore to have seen the army, but it was not thought safe as the *looties* might have met us, and given us some alarm, on our return, after we had quitted the field.

I have the pleasure to tell you that we are all pretty well. We have some little complaints, but I trust we shall continue as we are. Lord C has a great deal of business and of course is much more confined than he has been used to. Your grandchildren are growing astonishingly fast. I think they will soon be taller than either your Ladyship or myself. I shall send their exact height at the end of my letter. They are thin, which must necessarily follow, but in good spirits. Charlotte bears the climate better than her sister. I wonder if her being a Florentine makes that difference. Signora Tonelli is pretty well, too, and her singing enchants everybody. She is a most excellent presence and the more I see her the more I like her. Mrs Woodhouse, too, is I find an extremely good musician, which we have *found out* of her lately, as at first she never would play. The girls' education goes on as well as I could wish and I do not find in them or myself that degree of indolence, or idleness, which I understood pervades everybody here. You and I are not idle people, naturally. Those that are so, become much more so here. I go on, as in England, with all my operations just the same, and can amuse myself alone, as I used to do at Walcot.

I have had several leaves of trees drawn for you. I cannot say I have done them myself. It is very fatiguing to the eyes, and the glare is so disagreeable, that they require great care, and the delicacy of Botanical Drawing requires a great deal of attention. I had no more drawing paper left; therefore you shall have more bye and bye, when I meet with any of an extraordinary shape. You have heard so much of the Bread Fruit that I thought the Leaf would be worth sending, though it is of such an unreasonable size. I have tasted the fruit of it, which did not answer my expectation. None of the fruits here please us. We are told the ripe mangoes are excellent, but those I have already tasted are not pleasant, from being like turpentine. The custard apple and guava are the best . . . In short I do not find anything that is better than in England, except the moon. She is certainly brighter and gives more light early, than in England. The moonlight nights are beyond all ideal, and Signora Anna allows they are superior to Italy. You know Cassaicoli said, '*La Lunard e Italia e puis brilliante cheil sole d'Ingliterra.*'* I think he might say so here most truly. I have not been more than nine miles distant from hence and from the Mount there is an appearance of hills at a distance, but here you know it is very flat, sandy, and not pretty, yet everybody that comes from Bengal says we have the advantage.

Lord Mornington and Lord Clive go on in great friendship, which you will be pleased to hear, as that is not always the case with the governors of these places. We are in hope of great news in about two months from the army. I am now watching for letters from England, as I find we shall not have any more for many months. That is a most dismal thought. We are all at a frightful distance from one another. Butler and the coachman have been ill and are alarmed and return with this letter to their own land. The following is an account of the army, which I thought would interest you. Active infantry – 11, 061; European division – 4,608; Cavalry – 912; Active division – 1,766; Artillery Men – 576; Lascars – 1,726; Pioneers – 1,000; Colonel Robert's Detachment – 6,785; Colonel Brown's Detachment – 3,817; *Nizam*'s Cavalry – 7,000; *Nizam*'s Infantry – 6,000; 12 Field Pieces and Battery Train; 57,000 Bullocks provided by Government; About 90,000 followers of different description, besides women and children.

* 'The moon in Italy is brighter than the sun in England.'

February 20th, postscript to above letter

Since I wrote the above, I find that the *Princess of Wales* is a single ship and therefore it is best not to send my things by her. Therefore, my Leaves will wait a straight journey or three weeks for the next ships from Bengal.

Once more, *adieu.*

February 15th, Henrietta to George Herbert, 2nd Earl of Powis

My dearest brother – I believe as to public affairs, all goes on well. Lord Clive is much liked. The idea of *his management* is much diminished. He is thought a useful man by Mr Webbe. Yet I understand that he is not thought better of in regard *to principle* and that Webbe has spies over him and that he cannot do any harm. He made great advances to Lord Mornington, which have not succeeded.

Lord Mornington is so much afraid of his person that notwithstanding he has a guard of a company of infantry and twenty of the Body Guard, which is as much as is ever employed as a rear guard to the *whole army*. He has taken fright and is going into the fort where there is a bad house, though large and chiefly occupied by the writers and public offices except for a few rooms. He has added that all there are to be *turned out* and all the *papers and records to be removed* which can only be done to the Admiralty where by his *arrangement with Lord Clive we were to go* in case of any siege or attack which though improbable is not impossible. Now we are left out. He says the walls we have round the yard, which Lord Clive has just built, is a *sufficient security for us*. It has occasioned great confusion. All the ladies whose husbands are gone with the army who are living in the country houses are taking fright and going into the Fort, which is very hot, and people cannot get rooms. You can see by this he is not likely to be very popular and the removal of papers and offices is by no means an easy thing to settle.

When I think of you at Edinburgh and myself many thousand miles off with all sorts of heat and the idea of the *river*, which will put itself before my eyes, I am not gay nor is Lord C more so than myself *internally*. We are, however, perfectly comfortable in our selves and both mutually wishing ourselves at home again.

General Harris, our Commander in Chief, is a poor *fool*, extremely *good and all that*, but has neither much knowledge nor much activity. That is the only thing that is alarming about the war. Everything else is in high order. This is my private dispatch and will be sent with more that are to go overboard if they are taken.

God help you my dearest brother.
I long so much to see you again, that I hardly dare think of it.
Your ever affectionate, H. A. C.
February 15th

On February 22nd Charly noted that 'the mosquitoes bite us most shockingly. I think they are much more troublesome than they were when we first came here.' From March 4th to March 25th the whole of the Clive family and servants contracted a fever beginning with pains in the bones and ending in an eruptive rash. Lord Clive speculated that the causes of the fever were somehow connected to the failure of the rains. The stagnation of the water in the river emitted smells that were particularly offensive between the Garden House where the Clives resided and the fort.

In April, Henrietta and the girls were allowed to make small excursions near Madras. They visited a Malabar pagoda, where they were forbidden to enter for fear of their polluting it. At Bonansalie, they were once again barred from entering a Hindu temple: 'Friskey ran into it,' Charly wrote. 'Some man ran after her, and pulled her out.' They went to a feast in honour of Vishnu at the village of Sydrapet, where they got out of the carriage and were given flowers and fruit: 'After the devotees had said their prayers, they brought out Vishnu with his wife on one side and his brother, Ramswamy on the other. Vishnu had golden hands and his wife had a golden rod to chastise the wicked.' In Madras the Clives gave a ball and climbed to the top of the Mount where Charly undertook to count the steps. Once they visited a bungalow twenty-one miles from Madras where Henrietta thought she saw the print of a tiger's foot and was told that three tigers were about in the hills. The amateur theatrical group produced Shakespeare's *King Henry the Fourth* and their physician Mr Thomas acted the part of Sir John Falstaff.

Miserable in Madras

'A most indescribable wish to go and see.'

Charly's journal entry of May 10th reported the end of the War with Tipu Sultan: 'The news of the fall of Seringapatam is confirmed. It was taken on the 4th May. Tipu is killed; Major Allen found his body, it is said, covered with the slain. He was trying to escape to the palace. His sons and wives have been taken prisoners; the eldest, Futteh Haidar surrendered himself, and the army commanded by Coomer ud Deen to General Harris, a few days after. His throne is said to be worth three lacs of *pagodas*, which in English money is £120,000! We went to the fort to see the *feu de joie*; first the ships fired twenty-one guns each, then the troops fired, and lastly the guns of the fort, and Black Town.'

Henrietta, too, seemed to be caught up in British self-congratulation.

May 16th, Henrietta to Lady Clive

My dear Lady Clive – We are in great joy at the taking of Seringapatam, which was done in a most competent manner on the 4th May and happily with the loss of very few men on our side. You know by this time that Tipu was killed on the breach. His sons are prisoners and the other chiefs have surrendered. The war is therefore quite at end and most gloriously without the town being pillaged or any insult to the inhabitants. [Whether Henrietta actually initially thought this, or if she was protecting her mother-in-law from from the reality of the post-battle destruction and pillage, is not clear. The truth of the matter was that Colonel Wellesley had to put martial law into effect to bring order to Seringapatam.] Lord Clive and Lord Mornington are going to settle all their affairs at Seringapatam and I am in great hopes of going too. They are to proceed first, and if all is safe, we are to follow therefore you will probably have long accounts by our next letters of that place. I confess I have a most indescribable wish to go and see in the first place a victorious army of 40,000 and besides that a real native Indian city with all the chiefs and potentates that will accompany us assembled in great state upon the occasion.

You will have pleasure in knowing that everything goes well here. Lord Mornington and Lord Clive are as much together as possible in friendship and acting in complete harmony, which has not always been the case between these governments. I am happy to say it.

Daily life continued: Harry stepped upon a snake in the garden in the dark and Charly was so frightened that she threw down her lantern and ran screaming into the house. The snake charmers played their pipes and out crawled a snake, said to be 'the very one', which was immediately killed.

Undated, Henrietta to George Herbert, 2nd Earl of Powis

My dearest brother – I wrote to you by the last over land dispatch on the 12th May and again sent a few words with an account of the taking of Seringapatam and all the *Gazettes* by a ship. The plunder of Seringapatam is immense. General Harris will get between £150,000 and £200,000. Two of the privates of the 74th have got £10,000 in jewels and money. The riches are quite extraordinary. Lord Clive has got a very beautiful blunderbuss that was Tipu's and much at Seringapatam. Some of the soldiers have got 20,000 *pagodas*; some have ten thousand *pagodas*, and one a large box of pearls. I should like to have the picking of some of the boxes. There was a throne of gold, which I am sorry to say they are breaking to pieces and selling by parts. Lord Mornington has presented me with one of the jewelled tygers from the throne.

We have been in expectation of going to Seringapatam. Lord Mornington and Lord Clive are to go together and I am to follow with my ladies. But Lord Mornington has people about him that did not like to go and frightened him about his health so that the journey was put off several times and now seems quite at an end. I believe it will be better for us as we may go in a cooler season and move at once. But the climate is so cool that it was very tempting to us who are expiring with heat. The thermometer is at 91 in my room.

The colours from Seringapatam are expected every day. They are to be received in form on the King's birthday and we are to have a great ball, which I hate. It is very dull and I long for a little human converse very much. I have written to Robert about many affairs and have enclosed it to you.

I have seen Major Allen, whose name you will see in the *Gazette* as one of the principal people at the Storm of Seringapatam. His account of the town and palace is very wretched. The multitude of people in it immense owing to Tipu's having obliged the families of all his chiefs to remain there as a pledge not daring to trust any of them. When his sons heard he was dead and believed to be found under a heap of bodies, the eldest who was one of the hostages in the last War* went to see the body and without showing any emotion said 'It is my Father.' The younger ones showed more feeling.

The room he slept in was small and grated with iron like a prison and he locked himself in every night. What a wretched being he must have been in continual dread of everybody. There were about 30 Europeans and native soldiers taken in some of the attacks and whose heads he cut off deliberately the day before the Storm took place.

May 30th, Charly's journal

It was decided that Papa and Lord Mornington should *not* go to Seringapatam.

June 4th, Fort St George, Madras, Henrietta's journal

At 5 in the morning I presented the colours to the Madras Militia, and made a speech or rather recited it, as I had no hand in its composition, it being done by Lord Clive I think most awfully well. Then at half past 5 in the morning, in the square of Fort St George, the officers of the Presidency met Lord Mornington, Lord Clive, and the principal officers of the Supreme and Local Governments. His Majesty's 10th Foot, a part of the 51st Foot, and the Madras Militia, with their respective Bands, were paraded at the same place. Lord Mornington received the Standard of the

* The Mysore campaign that ended in 1791.

late Tipu Sultan and the Colours of the French Corps in the service of Tipu, which had luckily arrived two days before with Lieutenant Harris of his Majesty's 74th regiment from Seringapatam. Lord Mornington, with great joy and feeling laid his hand upon the Standard, bending it towards the earth. He then made a very good speech. Afterwards he embraced Lieutenant Harris and congratulated him. Then the Standard and Colours were carried into the church and deposited in the chancel. A Royal salute was fired from the Fort Battery and three volleys of musketry were fired by the troops on the Grand Parade. Later Lord Clive gave a public breakfast. At night we had a great ball.

It was one of the most pleasant and fatiguing days I ever had in my life. Lord Mornington said something to me that pleased me much. It was that it seemed appropriate there should not be a great victory in this country without a Clive being concerned with it. It was very handsome of him to say so.

Charly described the evening of June 4th in her journal: 'At night Mamma gave a great ball at the Admiralty to celebrate the King's birthday. At supper, the gentlemen drank the King's health, and gave six cheers. Mrs Harris sang "God Save the King".'

On June 14th Henrietta and the girls continued their pursuit of Indian religious celebrations. They went to Triplicane to see the Hussein Hassan feast where they got out of their *palanquins* to see a great many people (with sticks) grotesquely dressed, dancing round an immense fire, calling out 'Hussein Hassan'. In Charly's words, 'They seemed to be fighting with the fire, dashing their swords and sticks into it; they were painted white, and some had masks, and seemed quite mad. Captain Grant says they do not know themselves the origin of this ceremony; at least no Mahometan he has conversed with could give him any explanation. The ceremonies of the Mohurrum, vary in different countries and depend a good deal upon whether the sect is a Shia or a Sunni, the liberality of the Sovereign, and the proportion of the followers of Ali. Tipu Sultan, a strict Sunni, had curtailed the ceremonies much. At Hyderabad, it seems that the Shia's are numerous, and although the Nizam is a Sunni, he does not appear to trouble himself about these ceremonies, which they carry on in that city, to a great pitch in pomp and splendour.'

July 3rd, Henrietta to George Herbert, 2nd Earl of Powis

My dearest brother – Lord Mornington was praised for his successes at Seringapatam. He in turn acknowledged the 'honourable, generous, and disinterested support' that he had received from Lord Clive. I have something to say to you, which is only at present between us. Our lives are so very dark here and so really *triste*. Lord Clive does not dislike it, you know. He does not mind it for himself. He sees how very bad it is for me. There is an idea, spread about that we do not like company and therefore nobody comes near us except at my dull assemblies and his dinners. I believe they dislike me a good deal from Mrs White, a Salop lady having written a long history of my pride and formality, which makes people avoid me, though nobody was ever so civil to them before. Upon talking of this to Lord Clive, he very fairly said he saw how uncomfortable it is to me from the confinement to the house which the heat obliges you to and the dullness of that house and that if I felt, upon a little longer trial, unhappy or uncomfortable he would not wish me to remain here. This was said so kindly and his behaviour has been such that I will not do it till the last extremity, but really the solitude, the confinement and heat make me at times so low that I can scarcely support it.

I think there is no apprehension of our health being very injured. He is well. The girls grow fast and are well indeed much, much better than I had any expectation they could be from the first setting out. I am thinner and nervous but that is all. Lord Clive's situation would be sad without us. I certainly will not go till I can bear it no longer and he expresses himself satisfied on that subject. I mention all this to you because at this terrible distance from one another I sit alone and think like this and I make myself quite uncomfortable. There are some pleasant people here but many very vulgar indeed and that is not a very good thing for your nieces. When there are things to be done out of this house, they go to them. The people here are in general in a state much like Ludlow. In two months more we shall have finished the first year of our banishment.

On July 8th Charly stated in her journal that it was her Uncle Powis' birthday, 'so Mamma gave a ball'.

July 11th, Henrietta to George Herbert, 2nd Earl of Powis

My dearest brother – The weather is what is called cold. The thermometer is at 6 in the mornings at 66 degrees, the lowest it almost ever has been at Madras. It agrees with us. Your nieces grow tall and increase in weight and I do not now grow thinner. Signora Anna is the only one who is very often unwell. She has lately had a bilious attack with very low spirits, which is usually the case. I wish Lord Clive did not expose himself so much to the weather as he does. I am afraid he will suffer, but there is a new farm yard in addition to the garden which he attends as much as he can morning and evening.

You will be surprised to hear that Mr Thomas besides his other perfections has one that a person never dreamt of before. He is really a very good actor. There is a little theatre and plays enacted by gentlemen . . . in women's clothes most extremely well.

We are all going to William Calls, a very pretty place nine miles from hence for a week. Your nieces are packing up as if they were returning to England, which I believe they would perform with more pleasure.

We all wish you a Merry Christmas and a Happy New Year and that we were all sitting round the fire with you. I long for England more than I can say and am very sorry to see that Lord Clive's really becoming attached to this place. It not only distresses me but this whole establishment who are all as anxious as myself to be at home again. I really think my stay will much depend upon the state of Signora Anna's health while we are at Bangalore in the course of the summer. I say all I can to make Lord Clive think more of England than he does, as I am sure if the old proverb is right: 'Learning is better than house and land', I am sure health and happiness is better than money not to mention the sight of all, which I think, is worth all the luxuries of the East. Yet if I return, this increase of expense will, I fear, make him disposed to remain.

July 23rd, Henrietta to George Herbert, 2nd Earl of Powis

My dearest brother – a ship came in yesterday that left England the beginning of March but had no news, having left England without having gone to Portsmouth and having left all the passengers and brought their baggage, besides a poor woman who took her passage from Deal to Portsmouth. Think of anybody coming to the East Indies *by mistake*!!!!

Probert will be glad to receive £5,000 by this ship, which is much as could be expected the first year. The rest will be better I have no doubt. We expect £8,000 or £9,000. *Adieu*, My dearest Brother. How happy I shall be to see you again. I envy these people that are just setting out beyond all things.

Ever your most sincerely affectionate
H. A. Clive

August 2nd, Henrietta to George Herbert, 2nd Earl of Powis

My dearest brother – The letters are not yet gone therefore I have a little more to add. I had the greatest pleasure the night before last in receiving your letter by Col Monson. It relieved me from infinite uneasiness from William Strachey's account of Robert. Since I wrote my last, Lord Clive and I have had more conversation about our stay here. He dislikes it as much as I do. He has said so in a letter to poor Probert (whose situation seems a very despairing one) and I think he is not quite happy about his health. He is not ill but grows thin very rapidly indeed, and I have given my opinion of the wish for all and how little the *money* is in comparison of our *health* and he has gone so far as to talk over how we should live if we *returned to England soon*. I cannot help thinking that another year will be as much as he will stay in which case unless the children's health requires it I shall not think any more of the first part of this letter.

Charlotte has been bilious and *yellow* lately, but is now well. Really we suffer more than they do, as they grow fast. I was not surprised that they are thinner and I am much diminished, yet not ill. The complaints of Lord Clive outlined to you sometime ago could be whether it is owing to that he is so much thinner I do not know. It is all uncomfortable and he feels more and more so and is tired of it. In October we shall have saved all the expense of coming here. Therefore there will be only the old debts, which will be something. Another year saving in England and here will be considerable. I do not like to name a time, yet I think before two years more are gone we shall be in England. It is a frightful time, yet I cannot see much hopes of its being sooner, January being the best time for leaving this place. I long for that time more and more every hour and indeed so does every one belonging to us. How kind and good you have been to Robert during his illnesses . . . Mr Strachey's first letter arrived Tues in good measure. Col P came two days afterwards and I am now quite happy. What a pity it is to waste our lives and perhaps our health so far from you and my Boys. God bless you again and again. How glad I shall be to see you again.

August 5th, Henrietta to George Herbert, 2nd Earl of Powis

My dearest brother – I have this very moment received your letter of February 25th 1799, for which I thank you much. I am much obliged to you for the account of Robert and for the pleasant description of them and their disposition, and for all your kindnesses to them. I have always expected that Robert's mind would sometime or another open though it was later than Edward's and that he will turn out . . . I am very glad Edward is pleasant and growing too. I was a little afraid he would never reach the gigantic size of his Papa. It diverts me to see that since he went to Eton he has left off calling me Mamma. I am now his Mother . . . perhaps Bonaparte has got some of *my manuscripts.* Foolishly I never kept an account of what letters I wrote to England at the beginning of this year. I now keep *a book*. . . The fleet is *certainly* to sail on Sunday that is the day after tomorrow which it has been to do so often that I am quite tired of hearing of it . . .

August 9th, Henrietta to Lady Douglas

My dear Lady Douglas – I need not say how much pleasure I had in receiving a letter from you dated the 24th October. It is terrible to think of the chasms in one's correspondence and that letters are such ages in coming to me. I assure you that I rejoice so much at the sight of a letter that I am sure you would out of common *humanity* have pleasure in occasioning it and every detail concerning Bothwell and Dalkeith really give me sincere pleasure. If there is beauty in *contrast*, my life is now beautiful as it is just the reverse of what it was in Scotland. You know I said a few words to you with my reasons for coming here one *sad* morning at Dalkeith and strange and absurd as it appeared to most people that I should choose to come here I know you understand me enough to make me now say that I am glad I came. I do not amuse myself as I might do in *better places*, but I feel it was right and that there are hours when myself and my girls are of use and my *reason* is satisfied and I only wish for the most happy day when I shall once more get into a ship (think what a wish for me) and sail towards England.

The people here are in general not much *enlightened*. There are a few women that are *good* and many clever men, but the war dispersed them in general. I believe the women are afraid of *me*. I do not know very well why, as I am most *outrageously* civil but they are alarmed. I live a great deal with my girls. We have for some months occasionally had a house at the Mount and now on what is called the Island [about five miles from the Garden House]. It is a fine exercise; for I am really at the best of my health and amused myself as well as circumstances would permit with my works in a morning and walking in the evening with my damsels. In former wars Tipu's *looties* came down to rob and kill, but as there were troops at the Mount I was bold and by that means had the place to myself. This continued till the weather was too hot. When the thermometer was 96 degrees in my room and at 102 degrees on the veranda, I was obliged to come back to the great house and my formality. Now I can go to the Island where my girls are established and walk by the seaside by moonlight.

I cannot sit and be idle nor can I bear to have *visits* from people I do not care for by way of something to do, so I puzzle about something. I am beginning *Persian* and hope in all due time to be able to read Hafiz and all the learned books. Then I shall be romantic and so extremely flowery in my discourse that I suppose I shall not be able to give a rational answer to a common question. It amuses me much while I am learning my verbs I cannot *think of England* and what you are doing now which so often comes across my mind that I am glad to put it out again. My girls are going on as I could wish. They are not indolent with the heat and indeed improve as much as they could do in a colder climate. Harriet will be I am persuaded a remarkable good player on the harp for *a lady.* She loves it and takes infinite pains in other respects. They do well. Signora Tonelli is a treasure to me in every way.

You have heard of all our victories in this country. I am almost tired of hearing of Tipu Sultan and all belonging to him. People think of nothing but pearls and emeralds. All the officers send heaps to their wives, but I do not think they are very fine, at least the few that I have seen. It is a very extraordinary event certainly, that five months ago at the beginning of March, the army passed the frontiers of Tipu's country and that within that time, he is dead, his country divided, the lawful sovereign restored and the English position secure for ever in all human probability. The only people that expressed concern at Tipu's death were his immediate attendants and followers. He was hated and feared by everybody.

Tipu's sons never saw him, at least so seldom that there was no acquaintance or friendship between them. The *first time* they had been in his great drawing room was after Col Wellesley *was living in it.* As they grew up they were removed out of the palace. On the journey to Vellore, where they are now living, they said that they had never been so comfortable. They, too, were as society amongst one another. The oldest appears to be, I hear, of a much more tyrannical and disagreeable disposition than even Tipu himself and not much reconciled to his confinement. The only difference is shown to the legitimate son. He is a little boy; but they made him king, and pay some respect to him.

I was terribly disappointed with the account of the *zenana.* I expected it to be like the *seraglios* in the *Arabian Nights*, but I am told it is only a number of small rooms not unlike the likes of a convent where each lady lives in *one* room. I expected to have heard of fountains of marble spouting up rose water and of cushions of finest embroidery. But not at all – the rooms were as dirty and as poor as possible.

Some astrologers told Tipu that the 4th of May was an unlucky day to him and he was advised to take care of himself. He went through some ceremonies in the morning to avert their bad prognosis. Is it not very odd? Under his pillow was found a little book, which contained all his *dreams.* I should like to see it. I believe many people's dreams might be as amusing as his, but it is an odd thought to write them all down.

I have sent you a bottle with some seeds which I hope will flourish and that you may sit upon the bench and be shaded from the *southwest corner* of the SW hot house by the southeast *pot* of Indian creeper. Some are trees and from the Cape. The others are from this country and creepers.

Adieu, my dear Lady Douglas, with all sorts of good wishes to all belonging to you in the hopes of hearing from you in this distant abode and of seeing you again some happy day.

'That two months of War should have produced the changes in our situation is hardly credible,' Lord Clive wrote to the Earl of Powis, after the fall of Seringapatam. 'From a state of constant inquietude and exposure to the intrigues and attacks of an irreconcilable enemy whose position in the heart of the peninsula made him always formidable, we have attained to one of position and absolute security with the means of establishing and enforcing the maintenance of peace throughout the peninsula.' He pointed out that additionally, 'We have obtained a trailer line of fortresses.' Along with the letter, he sent a blunderbuss made at Seringapatam and promised him 'a most beautiful mare of Tipu's'. Lord Clive also described his wife as 'becoming slim and is just the weight she was when we were married'.

The heat remained trying. Henrietta, waiting for the rains, held firmly to her intention to travel in South India. Fighting her ennui, she made plans to visit not only Bangalore but also Seringapatam. She and the girls attended yet another *nautch* given by the wealthy merchant Arnachellum Chitty in honour of his daughter's marriage. There they admired eight Hindu and two Moorish dancing girls; 'one tumbled backwards and picked up a ring, which was on the floor, with her eyelids'. Charly rode on an elephant without a *howdah* and found it to be a likable experience 'though when the elephant knelt down, it was not so pleasant'. Friskey had four more puppies and Flirt seven.

August 16th, Henrietta to George Herbert, 2nd Earl of Powis

My dearest brother – I keep all the dates and the names of my correspondents in a book. Therefore I am certain I cannot mistake, and though you have not heard from me, I assure you I have not omitted any opportunity of writing. Since I had your letter (that is yesterday) we have had an overland dispatch from Bombay with great news from Italy, Ireland and every other place. Before this time you have heard of the taking of Seringapatam. What a wonderful people, we are really, having the command of the whole world. It makes me very proud of being an Englishwoman.

Signora Anna I hope will do well by degrees but the absence of people with the army has been bad for her. Now that they are returning I hope she will do better. She is a most excellent person and your nieces improve extremely with her.

I think Lord Clive much better than he has ever been. There is now much less business, the war ending so well. We shall be quiet soon. Lord Mornington is to return next month, I believe. He seems anxious to get to Bengal but is terribly afraid of his health.

Undated, Henrietta to George Herbert, 2nd Earl of Powis

My dearest brother – The bankers and merchants are losing some 700 *pagodas* a month by the delay of the ships. We have got Meer Allum here. He is, as you know in the *Gazette*, the Commander in Chief of the *Nizam*'s army. He is to be received by the Governors in form. They are to sit like the two Kings of Brantford* was upon two yellow satin chairs under a canopy to place him in the middle. It is a ceremony I will see.

* Perhaps a reference to Joseph Brant, a Mohawk leader and British military officer during the American Revolutionary War. Brant met many of the most significant people of the age, including George Washington and King George III, founded Brantford (in Ontario) around 1784 and, on numerous occasions, tried to intercede between British, French and American forces. In his constant negotiations with heads of state, Brant was clearly duplicitous; wearing whatever 'hat' suited his sense of whom to trust and which way to turn. Likewise Meer Allum was duplicitous in his relationship with the British and the *Nizam*.

Lord Mornington has his *coronet* as large *as the life* placed upon the back of his chair and another on the top of the canopy which is all yellow and I think will be very *unbecoming* to their Lordships. Lord Clive has no coronet, but a plain chair. It is very comical how Lord Mornington likes all sorts of parade and show and such sort of things.

Charly described Meer Allum's arrival 'in a gilt *palanquin*' and described him as being 'dressed in muslin, with no ornament but a pair of small pearl bracelets'. He was accompanied by his son Meer Dowraun 'who is an enormously fat man, [who] wore a fur turban, with a sort of flower of table-diamonds; his dress was trimmed with fur. He came upon an elephant.' On August 28th, Charly commented sadly that 'Our poor dog Fanny died of liver complaint; and Friskey's puppies so ill, that we were obliged to have them drowned.' On August 29th the girls played their harp and pianoforte for Meer Dowraun who 'had several rows of very fine large pearls, intermixed with emeralds round his neck; rubies and diamonds on his head, and emerald bracelets'.

Undated, Henrietta to George Herbert, 2nd Earl of Powis

My dearest brother – I had the great pleasure of your letter of the 20tieth April yesterday with one from each of the boys. Thank you a thousand times for the goodness it contained. Your account of the health and tempers of my Boys is very pleasant to me. It gives me great pleasure that you have them both in hand and that they are so much with you and that you appear to like them. It is the only consolation we can have for losing sight of them at this time, which indeed is painful to think of, and I must sincerely wish I could find any time when we might hope to be released from this banishment.

I am very glad to find Probert is so much better as to be able to go about. I am just returned from a wedding. I attended Mrs Wodehouse to church and she is now Mrs Rothman and going on Tuesday or Wednesday to Bengal. We are all sorry to part with her and shall not think of anybody in her place. He is a good sort of man, but I have not quite liked him so much just now as we did at first. However, I hope it will all end well. General Harris is now just arrived and therefore Lord

Mornington will probably keep his determination of going on Wednesday next to Bengal which will not afflict the greatest part of this country. We are preparing for a great fête to be given to General Harris, which was to be done by Lord Mornington but now will be done by Lord Clive.

We have Meer Allum and his son. They came to see Lord Clive. Meer Allum had a great curiosity to see *English children*. Two nights ago we came to him and the girls played and Signora Anna sang which he said he admired very much but I doubt if he understood much or comprehended. The experience of music that we have heard here and the songs of the dancing girls are not good . . . We are to have them, and I believe the *Nawab*, at the ball, with all the splendour of the East of which they have much more experience.

On September 5th, Charly dutifully mentioned without elaboration the event of Lord Mornington's departure: 'Lord Mornington returned to Bengal.' The Governor-General sailed for Calcutta in the HMS *Sybille*. On September 6th Charly wrote of an entertainment given by Captain Malcolm for Meer Allum at the Theatre. 'It began by an exhibition of scenes. 1st: A wood seen first by moonlight, then 2nd in a thunderstorm: 3rd A drawing room: 4th A street: 5th A little cottage and aqueduct, prettily illuminated: 6th A grove: 7th A garden: 8th: A gallery ornamented with statues, a view of a garden in the distance. Meer Allum was so pleased with one in particular, where a church was seen in the distance, he wished for his horse to gallop to it. We had afterwards dancing-girls. The fête ended with a ball, and supper, and some very pretty fire-works.'

Then on September 9th Charly described yet another gala: 'Papa gave a great ball to celebrate General Harris' safe return from Mysore, and the capture of Seringapatam. The ballroom was erected for the occasion in the garden. Meer Allum and Meer Dowraun were present. The garden was illuminated. At the upper end of the room, there was a transparency, representing the storming of Seringapatam; and before supper fireworks, and figures in them representing ships fighting, a dog, a tiger, a carriage drawn by horses, and two figures "Tipu" "Sultan" written below; a tree on fire. Towards the close of the evening, Papa presented Meer Allum, his son, and suite with jewels and trinkets. Meer Allum did not remain for supper (which was in tents). His son stayed to the end of the entertainment, which lasted till 4 in the morning.'

Charly's journal entries for the remaining days of September are brief and to the point: '*September 20th.* We went to a dance at Mr Wescotts. It had rained so hard in the morning; there was a great deal of water in the roads and tanks. Mr Brodie's pigeon house was struck with lightning.' '*September 21st.* We went in our *palanquins* to a village on the road to Pondicherry. In the middle of a great tank is a *pagoda*, with an altar . . . ornamented with figures. There were two or three other *pagodas* and a *choultry*. Everything appears very clean and neat; the inhabitants, *Brahmins* gave Mamma a wreath of flowers for her neck.' '*September 27th.* A violent storm of thunder and lightning occurred, during Mamma's assembly.' '*September 29th.* The *Sybille* towed in by the *Suffolk*, as she had lost a mast in the storm of the 27th. General Stewart and his suite were on board her.'

October 15th, Henrietta to Lady Clive

My dear Lady Clive – I shall not let the ships go without saying a word to you though the chance is that you are a very long time before you will receive it as we have not yet heard of the arrival of the *Dover Castle* in England, which left this place this time last year. Therefore it is most likely you may be many months before you receive this epistle. We are much disappointed in not having the letters from England. The ships that left in June are supposed to have gone on directly to Bengal from the Season being far advanced. They were seen on the 29th of the last month by a vessel, which told *another* ship and we have heard it here. The monsoon being expected everyday from tomorrow, as you know well. No ships will come in here any more. It is a sad thing to see the Road without a ship for two months. We shall probably have the letters in a fortnight or three weeks from Calcutta.

Did I tell you in my last letter that Mrs Woodhouse was going to be married? She is so now to Mr Rothman, one of Lord Mornington's secretaries, a very good sort of man with a good fortune and will probably increase it. He is not young and has been here many years. She went with her spouse to Calcutta so that we have only Signora Anna with your granddaughters who go on as usual to perfection. I assist as much as I can and so we go on. We are still at the Island, which probably was not a place you ever saw as I doubt if its merit was known or that there were any houses on it at that time. It is near Mt Thomas, but across the river. The air is perfect and so fresh that I delight in it. The girls are in the most perfect health and spirits growing both tall and stout. They will soon arrive at the size of their grandmamma, Harriet being now 4 feet 10 and 1/2 inches and Charlotte one inch shorter. In the last three weeks, Harriet has increased three pounds in weight. Lord Clive is quite well and I think looks much better than he has ever done since he came here. I am so, too; except now and then I still grow thin which though you know I can *bear it* I do not wish to do too much. The cool Season will do us good. I did not ever think till I came here that I should *long* for a *rainy day*, which I assure you I do extremely.

October 18th, Henrietta to Lady Clive, continued

The long expected ships are gone on to Calcutta. The monsoon is expected every day but at present there is not any appearance of it. We must wait for letters with as much patience as we can till their return from Calcutta. It is a sad disappointment to us. With every good wish to you and all belonging to and with you from every person here particularly Lord Clive and the girls who are now really growing great girls.

Adieu my dear Lady Clive,
Your affectionate daughter.

During October, Charly indicated that there were few activities. Her time seemed to have been spent between the Island and Garden House. On October 25th she noted: 'no event, but the arrival of Lord Mornington's picture'.*

* A portrait of Mornington painted by Thomas Hickey after the surrender of Seringapatam. It was hung in the Madras Exchange along with those of Cornwallis and Eyre Coote.

Undated, Henrietta to George Herbert, 2nd Earl of Powis

My dearest brother – I did not write by the last overland dispatch because I was at Ennore or rather at Pulicat* where Lord Clive went on an expedition that was pretty equal to any. We went to Irum, which is usually inhabited only in the land winds on account of its being surrounded by water, just as the Monsoon began. We had one expedition by *water* and *palanquins* in a most decided rain in an open boat that *was nothing*. A few days afterwards we set out in spite of some black clouds and some rain to Pulicat. We arrived in *palanquins* and crossed two rivers in perfect safety. We were received very hospitably by the Commandant and saw the remains of the Dutch fort in a fine shower. The next morning we were all to go to the lake. It poured with a great deal of wind and considerable waves. We females declined going with Lord Clive who set out in a great unwieldy boat and men that were never used to anything but the surf at Madras. The boat could not sink as it is made to resist all dashing waves. He was to return at the latest in the evening. We were foolish enough to go in another great boat to fish, but were wet to the skin in half an hour and glad to get home.

Lord Clive did not return that night. I had great uneasiness . . . The rain was incessant. The squalls were so violent. The river so much increased that in another night it would have been impassable and the only chance of getting to Ennore was by water. Lord Clive did not arrive at Pulicat until 8 the night following. He was 30 hours in the boat. It was impossible for his party to land on the Island. The Dutch people have talked of nothing else since and I am persuaded will do so for sometime. I assure you I was in very great alarm.

Your nieces are growing very much. Harriet will be a large person I believe. It is very extraordinary but they are never so well in this house at Fort St George as in any other place. We have colds more or less now but that is not to wonder at. It is nearly decided that I and my girls go to Bangalore in March and remain there till August or September. It is quite cool at that time and will be very pleasant. I hope Lord Clive will come to

* Small towns a few miles north of Madras at the mouth of the River Cotteliar

us there in the summer and go on with us to Seringapatam and from thence by Madura and Trichinopoly is my scheme by which means we shall see all the great horn and the most beautiful country besides, avoiding the land winds. Captain Brown will go with us as we shall have tents and camp everyday and from Bangalore may go on any little journeys where there is anything to be seen worth our observation. The life here is so dull and so much the same that a little change is absolutely necessary to keep on being alive.

I have sent a letter to Probert enclosed to you about *my* affairs, which are certainly flourishing. I am very rich and have a great increase British pounds 800 (£800) in all here and British pounds 200 (£200) in England as I had settled when I left it for things to be sent. British pounds 800 here *sounds* prodigious but really every thing as to dress is just two thirds more than in England and I have had as yet but one small collection of things sent out.

November 29th, Henrietta to George Herbert, continued

I do not think I have anything more to add at present. We are all well. Signora Anna is the person that complains the most and has almost said that the climate will not do much longer. She is now unwell and low and I believe has not made so much as she expected to do here. I have told Lord Clive of it and very much doubt her remaining.

You will be glad to hear that Lord Mornington has said at Calcutta that Lord Clive and he lived here like brothers, which came round to me by William Rothman. I believe he is very anxious Lord Clive should remain here as long as he does at Calcutta and I believe feels much about him in regard to his good conduct and assistance to himself. He said that if it had not been for that Seringapatam would not have been taken. My Love to my dear boys. I shall send them some little odd things by the fleet.

Charly's journal added a few more details about her Papa's adventures: '*November 1st.* Having no tidings of Papa, we were very near remaining the day at Pulicat, but as the weather was getting worse, and the night passage would not be safe, we started and went by the seaside and saw the wreck of a sloop from Vizagapatam. There were not two planks together. Two boats sunk in the night, and their crews lost. We crossed the river at Ennore in a ferryboat. When we arrived, we heard of poor Friskey's death the day before.' '*November 2nd.* Major Grant came from Madras to breakfast with us, and after breakfast a letter arrived from Papa to say that he had arrived at Pulicat. They arrived at Irum at 5 o'clock the day they started. For thirty hours, they had nothing to eat but a pamplemousse. Major Grant came over, in the full belief that they were drowned. They arrived at Ennore very tired. Major Grant went back to Madras. ' '*November 3rd.* We returned to Madras, via Tripatore, where there is a fine pagoda.' '*November 5th.* We went to a breakfast at the Patheon, given by Colonel and Mrs Floyd. The Star and Badge to be presented to Lord Mornington from the army was shown to all the party. They were very handsome, especially the Badge. We went into the Theatre to see some jugglers. Lord Mornington sent Papa a severe reprimand for his Pulicat expedition, adding that Madras would not do without a Governor or Lady Clive without a husband.'

1800

Travelling the Great Horn

'Not with seven leagued boots but with elephants and camels like an Eastern damsel with all possible dignity.'

From the fair copy of Charly's journal made by W. H. Ramsey in 1857

By the beginning of 1800, Henrietta's passion to travel within the India of her imagination had evaded her. Unwell with one of India's indigenous fevers, she remained confined to Madras which was now beset with January rains. Determined to experience her own India, she held steadfastly to her need to realise her simmering 'indescribable wish'. By the end of January her prospects to travel began to look more promising.

January 22nd, Henrietta to Lady Clive

My dear Lady Clive – The night before last I gave a great ball for the

Queen's Birthday and your granddaughters danced from ten o'clock till near three in the morning and could have gone on a good while longer. I confess I was not easy about them last year, but now they seem quite stout and I hope a little change of air during the hot months will be of great service to us all and we think with some pleasure of going to more distance from this place and seeing a little more of the country.

It is impossible to imagine the sameness and dullness of this place [Madras] and the confinement in the morning is a very unpleasant circumstance to us. We had a few words in general of the good health of all the family from William Strachey by the last overland dispatch, which was a great happiness to us, yet we long for letters from everyone. In particular at this horrible distance every little circumstance is very interesting and it is *many* months since I had a word from you. I cannot help thinking of a good fire and the little worktable near it where I used to sit at Oakly Park, with nieces and children at another table, with great envy and had rather see one of the old oaks than the finest Banyan Tree in India.

The fleet carries home General Harris and his family all covered with money and jewels from Seringapatam. Mrs Harris is a very good woman with a great many children and has taken the greatest care of them here and will now I believe be much happier for all the honours that will probably attend the General such as Peerage Lord if that is to be the case in England. Most of the people I know the best are going at the same time which will not render this place more agreeable.

Charly's diary gave some indications of the happenings at Madras for the next few days:

January 26th Flirty's bad health caused us to send her home under the care of Mrs Kindersley. She appeared in the procession that attended General Harris on his departure; she was carried by one man and her basket by another.

January 27th The elephants taken at Seringapatam went off today, a present to the Nizam. One had a golden *howdah* and cloth worked in black spots, to imitate a leopard; the other a silver *howdah*, and cloth similarly decorated.

January 31st, Henrietta to George Herbert, 2nd Earl of Powis

My dearest brother . . . I am now at the Mount for change of air. Our last expedition was not so good. When I wrote last, rains came with violence and we were obliged to come way from William Call's, which Lord Clive has taken for a few months . . . I hope we shall set out to Ryacottah and Bangalore in March.

Lord Clive will once again be denied the opportunity to travel as he is to remain in place to look after great works that are going on in the Government, no less I believe than the regulation of the Judicial and Civil establishment all over this country. Therefore there was a great doubt if Lord Clive could leave this place for a week without the Government being in charge of the *council*, which was not approved. The power being great and there are many *obvious objections* (which you will understand) to the power being in any hands not *quite white* which must have been the case. It seems that it might for a few days and that he may visit us and see a little of this country, which I am sure will be necessary for his health; when we are gone the house will be even less cheerful than it is now.

We expect great pleasure and health to attend us. At least it will be variety.

I am now under the disagreeable necessity of hunting for a maid amongst soldiers and sergeants' wives. Two I brought are disposed of: Lee's sister is married and a fine Lady and Thomas's wife nursing a child. Sally is with me, but I fear in a bad state of health and has been scarcely well enough to attend me more than a few days at a time for some weeks. I am afraid she will not be able to be of much use on our journey. Therefore I have your nieces only to assist me.

I assure you, seeing General Harris and all those people setting out was a sad day. We gave a great breakfast to them and all the settlement. The streets were lined with troops and it was really a fine sight and one could not help wishing oneself in the same situation.

Lord Clive is well and is in good spirits. The girls I do now feel perfect. I long to hear from you and above all to see you. The fleet sailed the 26th January; therefore, you may know when to expect them. God bless you.

My love to my dear Boys. How I long to see you all again.

Ever, my dearest brother,
a thousand loves to you, affectionately
H. A. C.

Henrietta undoubtedly was busy with preparations for the journey; there are no journal entries for February from her and only one from Charly: '*February 3rd* We went with Papa to the Garden House and breakfasted in the Octagon, a pavilion at the end of the grounds, that has always belonged to the Governor. The *Nawab* claims it, and as Papa does not choose to enter into any discussions with him, he relinquishes it.'

Finally in March everything was in place for the four female travellers to set off on their adventure. The journey itself got underway with great fanfare on March 4th, as indicated by Charly in her journal: 'After having seen the Body Guard reviewed, we commenced our journey in *palanquins*, and took possession of our tents (which had previously been pitched) by the Race stand, seven miles from Madras, and about one and a half miles from St Thomas's Mount.

'Fourteen elephants were employed to carry our tents, which consisted of two large round tents, six Field officers, three Captains and several smaller tents for the cavalry, infantry &c. by whom we were escorted. Four elephants were employed in carrying a part of our baggage; two were not loaded that had been trained for carrying *howdahs*, which we sometimes rode when the weather was not too oppressive. We had two camels, which were mostly used for carrying messages, and one hundred bullocks to draw the bandies in which all the rest of our baggage was to be conveyed.

'Our party consisted of Mamma, Signora Tonelli, my sister and myself, Captain Brown, and Dr Horsman. Papa, Major Grant, Mr Thomas &c. only came a short way with us, as it was impossible for the former to be absent for any length of time from the seat of government, without resigning his situation till his return; which was very unfortunate for us, as by that means, we had not his company farther than Chingleput.

'Mohammed Giaffer commanded the detachment of the bodyguard, consisting of 30 men; and the infantry were commanded by a *Soubadar* and a *Jemadar* and amounted to 66 men, including 16 boys, who had been selected to act as our orderlies.

'We found it necessary to take all our servants, for travelling in India is not like travelling in Europe, as were obliged to take every article for cooking &c. &c. that could possibly be wanted. This of course occasioned a great number of followers, as all our servants took their wives, and those of higher caste their slaves to prepare their meals, which do not give great trouble, as they only eat boiled rice and curry, the latter of which is made up of meat and vegetables, which they never vary, and only drink water. When every soul was assembled they amounted to 750 persons!! . . . which is not in India a very great number, and it is not to be wondered at when all is considered.

'We remained at this place the next day and saw Lord Wellesley's bodyguard reviewed. They were then under Lieutenant Daniels command. I saw the great superiority the Madras bodyguard had over the Bengal; they had been trained under Major Grant's orders and Lord Wellesley testified his approbation by increasing their number, and ordering a body of them to follow him to Calcutta, chosen out of this fine corps, and which were not ready to embark.'

On March 6th the four wayfarers were awakened 'in a truly military style by the reveille being beat round the tents at four o'clock in the morning'. Not long after they recommenced their journey, breakfasting in Mr Smith's Choultry at half-past seven at Vandalore. Charly elaborated: 'The latter part of this journey had been through a jungle, and after being accustomed to the flat situation we had but just left; we were well pleased with the hills, though those, which we passed on our road, were not very remarkable. It was not till the middle of the day that we reached our encampment at Calumbankam about two miles from Vandalore Choultry. We had been detained by one of the largest elephants becoming very riotous, and by passing his trunk under the legs of two other elephants he had thrown them down, which occasioned great delay, as it was some time before they could be properly loaded again.'

The heat was intense; in the tents, the thermometer was at 94. Somewhat ruefully Charly commented: 'We were not for the first few days in good train, and did not proceed regularly till we got a little more accustomed to this method of travelling.'

Charly described in some detail their tents: 'Mamma had a Field Officer's tent, Signora Tonelli had another, and my sister and myself had one placed between them. Sally Rubbathan and Charlotte Fisher were in a Captain's tent close to us, Marianne had a private's. This was enclosed by what in India is called a *Knaut*, and which the native princes when they travel in India have always around their wives encampment. It was a kind of tent wall that went all round us and sentinels were placed at the entrances.'

Their first day's journey was 16 miles. Afterwards, in the cool of the evening they walked to a tank surrounded by banyan trees. 'We thought them beautiful,' Charly wrote 'and had not seen anything which reminded us so much of English oaks.'

March 7th, Henrietta's journal

Set out at half-past four and arrived at Chingleput at half-past seven. The first part of the road was rough but the approach for the last five or six miles was beautiful. I drove the *bandy* for the first time without any difficulty and was much pleased with the appearance of the country. The distant hills – broken, rough, and strong – were very much like those at the Cape and near the Mount. There was a pretty tank on the right about five miles from Chingleput. As Lord Clive and myself had gone on faster than the rest of the family that followed in their *palanquins* we got out of the bandy at a Mussulman burying place and remained under some tamarind trees till they came up. Captain Wilks told me that the way one distinguished between the tomb of a moor man and woman is that the first is always raised and the second hollow at the top. The Sultan brought a pomegranate and some mint, the only productions of his garden. Soon after, the *Amildan* arrived with tom toms on each side of a bullock (something like little drums) with dancing girls and wreaths of flowers which he put on our shoulders and gave limes to Lord Clive. We proceeded attended by all these people to the town at the end of which William Hadee, Collector, met us.

The lake is beautiful surrounded with hills putting me much in mind of Switzerland in miniature. I went to the Commandant's house and thence to the Raj Mahat, the remains of part of an ancient palace of the Rajah of Chingleput. This building is in a very strange shape and has a room surrounded by a sort of veranda. The staircase, if it is to be called so, is so narrow as scarcely to allow a person to go up and the steps just wide enough to allow a foot each turned out to tread on them and in total darkness. The view from the top of this building is very extensive and fine. Though the lake now appears so fine, last year there was not any water in it at all. They hunted boars upon its bottom. The fort has been partly repaired and partly is in a decayed state. At the entrance of the fort there is a *choultry* and beyond it a *pagoda* and under which is the gateway through which you pass before you come to the drawbridge. The commanding officer's house is very pleasantly situated over the lake and there is good room in it.

About 12 o'clock I went to the encampment at Attour, two miles W of Chingalput. Owing to some great mismanagement of the elephants our baggage did not come up till after eleven and it was one o'clock before my tent was pitched. A great many tumblers and rope dancers came and performed very well before the tent, particularly two or three very pretty things. One man was carrying a girl on his shoulders and she carrying a large earthen vessel supporting it with one hand and the other extended. It was a good exhibition for that sort of thing. The Commanding Officer dined with us in camp and Lord Clive set out to Carangooly in the evening with William Hudson.

March 8th We set out very early in the morning to Carangooly. The road grew wild and uncultivated, except near the village. We passed a pretty *pagoda* upon a high hill. About two miles from William Hudson's, we were met by dancing girls with tom toms, who attended us to his house. The lake is of great extent and surrounded by distant hills. There is a view of the ruins of the old fort. The view was very striking as we approached the village built by William Place. It is uncommonly neat and enclosed within gates. Each house has a veranda and nut trees planted before them. The inhabitants are the different people employed by the Collector. Trees line the small streets on the right hand, cropping the road. There is a bungalow built by William Hudson. New seeds that we had given him perished there, not having been sufficient water for more than the common uses.

I felt here the comfort of a house in comparison with a tent. The heat was not disagreeable. The hills rise immediately behind the house. In one of them a few months ago while Mrs Cochbasse was sitting in the veranda, a tyger was seen walking quietly across. She was the first person that perceived it. He made his escape to another hill and it was two hours before he was shot. He retired into an aerie in a rock and it was a considerable time before he was killed though there were many people with a variety of arms. William Place's house was bought, by the East Indian Company, for the use of the Collector. On one side is the collection, where all the clerks write and all causes are tried, as well as the papers and commanding a much finer view than the house built by William Place. It was begun years ago, as well, as the garden. The trees grow well.

After dinner I went with Lord Clive in a *bandy* to the old fort. It was attacked and destroyed by Col Moorhouse in the year 1780. The gateways are completely destroyed. There are small remains of the *Killadar*'s house and a building where Haider shut up the inhabitants before he carried them away. William Hudson had begun a plantation of tobacco and other trees but the nursery is to be made near Vellore – this one not being thought sufficient, and that one nursery of a considerable size, is better than many small ones.

The village of Carangooly is neat, but not so much so as the first village. There was a fine tobacco centre and several paddy fields in great vigour. We returned by the works made to dam up the bed of the river and to form the tank. The sluices were opened that I might see the rapidity of the cascade so that though there was so much water last year it was dry during the monsoon. William Hudson gave me some specimens of a black hard stone used for building. It had much the appearance of basalt. He called it granite. The air was particularly fresh and delightful and very different from that of Madras. The country is perfectly healthy.

On March 9th, Lord Clive left in the evening after they had dined and returned to Madras, travelling all night that he might arrive at Madras to breakfast the next morning. The travellers would not see him again until October. Perhaps because of the parting, Henrietta's journal had more complaints than were usual for her: 'The sun was in our faces. The *palanquin* boys did not carry me well and I was most completely tired. The heat was intense in my tent all day.'

In order to avoid the heat the march usually began before daybreak with a boy carrying a lantern by the side of each *palanquin*. Henrietta drove her own *bandy* when possible, and at every opportunity she collected botanical and geological specimens.

Charly's March 10th journal entry described their early morning departures: 'As we were by this time more accustomed to our travelling, we went on in a very regular manner after this period. The general was beat round the encampment, and in an hour afterwards, we were in our *palanquins*; the ground was cleared, and the baggage all followed in about an hour after. Two *Dragoon* rode first, then a *Chobdar* on foot, with his silver stick; who was followed by a *Hircarah* and two peons. Mama's *palanquin* led the way, next came my sister's, then mine, Signora Anna's, Captain Brown's, Dr Hausman's, and our female attendants; Jemadar Giaffer with two Troopers, followed the whole. When the weather was fine, Mama drove one of us in the *bandy*, and the rest of the party mounted elephants for variety.'

Frequently, Henrietta, Anna, Harry and Charly stopped to visit *pagodas* and to learn about their gods. One of these occasions Charly described, 'as the most extraordinary things I ever saw . . . the priests covered us with flowers which I am afraid we did not receive with proper respect, for we were much tempted to laugh at the solemnity, with which they treated these frightful stone and wooden figures. We were also entertained by dancing girls . . . We returned from these curiosities through a magnificent *choultry*, supported by one thousand pillars. We were told it was built in imitation of the one in Madura . . .'

Although they continued to enter the Hindu temples whenever they were allowed to do so, more and more the travellers seemed to express a preference for Muslim edifices, finding them less overwhelming. In the evening they continued their journey and 'were shown the principal Moorish Mosque, which is pretty from its neatness'. Charly reflected that 'perhaps it appeared pleasing to us from the contrast we drew from what we had seen in the morning of a different style of architecture. There are but few Mussulmen in this town, and the Mosque is not therefore of any particular beauty.'

March 11th, Henrietta's journal

The country is beautiful and put me very much in mind of Maidenhead. At little Conjeveram I was met by all the tom toms on foot and upon a bullock with *polygar* spears and an elephant, that salaamed most politely as I passed. The multitude of people was quite amusing, but the noise and the dust were very great. Upon a very white pretty *pagoda* there were many monkeys very ugly with reddish furs. They came and chattered upon the wall as we passed. I went to the Collector's house to breakfast. It is very pleasantly situated in a garden. The upper story was large enough to contain us and we remained there all day. The streets are much better – wider, and cleaner than any town I have seen in India. There are trees planted before the houses, which are decently built, and the inhabitants are clean and have the appearance of comfort.

I went to the Great Pagoda. It covers a great deal of ground with all its *choultrys* and houses and a tank that is very large. I could not discover when the *pagoda* was built or by whom. They seem to have no tradition of it or of any of their buildings. The steps are steep and the staircase totally dark. I went up the two first stories with great surprise. The ladder was more than I could handle. I went up a few steps, but my head grew so giddy I was obliged to return. Signora Anna, the girls and everybody else went to the top. The view is very extensive. We saw a good country with a great deal in cultivation. The hills at a distance are wild and fine and I was much pleased with the whole scene. From the top there is a more commanding view, but I saw as much as satisfied me.

In the evening I went to the *pagoda* at Little Conjeveram with all the tom toms with us. Mr Hodgrove had ordered them. The priest came out with flowers and limes. This morning the priest had not prepared this as usual. I heard that Mr H's peons scolded them and they (as we suspected) brought some that were a little dead from their god. At the entrance of one of the great Swami's houses there are two colossal figures of granite with four arms, each which are supposed to be the guards for the temple. Mr Place gave a large gilt pillar to hold blue lights, which is placed before the temple. There were many monkeys: some came down to be fed; one had a young one carried upon its heart. They were very ugly. After coming from the *pagoda* in the morning I went into a small neat mosque built over the tomb of a holy man, his mother and servant who had been dead one hundred years. There was a little table before the tomb with some perfumed sticks burning and some flowers. It was neat and pretty and much superior I think to the Hindoo Gods and monsters.

March 11th, Henrietta's journal

We proceeded as far as Avaloor *Choultry*, and entered upon the *Nawab*'s dominions which we found in a very different state as to the appearance of the country, which is thinly inhabited, and but poorly cultivated, and in most parts appears barren and miserable. The difference from the Company's territory, which we had just left, was very great, and evidently proves, which is the best managed.

Charly added a few details in her account: 'The *Nawab*'s *Dewan* came from Arcot here to meet us, and prepared a *pandal* for our reception. He did not come in very great state, but his dress was very magnificent, as well as that of his son, who accompanied him, and who appeared to be about 12 years of age. The *Dewan* . . . made us a present of a dinner (an act of civility). He encamped near us, and paid us another visit in the evening and was uncommonly civil.'

Arcot: March 12th–14th

'We saw the 25th Regiment of Calvary reviewed . . . they are reckoned a very fine body of men, being all very young, and not having been long in India, did not appear to have yet suffered from the heat of the climate.'

March 11th, Henrietta's journal

From the moment we came into the *Nawab*'s country the appearance of everything changed. The country was fertile and the people poor. A little before we came to the *choultry* one of his highnesses calmly made his appearance, not riding remarkably well or very well dressed . . . His followers were many and made more noise than could have been supposed even by Musulmen . . .

Arcot had special relevance for Henrietta as it was the scene of the battle that the young Robert Clive of India took almost single handedly in 1751. Orme had written of that event, 'Thus ended this siege, maintained fifty days under every disadvantage of situation, and force, by a handful of men in their first campaign, with a spirit worthy of the most veteran troops.'

In the evening Henrietta, Anna, Charly and Harry went to see the fort which was in ill repair. Charly noted their attempt to see 'the famous breach made in the wall of the fort when Grandpapa invested it in the year 1751, but as it was dark we could not be satisfied as much as we could wish, and I regretted our not being able to see it by daylight'. Afterwards they were shown a beautiful mosque. Charly wrote: 'A priest was employed in the mosque whose duty it was to strew fresh flowers on the graves every morning and evening, a duty the Musulmans ever pay the dead, who in their lives had performed actions which claimed their gratitude.'

They also paid the *Dewan* a visit. Charly described their reception in 'a room beautifully illuminated and perfumed. He (the *Dewan*) was magnificently dressed in white, trimmed with gold and green embroidery; his son was dressed nearly the same.'

March 13th, Henrietta's journal
Before I arrived at the cavalry cantonment near Arcot, I was met by Colonel St Leger, Colonel Blaquiere and Captain James Grant, with some of the 6th Black Regiment of Cavalry, just raised by the former, and some of the 19th Dragoons. Col St Leger's *Soudabar*, as he came to receive me, came in between the body-guard and my *palanquin*, which Giaffer could not suffer, but brought his troops round directly between them and myself. I had the whole Guard [26] with the addition of Col St Leger's and Col Blaquiere's, which came on each side; and though the honour was great, the heat and dust were by no means pleasant. The house is large and pleasantly situated, so as to receive any air that blows, and had a large verandah round it. Col St Leger was so good as to give up his house entirely to me.

March 14th The morning was extremely foggy and unfavourable at first, but it soon passed over and was very cool and pleasant. It is impossible to say enough of the regiment. The men ride better than any I ever saw before. The horses were of a larger size than common and the whole in good condition; and though I expected much it was more than equal to my expectations. The Gallopers* were the first I had seen with cavalry. They went at an astonishing rate, and fired with equal expedition. It is certainly the most perfect regiment I ever saw, yet I think those in the charge of the Bodyguard last year halted with a more perfect line. The old *Soubadar* of the Bodyguard, who was there, said it was beyond all praise. The officers of the 25th breakfasted with Col St Leger.

I heard that the people are so much convinced of the mildness and advantage of the English Government over that of the *Nawab*. The taxes are now so high that many are gone into Mysore, and many to the west, and many to the Company's districts. When the *Nawab*'s son came here six weeks ago, all the richer people went away directly. He came to receive presents and very often if what is offered is not thought sufficient the Prince has no scruple of asking for more money. He was however very disappointed and got very little plunder.

* Field guns

On March 14th Charly wrote succinctly about seeing the 25th Regiment of Cavalry reviewed: 'They are reckoned a very fine body of men, being all very young, and not having been long in India, did not appear to have yet suffered from the heat of the climate.' That night the travellers slept in their tents, as they were to resume their journey the next day.

Vellore: March 15th–17th

'It was late and it soon grew dark, but I was determined to see as much as I could for a place so remarkable in the annals of this family.'

The travellers found the situation of Vellore, surrounded by three strongly fortified hill forts, magnificent. The four eldest sons of Tipu Sultan were kept there. According to Charly's account: 'The town itself is strong, the ditch is no little defence to it, as it is filled with alligators, which constitute in themselves a good defence from an enemy . . . We went into the fort in the evening and walked round the ramparts, from whence we saw the alligators.' From Madras, Captain Sydenham sent Charly a rundown of the principal places to visit on the way to Mysore.

March 15th, Henrietta's journal

I left Arcot early in the morning and came to Vellore.

The country improves much, and the last few miles is through an avenue of old and large Banyan trees . . . Col Doveton met me at the end of the town upon an elephant. The *howdah*, which he had made to hold myself and my daughters, was so constructed that we could sit with our feet down, and not as the natives use them. I passed the fort to go to Col Doveton's country house, where we breakfasted; there is a large garden, with a great variety of trees, green and flourishing, which is not generally the case in India. There are two buildings in the garden, where we slept; the tents were pitched beyond. Col Doveton from having the charge of Tipu's four sons cannot sleep out of the fort. In the evening I went round the fort. It is exactly a mile in circuit by the ramparts, and appears extremely strong. The country is much more beautiful than I expected, and the surrounding hills high and rough, like those at the Cape, the valley much cultivated, with many trees and topes. I believe I saw an alligator in the ditch surrounding the fort, which is supposed to be much infested by them. I intended not to have remained beyond this day at Vellore, but the heat had affected Charly a good deal. Therefore I was under the necessity of remaining another day.

I had declined seeing the Princes, but Col Doveton told me that the three younger ones had been particularly anxious during the last week for my arrival, therefore it was thought right for me to receive them. The baggage was obliged to be changed, as one of the elephants' backs was hurt, and the division of his load took up a good deal of arrangement.

March 15th, Vellore, Henrietta to Lord Clive

I was in great hopes to have heard from you yesterday and I *depend* upon it today... We went in the evening to see the fort. It is a sad ruinous place. The mud walls are still remaining sufficiently to show the extent of the fort and the view in crossing the river (which like all the rivers in this country, a bed of sand, except in the monsoon) is very pretty. There are mosques and some buildings amongst the trees, and a background of wild mountains. The fort is most extremely narrow, populous, and dirty: everybody looking poorer. All is desolate. Not a good specimen of a *capital.* From thence to a house building for his Highness, where our white and gold friend received us. It has a tank behind it and the room is a hall supported by white *chunam* pillars and hung with lamps more like my ideas of an Eastern Hall than any I have seen.

From thence to the fort and saw the breaches made in the wall by your father. It was late and it soon grew dark, but I was determined to see as much as I could for a place so remarkable in the annals of this family. The dust and heat were prodigious. I was much tired, but had great pleasure in seeing this interesting place.

March 16th, Henrietta to Lord Clive, continued

We breakfasted in the commanding officer's fort-house. During the day we saw a palace which is building for Tipu's and Haider's wives (about 500 in number) . . . They're to be allowed two apartments each, besides a verandah, which must appear very magnificent to them, after the confined space they have been accustomed to live in.

I went at seven o'clock to the fort, and an old *pagoda*, magnificent and well-carved, constructed of granite now converted into a military storehouse. The sculpture is much better than any I have yet seen, some of the open work is extremely neat, and well executed. There is a tyger cut in granite, and the stone is so hard that though it has been attempted to take a bell out of the tyger's mouth, it could not be done, but part of the jaw was broken without moving the bell. It is thought to be very ancient. Col Doveton has established a school, for the children of the soldiers of the Scotch Brigade, who are in garrison here; and to take care of the four Princes, Futteh Haidar, Abdul Khaliq, Moyen Uddeen and Mousa Uddeen.

I breakfasted at the commanding officer's house, and afterwards the Princes came to see me. Moyen Uddeen and Mousa Uddeen came from their house opposite on horseback; the countenance of the latter, the *Padshaw* (being a legitimate son) is extremely interesting; there is a great appearance of gentleness in his countenance. I understand that Col Wellesley was much pleased with his manners at Seringapatam. His brother's appearance was quite different; his spirited, and even fierce eyes, were extremely expressive of his character, which is violent and cruel. He has great pleasure in beating his servants, and tormenting animals; once he had a horse rubbed over with gunpowder, and then set on fire. Col Doveton has been under the necessity of interfering on many occasion, not always with proper effect. He is the younger of the two hostages, brought by Lord Cornwallis to Madras; he was then a child, but very acute and clever. I have heard that Lady Oakly was very kind and attentive to both the hostages; she said (through the Interpreter) to the youngest, that she would teach him English, and that he must teach her his language; he answered her, that she might teach him English, but she was too old to learn his language.

A short time after they came, Abdul Khaliq arrived, who is illegitimate, his mother having been a slave; the other brothers look upon him with great contempt; of course, I got to receive him, and his brothers did the same, but they said to Col Doveton afterwards, that they should not have done so, if I had not thought he was their elder brother. He has a most sulky countenance, and really the appearance of a slave, unlike the general countenances of the Mussulmans; he was more dressed than the others, being in silver muslin, with a red and gold turban. The *Padshaw* has not worn any turban, only a shawl twisted round his head, since the death of his father, which with them is a sign of mourning. A little boy, brother-in-law to the *Padshaw*, came with Abdul Khaliq. He was very fair, but not pretty, and his gold turban, and bright rose-colour embroidered sash, did not add to his beauty.

They enquired after Lady Oakly, and spoke a good deal to Col Doveton, when after the usual ceremonies of *betel* and *ottah*, they went away. The mothers of both the young Princes were of high caste; one of them (the *Padshaw*'s) is dead. After they were gone, Futteh Haidar came; he had never been in any English house, or seen any English women, and had not till that morning expressed that he wished to pay his respects to me. Futteh Haidar is said to be very like his father, indeed he resembles all the drawings I have seen of him. He is fat, and has a most remarkable thick neck, like Tipu's; there is a most terrific expression in his countenance, and I fancied I could see as he looked round him a wish to have the English in his power. One of his attendants stood near to him whom he frequently looked at, and appeared to express something in those looks, which we did not understand. His manners were more polished, than those of his brothers, he having mixed more with the world. I really could have looked at him till I had been frightened; there is something so fierce in his aspect. He passes his time in reading, and in his *zenana*, in great retirement, in continual regret for having surrendered himself a prisoner. He says Purneah* deceived him by advising him to surrender, saying that it would be most likely to soften the English Government

* Dewan of Mysore, a Brahmin who had also been employed by Tipu Sultan

towards him; he could have occasioned much trouble, if he had not come into Seringapatam. He, however, could not have inherited the *musnud* by right (not being legitimate) yet it is supposed had Tipu died a natural death, there would have been a struggle between Futteh Haidar and the *Padshaw*.

They had each several wives. Futteh Haidar married a great-grand-daughter of Chunda Sahib and has had seven children, who are all dead; one died on the road to Vellore, and the last since he came here. His wives' habitation is divided by a high wall from those of Abdul Khaliq, and there was lately a serious engagement between these *zenanas*. His elder wives overheard something impertinent said of them by the young ones of Abdul Khaliq, and resented it; stones were presently thrown from each party till the stones were exhausted. Then they sent their old female attendants out into the street to collect more. A message came to Colonel Doveton to inform him of this civil war, and he sent them word that unless peace was immediately established, that he should be under the necessity of sending in a guard which would disgrace them for ever. This quieted the fury of the combatants.

Col Doveton described Mousa Uddeen as very clever, as I have before mentioned, and ready for any expedition if he could possibly get out of the fort, or for any mischief. A few days ago he sent to desire Col Doveton would drive him to a great camel feast, where there are usually some thousands of people assembled, but he declined it. The *Padshaw* is more gentle and reserved in his manner, but it is a pity they do not attend to reading or some part of education; they only play like much younger boys.

Futteh Haidar says he was alarmed for the safety of his family at the taking of Seringapatam, but perhaps the reason I have before given may also have some weight with him. There is not the least friendship subsisting between the brothers; they never meet but in great form. Two of Tipu's daughters are here, and said to be very beautiful. In his pocket-book at the time of his death, Tipu had a list of the most beautiful daughters of his courtiers, to be enquired for. His wives were of all nations and religions. Some were Christians taken from Goa, and other places, where the missionaries had made proselytes. Col Doveton was lately under the necessity of enquiring the names of some of the ladies who had been taken from their husbands, who wished to marry again if they were dead, which the missionaries insisted upon being first proved, before they suffered a second marriage. It was a long time before the family would submit to this request.

The *zenana* is generally a square-building with high walls, consisting of a court with eight small rooms, and a verandah, divided into two stories, which are sufficient for four ladies, and their attendants. Futteh Haidar sent me a great many dishes of *pillow* which are usually prepared in the *zenana*. Col Doveton explained to me the difference between the wives of the Moro-men. They are all really married to the persons with whom they live, but when the ladies are of high rank, they expect, and their relations insist, upon having expensive celebrations of the marriage, which is not always done. There is no particular right of succession, but the Father names his heir, which is generally one of the sons of the elder, or of the wife whose marriage, has been publicly celebrated.

From Vellore, the travellers proceeded to Pollicondah. The intervening country was extremely flat but with a large tank at Chitterburry. The road ran nearly parallel to the Palaur River. On the left of the road they could see a high range of mountains, amongst which sat Coulasghurr, a large hill fort, garrisoned by the *Nawab*'s troops. Brinjeveram, a populous town, remarkable for its *pagodas*, was situated on the banks of the Palaur. Pollicondah was situated near a high hill, with a small pagoda on its summit. The road from Kistnagherry to Ryacottah was through a pass of the *ghauts*, but the ascent was gradual, and not difficult. Captain Sydenham had informed the party that 'the road is very romantic, in many places overhung by eminences, covered with thick jungle. The approach to the Fort of Ryacottah is as picturesque as the imagination can well conceive, and the eastern face of that lofty rock, crowned by a strong and extensive line of fortifications, towers above the intervening range of hills.'

Crossing the ghauts: March 17th–30th

'Part of the journey was performed upon elephants which we like much it being cooler than palanquins.'

March 17th, Charly's journal

We left Vellore, and breakfasted under a *Pandal* on our way to Pollicondah . . .

March 18th We left Pollicondah and went to Sautghur. We breakfasted in the garden belonging to the *Nawab* with two Armenian gentlemen who had the charge of it, and Captain Davis, who commanded 200 pioneers, who are engaged in improving the roads. The garden is two miles in length; the view was beautiful. Sautghur is at the foot of the *ghauts*; the hills are covered with stones of an immense size. Upon several of the hills there were batteries erected by Haidar Ali,* and there was a wall extending from the village up to the hills. Captain Davis and the two Armenians dined with us, and after dinner we went in *palanquins* to see another garden of the *Nawab*'s where there are vines, apple and peach trees and the finest guavas I ever saw. We went into a wood; our encampment in a tope of tamarind trees was cool and pleasant.

March 19th, Henrietta's journal

We left Sautghur, and went up the Padinaig Durgan Pass; it is so steep that we were obliged to walk part of the way. Captain Davis came with us and we encamped in the banyan tope. When we arrived at the top of the hill we found no tents, the sergeant said he was afraid of tygers, and had

* Haidar Ali was a military adventurer who by 1766 had consolidated his power in Mysore by seizing the throne of the Hindu Wodeyar rulers. In 1780 he and his son, Tipu Sultan, invaded the Carnatic with nearly 100,000 men and defeated the British at the Battle of Pollilur. Tipu later depicted this triumph in a painting on an outer wall of his Daria Daulat Palace at Seringapatim. Haidar Ali died in 1782.

remained below. The thermometer was 87 degrees in the round tent, and 91 degrees in the sleeping tents.

March 20th, Charly's journal

We remained at the top of the *ghauts* to rest; the thermometer was 66 degrees in the morning, and 88 degrees in the middle of the day, and 91 degrees in Mamma's tent. One of the elephants had a shivering fit, for which they meant to give him a hot curry. The views from the hills are very interesting and pretty.

The party found the old fort built by Tipu 'garrisoned by five Sepoys and a *havildar*'. Walking was difficult 'as it was so slippery in many places, so we did not accomplish our object'.

March 22nd, Charly's journal

Captain Davis came up the Pass, and passed the day with us; he told us that at Tripatore there were some dwarfs living, who never descend from their mountain but to pay the tribute, and no one goes up to them, as the change of climate always disagreed with both parties. An old *Begum* was living on the top of a steep hill, from which she had never descended for thirteen years; the only ascent being by a basket, from the steepness of the rock.

March 22nd, above the ghauts, Henrietta to Lord Clive

My dear Lord Clive – This is Edward's birthday. I wish him and you most heartily many returns of it *together*. He is now fifteen. Think of that and how happy it will be for us all to be assembled again and to see those dear boys before they are grown up and how much we lose of them now. Pray finish what you have to do at Madras soon that you may not wish to stay longer than is absolutely necessary.

I do not know when I have been so much pleased as by your letter, which arrived yesterday. All was quite right when your letter came, it being the longest I ever received from you in my life. I am very glad you are satisfied with what we have done. We all wish much for you. The whole scene is new and so much what you would like and the difficulties really nothing. The fatigue would be trifling if it were less hot. These three days have brightened both us and our animals and we are unwilling to quit it though it is very desolate and wild. We went yesterday evening to the pass of Padinaig Durgan. It is not very easy of access and we were obliged to scramble in our best manner. The view was very extensive of a country with scattered trees and rocks, scarcely the smallest appearance of cultivation and nothing very striking but all hills and little valleys. Their fort does not command the Pass. I do not envy the six *sepoys* that are there. Upon the whole I am disappointed as to the appearance of the *ghauts.* The Apennines are a thousand time more like a pass and much more inaccessible. I should imagine this is difficult without beauty.

There are scarce any inhabitants near the road. They are not yet accustomed to the English and are afraid of having their things seized by the regiments marching through the country. Therefore they live at a distance.

We have not vegetable except yams, which is the only thing we want. Captain Davis from the bottom of the Pass has supplied us today. We were spoilt on the road by such things. Even your garden cannot produce such large cabbages.

Charly has recovered her spirits and strength. Indeed the latter has not failed much and she is quite well with no more bleeding at the nose since we came here. She has water thrown over her every day, which appears to be of great service. We are collecting every thing that you have not in your garden. There are no small trees to be found, but the cuttings I have, no doubt will grow, and I shall send them.

On March 23rd Charly found the landscape through which they passed on the way to Vinkatagherry 'very dreary'. On March 24th after they had descended the Pass, Henrietta, Anna, Harry and Charly climbed up to the hill-fort, a steep ascent of a mile and looked down on the Sultan's battery that had been built by Haidar when he took the place from the English which Charly characterised as having been 'effected in the usual military manner, by attacking it from a higher hill'.

March 24th, Henrietta to Lord Clive

We are just returned from Vinkatagherry and a more desolate place is not to be seen, I believe. The first five miles is the same sort of jungle that we saw inhabits the last pass, without trees and only small spots cultivated with rice. The fort is a ruin completely and the view tolerable desolate except a small tank with some teal on it. I saw nothing Christian-like. How Thomas Sydenham could praise it I cannot grasp. I am sure there is nothing to tempt one to remain there.

I am much afraid all Col Reed's avenues were cut down by the *Nizam*'s troops for firewood. If it is so, it is most savage. They say they even took the doors and gates from the cottages and gardens and sold them in their bazaars. So says Captain Davis who came here yesterday.

Part of the journey was performed upon elephants, which we like much it being cooler than *palanquins*. This evening we shall pick up seeds for you. Charlotte's nose behaves very well. Signora Anna complains very little. She is in good spirits and I am better for the cool nights and mornings. As this is a shabby letter, and not worth sending, I shall keep it to be finished at Amboor.

At Vaniambaddy on March 25th the party crossed the River Palaur, which they had frequently done since leaving Chingleput. This was the boundary of the Company's territory, and that of the *Nawab*. They occupied the entire *pandal* that had been erected when Lord Mornington had been expected through the country. 'It consisted of several apartments,' Charly noted 'decorated with flowers, and amongst them, the red lotus.' March 26th: The travellers found the road good and the country pretty to Tripatore, a large and flourishing town. March 27th: Along the way were sugar-plantations and they watched the process of making rum from sugar and observed people weaving muslin. Charly was delighted to pass 'through a tope abounding in monkeys'.

At Malpaddy on March 28th, Captain Graham, the Collector of the district, and his assistants came to meet them. When they arrived at Kistnagherry, a hill-fort, they visited a ruined pagoda dedicated to Vishnu. On March 29th while still at Kistnagherry, Charly reported that they saw '200 criminals in chains, those who had committed murder were distinguished from the robbers by a double chain on their feet'.

Captain Graham loaned the trekkers his house where Cockatoo, the family parakeet, was frightened at Captain Graham's month-and-a-half-old pet cheetah that 'runs about like a cat'. In the evening they walked to a tank, from whence they could see Ryacottah. The thermometer was 98 degrees. March 30th: In spite of the rain, they went out after breakfast to see a garden and the *Pettah* that Captain Graham ordered built. It had about 3,000 inhabitants principally Mysoreans. They saw several tiger skins. There were bears on some of the hills. Charly was disappointed to learn that Captain Graham disbelieved Captain Davis's stories about the Begum, and the pigmies (dwarfs).

Ryacottah: March 31st to May 15th

'We live like hermits on our Rock and it is very comfortable.'

On March 31st the travellers arrived at the strong hill fort of Ryacottah, a journey of seventeen miles from Kistnagherry. Ryacottah was the first hill fort to be captured by Lord Cornwallis's army in 1791, and was ceded to the British by the treaty of 1792. General Harris's army camped beneath it before entering Mysore territory in 1799. On a clear day from the flagstaff on the summit of Ryacottah they could see an extensive view of the adjacent country, and a variety of hill forts both above and below the *ghauts*. Kistnagherry, which had appeared as a lofty mountain, when below the *ghauts*, from this elevated situation, was now far below the horizon. The base of Ryacottah had been affirmed to be on a level with the summit of Kistnagherry.

Thomas Sydenham in a letter to Charly advised her as to a useful method 'to ascertain the situation of all places against any hill they might ascend'. He encouraged her to take up 'a map of the country, a pocket compass, and a spyglass. By referring to the former, and the bearing of the compass, you will easily ascertain the situation of any place expressed in the map. The natives are by no means intelligent in showing different places round any central point, because they know nothing of their relative bearings. By adverting to your map, and compass, you can correct, or corroborate, their information.'

Col Mackay lent Henrietta his country house where monkeys were prevalent. The temperature ranged from 75 to 92 degrees.

April 2nd, Henrietta's journal

The road to Ryacottha is very beautiful and perfectly wild, rough and savage. About eight miles from Ryacottha is a pleasant spot with a *pandal* built for Lord Mornington. The approach is long and winding and difficult for a carriage, but the view makes ample amends when you are arrived at the fort. The house is very pleasantly situated. There is a large room with an open veranda with pillars and a detached building consists of three rooms and two smaller ones where we shall sleep: four in the large ones, I only in another, and the fifth small room for the musical instruments. Col Mackay has a harp and a pianoforte. I do not know if he *plays himself.* I think we shall be very comfortable here.

April 6th, Henrietta to Lord Clive

We are all gasping with the heat and growling not a little that we are as hot as you are at the Garden House. Last night we had rain and thunder, but today we are very much oppressed. I really have suffered more for these last three days than I have for several months.

Poor Captain Brown has been complaining for a few days and yesterday morning overwhelmed with a violent inflammatory fever. He had had a headache and went to bed the evening before. Dr Hausman says that he was in considerable danger and he was obliged to bleed him instantly as he was really delirious and he says in a frightful state. He is better today but not able to lift up his head from his pillow. Dr Hausman thinks it will be yet some days before he will be well again.

Signora Anna is complaining. I wrote you word she was poorly. She is weak and I think a little feverish. Dr Hausman has a great dislike to saline draughts but we proposed them to him for her. The weather is much against her certainly and she is low. My cold is better and the girls quite well, writing to their grandmamma and their brothers.

It is supposed the little monsoon is beginning and then we shall be better. Night before last Charly spied a snake travelling between her room and mine. A general alarm was given and the bodyguard called upon to dispatch it, which he did immediately. This put monsters into all heads. Signora Anna began to search her room where she found a little scorpion. The same night my night sleep was attacked by a huge cockroach, which I found, perched upon my pillow. This is enough as you may suppose to occasion grand searches every night in all the rooms.

Captain Graham has brought his little tyger but I do not feel disposed to accept it though it is now so *good* that I can take it up and play with it. We have two antelopes that are pleasant playthings for old and young. I have fruit sent from all places. Some came yesterday from Bangalore and some excellent grapes and some purple ones really delightful to see and eat from Salem – such a plantation of celery in a basket from the same place. I have roses from Kistnagherry, for this place does not produce a flower of any sort. You will have a parcel of grapes sent today from Colonel Mackay. We often wish we could show you little odd views and trees' fruit. The girls desire many loves to you and as Cockatoo is in perfect health and high spirits, they are quite satisfied with everything.

Adieu, my dear Lord,
ever your very affectionate
H. A. Clive

April 8th, Henrietta's journal

Captain Brown is better. He could not sit up yesterday but will, I believe, today. Signora Anna is better, but very thin. The heat is still great. An officer died upon the road and was brought up yesterday morning from Bangalore, but he did not die of heat or bile but of drinking. I believe he was found dead in his *palanquin*.

April 9th We went to the top of the Rock. There is a road a considerable way up that is not difficult for a *palanquin*. There is a gateway which is supposed not to be so well placed as that formerly made by Tipu as an enemy might now come up under the shelter of the rock within a few yards of the gate. The view is very wild and extensive. There is a small house not far from the gate built by Captain Lennon who commanded there and had hope of repairing the fort under the orders of Colonel Reed. There is a small tank near the house and two more at a small distance. The flagstaff is considerably higher than this part of the rock but not very difficult of access. I breakfasted and dined there and returned to the lower fort in the evening.

Colonel Mackay showed me several coins of old date and some very beautiful round stones perfectly polished and white and of a grain much finer than marble which were given to him at Madras by a Dutch Merchant who said they were often found in the centre of cocoanut trees. I shall endeavour to procure some if possible.

April 9th, Henrietta to Lord Clive

We are all invalids more or less and suffering much from the heat which is really terrible. The thermometer is as high as with you but we have the advantage of purer air. Yesterday Charly had a little return of the fainting she had at Arcot. It went off almost directly but she is weak and languid today. My cough torments me and is partly nervous, I believe. As you know, it is sometimes and prevents me from sleeping. Yesterday I had one of the nervous faintings I used to have in England and, indeed, I have felt very nervous and uncomfortable for some days. I am quite weak, low, and nervous.

Captain Brown is not quite so weak today. He came here yesterday and I believe moved too soon. He is very thin and weak without any appetite. Signora Anna and Harry are the best at present.

April 11th, Ryacottah, Henrietta to Lady Douglas

My dear Lady Douglas – I am persuaded that there is a letter for me from your good pen upon the ocean though I cannot tell when it will arrive; I must write to testify that I am alive. We females suffered so much from the heat last year without positive illness that I left Madras a month ago and by slow journeys am arrived at Ryacottah where I am living in the most wild place, without being dismal, that you can imagine amongst the *ghauts* with such rocks and mountains that they delight me. The heat has been very violent. For some days now we have enjoyed rain and are reviving. I never knew the *blessing* of a *storm* till I came here. Here it is more watched than the sun is in our blessed climate.

The country is pretty in many places – in some very flat and as if it had really been gained from the sea, and that I am now upon what were the banks of it living in tents. The change of scene makes it very delightful to the girls and I was amused. Though we travelled twenty-six days, we were not tired of our journey.

It is really melancholy to think what a time passes between the arrival of each fleet. I have only had three letters by chance conveyances since last August. It is now April and I know that letters were sent to the packet in September. It is a constant expectation of news and as continual disappointment. If we had a regular correspondence how much easier our minds would be. I cannot help sometimes making up monsters in my own mind of what may happen by these terrible delays.

Absence does not make any attachment in England the less, though I am determined to think of it as little as I can while the fates decree that I am to remain in Asia. Certainly I ought to be tolerably contented. Everything in which Lord Clive is concerned goes on well. I am told there will be essential service rendered by him and regulations made that will be for the permanent good of the country. What I hear of the Nahir Princes and their government is so horrible that it is impossible the people should not rejoice at any change that takes them from their tyranny. As for his Highness the *Nawab* of Arcot, he is the most shabby potentate upon earth in mind and appearance and his country starved and pillaged.

April 13th, Henrietta's journal

In the evening we had rain and the following day, which cooled the air, but it is now as hot again as ever. Therefore tomorrow we shall be established upon the hill for a few days.

Charly is weak and at times low and looking pale but no bleeding at the nose. Sometimes her spirits are good but not equally so. The removal to the hill is a pleasant change for us. The monkeys delighted us *all*.

On April 14th Charly's journal characterised the monkeys as 'great thieves, slipping their fingers through the Venetian blinds, and carrying off everything they can reach; they one day came into the dining-room, which is open to the verandah, where preparations were made for dinner, and carried off all the rolls that were on the table'.

April 14th, Henrietta's journal

After having sent off my letters to go by the fleet I went up the Rock to inhabit a small bungalow upon the upper works for cooler air. About two or three weeks after I was there a comical imposition was attempted. The people say that the hill is inhabited by some goddess sisters who bathe every Sunday night in the largest tank on the rock. About eleven o'clock at night, the greatest disturbance was heard. Large stones were rolled down from the upper part, which fell near the batteries' tents. The Black servants were terribly alarmed and so were the girls and Signora Anna. The servants said the gods were angry and that some of the town people spoke languages that they never knew before and all were terrified to the greatest degree. I did not hear the noise. Captain Brown went up on the rock but could not discover anything. The first alarm was given by the sentinels at the upper part of the fort. And afterwards, though the guard understood a voice that said, 'Not stay.' Another voice was heard to say that if I did not quit the place in a week that we should all be killed. Upon examining the place afterwards there was found that a famous cave was just below the battery from whence the sentinel was alarmed and that by means of a long ladder which hung in this cave any person might with care get up to the battery. I believe it was a prank played either with a chance of getting money from me or from the servants in which I believe they succeeded. On the next Sunday night I had many of the bodyguard dispersed on the hill and never heard any more of the goddesses except that they had quitted the rock.

April 14th, Henrietta to Lord Clive

My dear Lord Clive – After being three weeks without seeing your handwriting I spare you. I am not a little pleased to see it yesterday. Your letters, though not so numerous as mine, are very long and unforgettable to me . . .

Charly is cured of all her ills by a dose of rhubarb and in spirits equal to any of her *friends* [monkeys] upon the Rock. Brown is a great deal better but has not attempted riding yet.

April 15th, Henrietta to Lord Clive

I am very sorry to find that you have had some rheumatism in one of your feet and have been wrapt in flannel. I am afraid you have been too much in the sun and that it is a little bile that has travelled to your feet. I cannot suppose it is *gout* and I do not like it that you should be unwell when we, your nurses, are absent. I hope William Thomas supplies you with novels and that you do not miss us very much. Harry has not been well, but yesterday took an emetic, which seems to have done her good. She is weak this morning but is looking much better. Charly's nose has behaved ill again yesterday, but she does not seem at all unwell and the cold bathing is begun again. Colonel Mackay had heard of you being rheumatic and has sent you a bottle of infallible oil from Malacca. I know that you are sometime incredulous, but I send it to you that if you are so disposed you may try it. Brown has been ill again and is creeping out and living upon broth. Still he looks very thin. Two nights ago he had a strong return of fever and headache and was a day in bed.

I am better and get up early as soon as it is light to perch upon an old wall a little higher than the house in a fine fresh air when the thermometer was from 6 to 7 o'clock at 71 and a half this morning. I believe it does me good. Any exercise seems too much. Many loves to you from the two animals [the girls]. We are now much amused and a little infested with monkeys. The day before yesterday they carried off a loaf just before dinner. I have a little blue *orderly* with a pistol and some *powder* to frighten them, as they are very impertinent. I wish you were here. I am sure you would like it much. The air is pure and the prospect not a little wild.

Ever my dear Lord,
your very affectionate
H. A. C.

April 16th, from Henrietta to Lord Clive

I have not seen Brown this morning, as he is unwell from having been too much out yesterday and had a return of fever and headache, but it is going off. I find he has heard from Grant that there is some alarm about the *Mornington*, which makes us quite miserable.

We live like *hermits* upon our Rock and it is very comfortable. I went out early this morning again. Sally had a fall yesterday while she was riding and in the charge of Giaffer who was frightened *to death*. The horse escaped and was followed by him twelve miles to a *droog* where it fastened itself in a tree by the saddle, which had turned under him, but it is not injured. He is to be starved a little and rode more.

April 20th, Henrietta to Lord Clive

I am quite in despair at the news which Brown heard yesterday of the capture of the *Mornington* in the channel. It is a most serious misfortune if it is true and cuts us off from all news of everybody for many months.

Captain Brown is to go next week to see Bangalore and the hill above Colar, which is the place for which I have the greatest fancy. Brown is a good deal better but is very weak still and requires taking care of himself.

April 21st, Henrietta to Lord Clive, continued

I have nothing much worth saying to you. We are all pretty well. Charly's nose bled a great deal last night, which we attribute to the heat, which was uncommonly great. She is weak today and Harriet is weak too. We watch in vain for clouds and rain. Tonight Brown goes to Bangalore . . . I have heard nothing more of the seven goddesses that are supposed to bathe in the tank from which we have water . . . Somebody hid themselves upon the Rock in order to frighten the people and rob us, but the servants are not yet quite convinced. We had not the bodyguard as sentinels, since we came here, at night, which we used to have. When Giaffer heard that the devil had been so loud and had stolen the fowls, he asked, 'What *devil do with fowls*?' which I thought a good question. We have not yet discovered how it was contrived, but from the direction of the stones, they came from an old ruined prison of Tipu's on the upper part of the Rock. I am very glad to hear you are almost well.

April 25th, Henrietta to Lord Clive, continued

I heard yesterday from Captain Brown at Bangalore. The thermometer was that day exactly which it is in this house. He says the palace wants little besides cleaning and as all the troops are ordered to Chitteldroog it will be quite empty. I am wishing much to hear from you, as much in vain I am afraid as far as the rain. Perhaps both may come together. We are all pretty well but in want of exercise, which is impossible to have. We have not much space here. Below it is too hot. The journey is sufficient to fatigue us.

Although we have not heard any more of the goddesses on the hill, we have discovered that there is an old unfrequented way by which I am persuaded the person came and which is just by the battery from whence the *sepoy* was frightened. The ladies always bathe on a Sunday. I shall have more trusty guards on the night than the *sepoys*.

April 26th, Henrietta to Lord Clive, continued

My dear Lord Clive – we are all pretty well in expectation of rain of which we had one shower yesterday with a great deal of wind and thunder, but it is not sufficient and it is very hot again today. I am nervous and weak.

Brown has sent me such a description of Bangalore that I shall like much to go to Colar as soon as we have had sufficient rain to make the journey tolerable. At present I dare not risk the heat of the tents in the daytime.

I am very glad that the directors have appointed Henry Clive. You certainly deserve that sort of compliment *at best* from them. The newspaper says you and Lord Mornington are to receive some *conspicuous* mark of approval. I think the best thing would be to send for you to England as I do not see any reward can be *sufficiently great* except that. If *they* were to consult me I should advise it with a *large additional income.* Don't you think that would be *very good* and right and pleasant?

I do not quite comprehend the house plan* from the description, but I conclude it is what you mentioned to me before we left the Garden House.

* Lord Clive is remodelling the Garden House in Madras.

I shall be very glad to see the plan and to know when it will be finished. If the girls have what you then proposed by the *music room*, may it be as much out of my hearing as it can because here I enjoy it *so much* that I shall be glad to have a cessation now and then. There are discordant sounds and a little scolding of Signora Anna, which altogether *is not amusing*, you know. All the other apartments remaining I approve much, being very unwilling to give up my little room where I have vegetated so long.

The rain will not come in spite of the appearance of the clouds, which have travelled round us for these three days. I am anxious to hear again from you though I had a letter a few days ago, as I am not a little anxious to move towards Bangalore for which we wait for orders from the Governor in Council.

May 1st, Henrietta to Lord Clive

My dear Lord Clive – we heard that Josiah Webbe was at Vellore which surprised me to find he was so gay as to have left Madras and I am afraid than an overland dispatch to my brother will not be in time as it was directed to him. He must have been at Vellore at the time it arrived at Madras.

We have no rain and are very impatient for it, as you may well suppose, and not a little for your answer about Bangalore. We are anxious to go there and Dr Hausman wishes much for it from our inability to use much exercise. I wish to go there next week at least to set out from hence and only wait till I hear from you. We are all pretty well. Charly's nose has not bled these ten days which is very pleasant to me and makes me afraid of going down the hill till we have some rain, as it is evident that any increase of heat brings it on.

I hear you are well. Thomas says so, though still with a large shoe.

May 2nd, Henrietta to Lord Clive

My dear Lord Clive – A thousand thanks to you for the letter and the plan, which I received yesterday. I am sorry to find that you have any remains of complaint and uneasiness in your foot. I am quite persuaded if you can come up to us it would be of the greatest service to your health.

We are expecting Josiah Webbe desiring to borrow my bearers. He must be Governor to be so in his time and to come to see us. I shall tell him so as we expect him [to be] passing this place and perhaps [he will] dine with me on my Rock.

I am much pleased with the plans which I see are just what you spoke about before I left you and approve of everything except I see that you take away my little dressing room. I doubt if the new room will be too hot for me. I think the garden room will be really magnificent and I begin to collect plants for you, which you will like. You do not say when it is to be built nor if the new great room is where the old one is.

Colonel Close is now sitting with us and speaking Mussulman and has been reading Persian. I think he will be a great amusement to me in these hot days.

The girls are very merry and desire their love to you.

Ever yours, very affectionately

H. A. C.

May 4th, Henrietta to Lord Clive

I have this moment received your express. Rain having fallen yesterday evening and in greater abundance around us, I had just settled with Brown that we would go in two or three days to Bangalore. Therefore your letter came just at the right moment. We will not be taken by Dhoondiah* most certainly. I had thought of him and Captain Brown asked Col Close when he was here if he thought there was any risk and he did not think there was any. Col Close mentioned his house to me and I shall like it much and am very glad we may move. Many of the followers have wishes made to move therefore it is not my own fidgety disposition though I really believe I want change of air or at least more exercise than I can use. Dr Hausman advises bathing and driving out which I shall do as well as I can, but that is not much exercise for me.

I am very sorry that you say that obstacles increase to prevent your coming here because though we are all well here I feel uncomfortable at the distance we are from each other and the length of time. What a pity

* After the fall of Tipu Sultan, Dhoondiah led an uprising against the British.

it is that Dhoondiah got out of his confinement at Seringapatam to torment this country. I have no doubt it will end in his destruction, but from the account they give me of his way of fighting it may be a long time before it is done.

I have an excellent Mussulman from Colonel Close. He was about Tipu and in great trust of treasure, I believe, or keeper of all the necklaces that I cannot now get in the jewel lottery. He understands a little English and seems a respectable person. The girls come to speak Moors and I see he is much amused with Charly and her disposition for speaking languages.

May 6th, Henrietta to Lord Clive

This morning Colonel Close arrived and found us breakfasting under a tent in the midst of Colonel Mackay's garden with peaches, some of which are just going to you. I consulted him about my movements as you desired and he says he cannot see the smallest risk in my going to Bangalore that Dhoondiah is more than one hundred miles now from Bangalore, that it must be known at least three weeks before he could at all approach. But he advises us to wait till Josiah Webbe comes up and goes to Seringapatam where he will see everybody and hear everything and may write to you directly. All this will be left for you to decide. I expect to see Josiah Webbe today at dinner. Colonel Close is just going off with my *palanquin* boys.

We had a violent storm the evening before last with wind beyond everything and a good deal of rain, but less than has fallen around us. Colonel Close was surprised with the girls' good looks. We thought of you and your ball while we were walking up the hills by moonlight with a fine breeze in our faces and rather thought you would have envied us as that you perhaps would have preferred sitting upon one of the rocks to the *yellow sateen chairs in the great room*. I cannot help the paper being so shamefully bad and my writing not being *very neat*.

I wish much you would send me a good whip for the lion. Anybody coming up in a *palanquin* might loan it for me.

Adieu, my dear Lord, ever yours very affectionately.

H. A. C.

On May 7th Charly wrote joyously that 'The Mornington packet arrived in Bengal', which is to say there would soon be mail.

May 7th, Henrietta to Lord Clive

I am so happy at having the letters safe that I do not know what to say or do. I am surprised not to have heard from my brother, but he is well. He is mentioned in some of my letters as being quite well. He is to *give fêtes* to the King and Queen and that he has Guntier the Confectioner for the *summer*. All this sounds as if he must be quite well and in good spirits.

Yesterday Josiah Webbe arrived and I talked to him and he will write to you from Seringapatam but he agrees with Col Close that there is now no risk in going to Bangalore. The preparations have made Dhoondiah turn toward the *Nizam* and by letters he has lately had he says he is quite satisfied that all is safe. Col Close said that Dhoondiah's Army was *nominally* 10,000 men but not so in reality, and not at all likely to attack your frontier. However at Seringapatam he will hear everything and will directly write to you. He was not at all well before he left this place. He had not kept himself well and had starved himself, which made him unwell.

I could not omit writing to tell you that you were *perfect* for sending an express and that we are quite happy to hear from these good souls in England. Poor Henry Ashton's executors have a mind to dispute the will made here with the legacy to Major Cragrie, which I am sorry for. He left her no ready money nor anything but a bare jointure. She will live at Ashton.

May 8th, Henrietta to Lord Clive

You are really so wonderfully good that it is quite charming two letters in a day. We suffered much yesterday from the land wind. The only thing that revived us was the letters. If you have my newspapers when you have done with them we should like much to have them.

Adieu, my dear Lord,
ever your very affectionate
H. A. C.

I am sorry to see my eldest son's handwriting is so much worse than the younger. We are in great want of writing paper.

On May 11th Charly received information on their intended route along with a letter addressed to Miss Charlotte Clive from Captain Thomas Sydenham in Madras: 'I am going to trouble you once more, with the perusal of an historical sketch of the Mysore country, which I have requested Lady Clive to have the goodness to forward to you. Another packet of information, containing an account of the principal places between Ryacottah and Seringapatam, is preparing, and will be shortly completed. Mrs Sydenham was so kind as *to let me have a peep* at your journal, and I was happy to find you had made such good use of your time. I perceive that your name is enrolled amongst those, whom curiosity has prompted to ascend the *Coverum* of the Conjeveram *pagoda* but I hope you did not follow the footsteps of T. Sydenham, who very imprudently, and at the risk of his life, walked round the outer cornice at the very summit of the *Coverum*. But this was done in his *juvenile* days, and we both know, that he is now grown more *cautious*, and *sedate*.

'On Friday last, I dined with Lord Clive at the Garden, from whence we proceeded to a grand ball at Mr Chinnery's. On Saturday we met his Lordship at Mr Webbe's who had a small party to dinner, in celebration of his birthday, and yesterday we spent the day at the Red Hills, and returned at night.

'The climate at Kistnagherry, and Ryacottah, will be a most seasonable relief after the heat, which you must have experienced through the Carnatic, and Barahmahal. The weather at Madras had been sultry, but a constant succession of southerly winds, and sea breezes, prevents the heat from being very oppressive. The thermometer in the house about noon is generally between 85 degrees and 7.

'As the homeward bound ships are positively to sail on the 15th of this month, you may conceive how busily Mrs Sydenham is engaged in her final preparations for the voyage. I request you will do me the favour, to present my respectful compliments to Miss Clive, and Signora Tonelli.

'I am, your obedient, humble servant,
'Thomas Sydenham'

May 13th, Henrietta to Lord Clive

My dear Lord – I thank you much for the letter I had from you yesterday after the leave to go to Bangalore for which we are all extremely anxious. The great heat affects us and we are certain that it is much cooler there and that we shall have more space. You cannot imagine how we have been annoyed in town and *land.* We shall make our journey as quick as I can that we get through the heat to a better climate. I think we shall meet Josiah Webbe in the road.

Charly is better but delicate and requires some care. If it is not hot she will grow better every day after we go from hence. We are working hard with Persian and Moosulman and the most excellent old Munshee from Colonel Close who was of consequence in Tipu's time. He tells me stories of Tipu that I begin to comprehend. The girls work with the Moor's language and in a few months they will understand it completely. It amuses me much. They desire many loves to you.

Ever, my dear Lord, yours very affectionately
H. A. C.

On May 13th the travellers went down from the Rock in order to start for Bangalore the next day. They went to see the Bull's Mouth, a spring in the rock that flows continuously from out of a bull's mouth carved in stone. No more was heard from the seven goddesses; the Hindu priests told the servants that the goddesses were so offended that they had left the Rock.

May 15th, Henrietta to Lord Clive

We are again descended from the fort and are now in preparation for the journey to Bangalore. I mean to set out tomorrow evening by which we shall avoid the heat of that day and only one in the tents which will be a great saving and shall of course get to Bangalore on the next. I am very anxious to find myself there.

On May 16th the party started at four in the afternoon for Bangalore accompanied by Col Mackay and Captain Graham; they soon lost sight of Ryacottah Rock, from the number of hills which surrounded it. They arrived after dark at Kattymungalum, where they found their tents pitched. Near the door of the dinner-tent Charly observed a collection of fireflies in a tree which 'appeared illuminated and, contrasted with the dark leaves, had a beautiful effect'. On May 17th they started in 'a very cold morning' and journeyed about fourteen miles to find their tents pitched in a mango tope at Attapilly where 'the water was very bad and muddy'.

May 18th, Attapilly, Henrietta to Lord Clive

As I am in a most blessed land I must write to tell you so. Yesterday evening we left Ryacottah and went to Kattymungalum. We had a very pleasant journey as we quitted the hills it became cooler and today it is quite *delightful*. The country is open and there are little streams occasionally, which remind one of the appearance of a common field in England. It was really cold this morning and the thermometer at 73. We are all revived and changed astonishingly. The feel of the air is quite different from any I ever met with in the Carnatic and indeed it promises to be delightful to us. We wish much for you, as you cannot imagine the feel it gives us of freshness and health.

Bangalore: May 18th to July 13th

'All being the only thing like India I have ever seen and perfectly unlike everything else except an old Japan cabinet . . . a complete idea of an Eastern palace . . . '

Henrietta, Anna Tonelli, Charly and Harry arrived at Bangalore at eight o'clock in the morning on May 18th, without any troops in attendance other than their own escort of *sepoys* and bodyguard. Captain Brown commanded at Bangalore. In 1791 Tipu Sultan, having vowed never to enter any place that had been taken by the English, had dismantled Bangalore when he thought it would not stand against Cornwallis. He had, however, left Haidar Ali's magnificent palace intact: the interior, painted by Delhi artisans, still glowed with patterns of flowers in rich reds, greens and gold. The travellers were delighted to stay there. In 1799 Tipu's palace at Seringapatam had not been long finished before it, too, was besieged by the English.

May 18th, Bangalore, Henrietta to Lord Clive

We came here this morning after a very pleasant drive. We set out at 4 o'clock and the thermometer was then at 70 and we were really cold. I even put on a shawl to drive. I cannot say how much we are pleased with this place. We shall go to the garden this evening; it seems delightful. The fort is as it was left by Tipu and very dismal in appearance, but the strength of the gates seems prodigious. There are many marks of cannon balls in the top of the walls and Captain Brown showed us the place where the troops got up the march, which is as it was then.

The palace has a large square before it so the entrance is on one side of one of the main courts, which is therefore not handsome, but the appearance quite pleased us. All being the only thing like *India* I have ever seen and perfectly unlike everything else except an old Japan cabinet. It is so contrived that there must always be a through air, but the wind be in whatever quarter it chooses. There is a large open veranda very high upstairs and open where we shall dine. There is a small room from that on the right hand. An old door goes into a gallery which is open on one side, at each end of which are two rooms: one for Signora Anna and the girls and the other's for me to sleep and sit. There is a court opposite to each gallery before our apartments that belongs to us as well as the rest and is not to be inhabited but by ourselves if we choose it. That opposite to the entrance is for Captain Brown and Dr Hausman. The fourth side we have not employed and have no opening into it.

The walls have been magnificent with gold, scarlet, and green and are still tolerably clean and good and there is not any glare. I am glad to have seen this sort of building as it gives a complete idea of an Eastern palace.

The number of interior rooms is immense with strange passages that lead to nothing.

The air is delightful. It is like nothing I have felt in the *East* and if Dhoondiah does not disturb us we are in perfect comfort here. Colonel Close wrote to Captain Brown today and says that he is still farther from us. After the Rock at Ryacottah this is really not only a palace but a *paradise* and I have not the least doubt it will make a material change in our health. The girls are well and much delighted. The appearance of this place makes me wish more than ever that you should come. What I have as yet seen is better than I expected. Many loves to you.

We walked in the commanding officer's garden, where there is a beautiful avenue of cypress trees, besides peach trees &c. &c. and we visited another garden afterwards, containing all sorts of plants. In the garden of the palace, among low buildings, which had been *zenanas*, we found many white rose trees. Mr Webbe dined here on his road to Madras.

May 20th I went the night we came here to the garden and it was agreed that if you were to see it, it would be difficult to make you leave it again. The *havildar* says that since 1791 not the least care even in respect to the watering (though there is a large tank on purpose above it) has been taken of it. The trees are magnificent for fruit trees and loaded with fruit. The garden that belongs to the Commanding officer is small but filled with fine cypresses and a great many rose trees and apple trees, enough to plant a large orchard. It was late before we had been round the garden that therefore I could not see everything so exactly as I shall by and bye. Josiah Webbe came here yesterday and as we dined later than usual we could not go out afterwards. We have some small squares that have some plants and very well contrived with small channels for watering them. It is very pleasant to me to gather a large handful of roses before breakfast.

There is a bath that I think when you are building such things might be very pleasant for you. Water was thrown over me. I tried it yesterday in great comfort. It is in a standing place raised with a little wall round it that the water does not spread over the room again or on the clothes and runs off directly. It is where Tipu was bathed and washed his head. There is *another apartment* which I am sure would divert you as it did us.

We are all pretty well as Josiah Webbe will tell you. Colonel Mackay has promised to collect some seeds of trees we like and will send them. He came with us here with Captain Graham, the collector. Notwithstanding all his *bows*, we like him much. He knows a good deal of natural history and plants and is very good about picking out those sort of things for me. I have tried to find some stones worth sending to you, but it is impossible. They are not worth it.

We are hoping for rain very much. It is hot in the room I have to sit in but the galleries or verandas are more delightful than anything I have ever seen and we wish we could transport them to Madras. The girls are well. Charly is a little thin but is now well. We are learning with all our might and shall bring back a great many stories of Tipu. He must have been a most horrid creature and not a little mad.

Many loves to you from the girls.

The history of Mysore that Captain Sydenham sent to Charly proved to be most useful to the travellers who were coming to understand more and more what sort of man Tipu Sultan was and the manner by which the British had assumed his world:

'By the treaty of Seringapatam in 1792 a vast portion of the extensive dominions of Tipu were divided amongst the allied powers. The provinces of Malabar, the Barahmahal, and Salem countries were assigned to the Company. The surrounding provinces to the north were annexed to the territories of the Nizam; and Benkipour, Sanoor, and the extensive province to the west and NW fell to the share of the Mahrattas.

'By the partition treaty of Seringapatam in 1799, the remainder of the actual dominions of the late Tipu Sultan were divided between the Company, the *Nizam*, and the *Rajah* of Mysore; so that by one of the most rapid and extraordinary revolutions which are recorded in the chequered annals of Indian history, the family of the ancient *Rajahs* of Mysore, have been placed in possession of a territory, far more extensive than the hereditary dominions of their ancestors. The Viceroy of the Mogul, or the *Nizam*, has recovered the large and fertile provinces which were first conquered by the original Mussulman invaders. And the

English Company had established their power on this side of India, with firm and permanent ties of Moderation, Justice and Magnanimity.'

In Bangalore on May 21st, Henrietta, Harry, Charly and Anna resumed their visits to places of local interest and continued their education into the various expressions of religion in India. They viewed a swamy bull of immense size and learned of the god Hanuman, depicted as an immense stone monkey. They were allowed to enter a Malabar temple since it had already been polluted by the Mahrattas and found to their amazement that one of the carved figures had five heads and many arms.

May 23rd, Henrietta to Lord Clive

I hear the 25th arrived this morning near this place and they are ordered to be ready to march. The country round this good place is a *little* bare and open. The roads will soon be good enough on all sides for me to drive. At present there are not many that are comfortable. You cannot imagine how pleasant the carriage and the *bandy* are to me and how much they have contributed to my amusement.

If there is not a good deal of rain I believe the trees in the garden will almost all die. There is an immense tank at the end of it, but it is nearly dry. The garden belonging to the commanding officer is I think much pleasanter than that of the company and is in much better order. They are near together with a fine mango tope between them. It is a great pity to see large parts and divisions of the garden filled with rose trees, but quite neglected and wild and other divisions of fine apple trees. If you would send some cuttings of myrtle it would be a very good deed. There is not any here and indeed fewer varieties of plants than I expected.

I enjoy the palace very much. I have not had so much room to walk about for a long time and there is constant breeze in the rooms we live in, but my bedchamber is very hot. If the weather does not change I must sleep in the tent.

Certainly the change in Harry is very great since we left Ryacottah. She has some *bloom* and looks fresh. Charly is rather thin though her looks are improved very much.

There is a sweetness and purity in the air that is beyond all description.

We have been today to see some of the manufactories of this place, which are chiefly of silk and some pretty.

I suppose you are very busy but I should like to hear from you. I am sure complete health is necessary to support the heats of Madras.

Adieu.

On May 25th General Ross dined with the travellers on his way to Seringapatam to inspect the fortifications. He stopped in Bangalore to examine the old fort, in order to decide whether the foundations would support the new building if it were repaired.

May 25th, Henrietta to Lord Clive

You must allow it was a little shabby to send a letter without a word with it when you might as well have said if you were well or not. I hear from Dr Thomas that you are so and that there are new novels arrived which I suppose you are reading instead of writing to me. Last night after I was gone to bed Major Copper came to Captain Brown and went on to Madras directly. He carries you some plants of raspberry and blackberry and some seeds.

Last night we walked round the rampart. It is dismal to behold it in its present state. Tipu blew up the stones and large pavement of brick when he destroyed it . . .

Adieu
and many loves.

May 27th, Henrietta to Lord Clive

I was very agreeably surprised by your letter while I was writing under the cypress trees early yesterday morning and just now the letters arrived for which we thank you much. I am very glad you give a better account of yourself than you did in your last letter that you have left off your large shoes. We are well and likely to be better as we had a fine rain last night in which we were all wet to the skin.

A Captain Dees is come with 300 or 400 horses, but the storm has put them into more confusion than Dhoondiah can ever do. They got loose and many are wandering about the country. The 28th has not yet arrived. We are very quiet here within the walls.

You are to have letters tomorrow from two ladies, *at least* I believe so. They take a great deal of pains with the Moors and me with my Persian. It is a great amusement.

Captain Brown has had the history of your expenses from Johnson and thinks that there is an appearance of there being a little too much. He has given me the enclosed paper and rather wishes you to enquire about it as they seem to draw for money at least they did last year sometime when it was wanted by which he says you pay interest unnecessarily. We are as economical as we can be. There is scarcely anything here to be bought, but I shall bring a little of the manufactories which they will make for me.

Adieu, my dear Lord.

May 30th, Henrietta to Lord Clive

I did not write to you yesterday because you had had a letter from a fair lady the day before that assured you we were alive. I have got two trees of sandalwood, about six feet long and one diameter. They are fresh and just cut down. Would you like to have any more as the *havildar* can get more if you wish it from Saverdroog. I shall try to get some young plants if possible to send you. We mean to send these trees bya bye through Ryacottah where they will take up a red wood tree from Col Mackay and the whole with the future rose and other trees will make a load for a bandy with the assistance of three antelopes, who are the greatest favourites and perfectly tame following us about. Captain Brown says it will be much better to send them all together as we want things here in return and he does not wish to part with any *lascars.* We wish much to have some common garden seeds sent here. Radishes, turnips, or anything: ours are nearly at an end.

We have had very fine rain for some evenings and a great deal of lightning. I will not tantalise you by telling you how the thermometer was this morning.

I should like much to send rose trees. They are so charming, but I doubt if it is not too hot in your country for them to travel. I hear of a great deal of sandalwood to be sold at Seringapatam, which they are sending in cars to Madras. Perhaps it may be good.

Colonel Close is to come here in a few days. General Ross goes I believe on Sunday to Seringapatam. We are trying to collect uncommon birds but as yet have not been very successful.

The garden is at present not in a state to be amusing except as a walk, being perfectly wild. The apple trees and roses would delight you. You will tell me what number and sorts you wish to have.

Many loves to you.

June 1st, Henrietta to Lord Clive

I have been breakfasting under the shade of rose apple trees in the garden in great comfort, and enjoying a very cool morning. I wish you could enjoy the fine air that we are at this moment. Yesterday we had an excellent pineapple arrived from William Call's late garden, in other words yours, which really was the best I have ever eaten in this country.

The girls are in good spirits as usual and delighted with every little bush in the garden. I see Charly will be very fond of plants and Harry as fond of feeding animals. She pays the greatest attention to the antelopes, which are very beautiful and quite tame.

In spite of all sorts of curtains and shades my eyes suffer a good deal which is the only unpleasant thing as I wish to employ them much. Pray don't forget the kitchen garden seeds. The Commanding Officer's garden supplies us now. Many loves to you.

The thermometer ranged from 70 to 81 degrees, during May and June. The travellers found the palace hot, so they used their tents at night, which were pitched in the beautiful avenue of cypress trees, in the commanding officer's garden. They continued their early morning visits to see celebrated shrines of the gods. Some of the idols, which were carried about during the Hussein Hassan feast held at this time were made of gold, and some of silver paper. Some represented mosques. It appeared that on this day the different religions joined together in this feast. On June 3rd Charly wrote in her journal: 'About twelve o'clock at night we went to see the idols carried about the *pettah*; some had blue lights, and some Bengal lights, and generally one man sang the death of Hussein Hassan, the others joining in the chorus, beating their breasts at the same time, and seeming quite in earnest. During the ceremony, there were people dancing round the fire, and calling out repeatedly Hussein Hassan Ali! Many were painted with charcoal and oil, and some with white and red. The boys had their faces painted red and white, with red and white sashes twisted together and white petticoats with green (Ali's colour) bells. They went about singing. The night was so cold, that it required shawls in the house.' Charly continued her account on June 4th: 'At twelve o'clock we went to see the ceremony at the Tank. All the little Mosques were pulled to pieces and washed, and then put together again; they are presented to the Tank by the people, who join in singing and dancing as if they were mad. When the ceremony was over, the shrines were covered with a cloth, and carried home without any procession. The boys continued singing, in their dresses of yesterday, and were by this time very hoarse. There was a fight, and a man was killed. Everybody collected money, and gave dinners to the poor, and to the beggars. It was half-past three when we got home. One of the elephants died suddenly.'

June 4th, Henrietta to Lord Clive

It would be cruel to tell you the height of the thermometer. Yesterday evening even my Welsh blood asked for a shawl. I had a delightful walk this morning at seven o'clock through the garden really walking as if round the shrubbery at Walcot to make me comfortable before breakfast. The walks are cleared of grass and we are very comfortable. If you were once to see the garden I am sure you would never leave it again.

I forgot I believe to mention that Captain Brown is *very anxious* for your answer about the trees as we are in want of stores or shall be by the time the *bandy* can go to Madras and return and he wishes to send the trees by that opportunity.

I see the Marquis of Wellesley in the *Gazetteer* from the overland dispatch. Is he to have all spots of tygers and flags and others nothing, either solid or ornamental?

I wish I could send you a fine whistling wind that I have round me at this moment. This country is well worth the pains of taking it. It will be pleasant to you to know the great numbers of the old inhabitants are returning here some after ten or twelve years absence. We met a large party a few nights ago and they say they come in every day particularly since we came here. They fancy it is a proof of the security of the place. Colonel Close and Purneah are expected everyday. Many loves from the girls.

On June 5th the 25th Regiment passed through on their way to Chittled-droog, for the approaching campaign against Dhoondiah. The travellers in residence proved of some use in aiding the passage of the troops. Captain Brown was active in collecting means for conveying (bullocks and elephants) and feeding them.

June 7th, Henrietta to Lord Clive

I am sorry to find that you have had a little more rheumatism and afraid that the Red Hills where you are tempted, I am sure, to be more in the sun than you ought to. We are in some measure the cause of it. All your improvements at this time of the year are bad for your health and the sun must be terrible at Madras. We are all well.

The 25th Dragoon came here two days ago and marches again tomorrow towards Chitteldroog. Colonel Close is expected every day with Purneah. I wish it was as necessary for a Governor of the Carnatic to see the country and judge of all things as it is for the Resident of the Mysore.

Josiah Webbe sent a *Gazette* this morning. What do you think of peace and a King of France? I want much to know what is likely to happen. We are anxious to see news of the *Madras Lottery*.* My fortune

* The Madras Lottery, established in 1797, raffled off objects to make funds to provide the native poor of Madras with such projects as hospitals and dispensaries. Funds were used for the public good.

is to be much increased by it. But the vile newspaper today does not give a list of the prizes.

We have been obliged to pick out a little *warm* room for the evening and have one that just holds us at the end of the gallery. This must sound very *strange* to you. All sorts of loves to you from the girls. It is pleasant to look at their altered faces. I wish you could do so too.

Adieu.

June 10th, Henrietta to Lord Clive

You have been sometime without writing which is not a little shabby, I think, considering so many fair ladies write from hence. Colonel Close and Purneah arrived this morning and came here with shawls and flowers. I do not know whether we are to keep them or not, but we are all in hopes it *may be lawful* as they are very beautiful. I shall enquire of Col Close what is right. We are all well. The rain is not come yet and is much wanted for the cultivation.

Colonel Close is much pleased with the number of the inhabitants here returned since he was here four months ago. There are great numbers and they are coming in fast. All this must be pleasant to My Lord, the Governor.

I have got fifty young sandalwood trees. They are very small and are for the present in the garden till you choose to have them. I doubt the safety of moving trees at this time of the year into the Carnatic.

We have now and then flying reports of Dhoondiah being beaten, but I am afraid without much foundation. The 25th marched on Sunday morning. Many loves to you from two damsels in perfect health and spirits.

June 13th, Henrietta to Lord Clive

I really do not think you deserve so many letters when you never write to me. It is three weeks today since I had one from you and I desired particularly that you would answer me about the trees for your garden as Brown is anxious to send away the *bandy*, as we shall have no wine if it does not set out soon. Be so gracious as to have a *permit*, I forget the right word, for the *bandy* to pass through his Highness's dominions. We are all well and very cool. Colonel Close and his suite breakfasted with me under some very fine rose apple trees in the company's garden and tomorrow we breakfast and, I believe, drive with him to a pretty place seven or eight miles from hence in way to Ooscotah.

Purneah made me a visit after breakfast in the garden and when they were gone it was so cool that we walked home at 9 o'clock.

We are much obliged to you for the seeds. There were no radishes, or carrots or much to my satisfaction, no onion seed. The girls are as usual. Col Close thinks them much improved since he saw them at Ryacottah. Your pineapples are the best ever I have seen in this country.

On June 14th Purneah sent the travellers a special invitation to visit his encampment. Charly wrote her impressions. She described his tents as 'having no draught through them and very hot'. She found that 'his troops, dressed in red uniforms turned up with orange, did not march well. Nor did the cavalry do much better; some went one way, and some another, without any regularity.' She considered it to be 'a singular circumstance that Purneah, a Brahmin, should have been employed by Tipu. Because he was very clever, he became much esteemed, and was, therefore, important to the tyrant, in governing his Hindu subjects. He was often in disgrace, but having charge of all the treasure, he was so constantly referred to for the innumerable presents and brides Tipu had to bestow, that it made him too necessary not to be restored to favour.'

June 15th, Henrietta to Lord Clive

It is a great deal to receive two letters on two days following after a silence of three weeks. I must say that yours are long and comfortable when they do come. I am sorry to find there does not seem any prospect of seeing you here in this place so like *England* and *Paradise* that I would give anything to see you here. You bear heat much better than we do certainly and I hope to show you two stout girls when we return and I wish you to think and decide when that time is to be that we may make all our little arrangements in case it is quite out of the question that you should come.

I do not think we ought to return before the end of August. The visible alteration in Charly in hot weather makes me wish to stay till the heat has a little subsided in the Carnatic. I think before that time we are not likely to be at all comfortable near Madras. The next consideration is how we are to return. We are all anxious that it should not be by the road we came both on account of the heat and that we may see as much variety of country as we can. Dr Hausman talks much about the Coimbatoor. Everybody tells me some place or another is worth seeing and I wish you to say what you choose we should do and then all may be settled comfortable to ourselves.

No doubt the Ameer Bagh is very comfortable. Much more so I believe than the Garden House except the room above our apartments, which I suspect to be very warm. My little bathing room will be delightful indeed. I am persuaded it is of service to us all and I am much pleased with the Governor having invented it for me. As for the great house, I am not in any hurry to inhabit it having, as you know, no great partiality to it. The ladies say they are no judges respecting the division of the rooms and desire you to do what ever you think best. I really am not much wiser on the subject than they are.

I do not know if Signora Anna will think her room satisfactory, which I suppose will be what was the veranda and *done last year*. I have found her much more difficult to satisfy in regard to apartment than I was aware she would be on the journey.

I am very glad your garden goes on well. I think I shall make some additions to it that you will like though there is not that great anxiety I expected to meet with. The pineapples are excellent.

We passed yesterday in a very pleasant mango tope with Colonel Close and Purneah.The troops . . . received us and a most comical set of figures they were. The commander of the infantry was a most majestic figure in *petticoats* with a large turban and a long beard. Col Close has decreed that we are to keep the shawls. He says it cannot be avoided nor they returned with any propriety that if I did not keep them they must to the treasury as they could not go back to Purneah but that I might make him a present in return which I did of two very good shawls I got here and a very handsome dress.*

* Members of the government and their families were not allowed to accept gifts

I am glad your Arab colt and mare [that belonged to Tipu Sultan] are so likely to turn out well. We heard of them on the road, but I was afraid they might not answer to you.

This morning received your letter of the 12th and immediately sent for the elephants. There is not any fodder for them nearer than fourteen miles, but they will set out today. However Brown says that unless you get a permit from the *Nawab* to meet them at Amboor they will be starved in his Highnesses country. He says that if an order is sent to the care of William Davies, the Engineer at the bottom of the Padinaig Durgan Pass he will take care it meets them or to Amboor.

So Josiah Webbe is setting out again. It is all malice he finds causes to travel himself and see strange countries and keeps the Governor to perform the part of a large mastiff guarding the great house in his absence. If you want collectors or *collectoresses* I think I should like to *extremely* . . . and grab over strange countries particularly near Hyderbad. I should delight in it above all things. It is hard that we poor females are not to get anything in this Asiatic world. You may be sure I will keep what you tell me quite secret.

Colonel Close is gone to Ooscotah [Ooty] but will return here soon. He is to make out a route from that he says will be very amusing round this place and to Seringapatam where I hear Col Wellesley and he have contrived everything they can invent to make the most pleasant house comfortable. Pray tell me when my increase of income was to begin. You told Brown it was to be but we do not know from what time and I should like to know.

Pray do not forget the permit for the elephants and the *bandy* with the wine. Col Mackay has sent you four jungle fools [birds]. Pray let them be taken care of for me and if they die, let them be very carefully stuffed, as I am in want of them for my collection and they are only amongst the *ghauts*.

Many loves and *Adieu*.

---

of jewels or expensive items. Presents of shawls and dresses were allowed and were usually exchanged along with a ceremony of *betel* and rose water.

Captain Brown has dismissed Sergeant Smith. He has been very often quite drunk upon the march and incapable of getting on with the tents. As Grant recommended him he had a scruple about sending him away till we came here though I have long wished it. I understand he has written to General Brathwith and Major Grant to hear him. Two days ago he came not positively drunk not yet sober and desired to see me to relate his grievances and how ill Brown had used him which of course I refused as I knew he never met with any European on the road that he was not incapable of his duty for twenty-four hours. I mention this as Brown has written to Grant about it and the man says Grant is keeping the sergeant-majorship for him at Madras.

The permits must be for the elephants, another for the wood on the *bandy* to pass, and to have forage for the bullocks. They set out today and take up the red wood at Ryacottah. Captain Brown is in such a pass for fear these permits should not be sent that I have had two messages since I began to write to remind me of them.

June 18th, Henrietta to Lord Clive

I intended to have written to you yesterday but as I was not very well I thought it was as well to stay till I was better. I had fever and many aches and pains all over me. I am better today but still on my couch and not perfect – though I did a great deal to make me so. The girls are in high health and nurse me extremely. We are in hopes of rain, which is much wanted and will be of great service to us all.

The elephants are gone. It was necessary to keep them a few hours more than was intended that Colonel Close might order forage for them on the road.

I did not answer about the grey colour, which I think will be excellent, if not a very light grey, for the Garden House.

Adieu. Many loves from my nurses.

June 20th, Henrietta to Lord Clive

As I am much better today I think I cannot do better than to tell you so. Yesterday I had great pain in my stomach, back and head. It is now gone and I am recovering fast though this day has been chiefly passed on the couch and I am not returned to my usual occupations. Dr Hausman's way is different from Thomas's but it succeeds very well and I have recovered as soon as it was possible. Within this half hour the plants are arrived. They are not yet unpacked. I hope to see them tomorrow morning. Thomas's news to Captain Brown this morning was that Lord Mornington is going to England with a *sapphire.* Josiah Webbe to Persia. I rather think a former Governor might be rewarding himself rather too much. The girls are quite merry. Many loves to you from the damsels.

June 23rd, Henrietta to Lord Clive

I have not written these two days because I had a mind to say I was quite well in my next letter but it is not yet the case. The pain that has plagued me so much in my stomach is not gone nor do I quite understand what it is but I am still prostrate on the couch and very idle. But a little more medicine will I hope make me well. The girls are in great health and spirits. Your plants all arrived safe except the geraniums, which were certainly drowned, as the leaves were quite moldy and touching the ground. I shall have great pleasure in watching them. I am afraid when we are gone everything in that way will go to ruin. Dr Hyzer (botanist) by his last letters to Dr Hausman does not seem likely to return here for several months and there is not any person here that is beyond a *Lascar* in knowledge which grieves us very much. The garden is beginning to be in order but it will all be lost for want of gardener.

Ever, my dear Lord,
yours very affectionately
H. A. C.

June 25th, Henrietta to Lord Clive

I am growing better, but am not yet well and do not quite comprehend why it is so. I have not been out of pain since this day seven nights ago. But it is neither rheumatism nor flu. Dr Hausman says it will go off when I use my usual medicine (exercise) which at present I cannot do from a great stiffness and soreness in my back and head. It is very uncomfortable and wears me very much. I have had all sorts of medicine to get rid of my ills.

I am happy to see the girls so well and they are, particularly Harriet, very robust. One is writing to you. You have a very fine cabbage going to you today.

June 26th Part of the 19th Regiment of cavalry, on its way to join the army and under the command of Major Kennedy, arrived in Bangalore.

June 26th, Henrietta to Lord Clive

I had your letter this morning and it did me good for I am still a poor creature. The aches still continue . . . Hausman says exercise will cure them, but while they remain it is difficult to use it. I do not walk easily and cannot go in the *bandy*, but the *palanquin* suits me more and I go out whenever I can but the rain sometimes prevents me though it is indeed a great pleasure. I thank you much for all your expressions of pleasure at our health and comfort and, not being in great spirits, I feel this much. I do not wish to move from hence to Seringapatam till just before or on my road to Madras. We are quite quiet and at our ease here and I understand that I am more at liberty as to drives and so here than I should be there and the rains are more violent than at this place. Though I have not been well, I do not find the least fault with the place and I feel it is especially necessary for me to be as cool as I possibly can.

I am very glad the Admiral is well and going on a secret expedition. Report here says it is to Manilla or Batoria. I think he will not refuse to bring me an odd seed or a pebble or some odd little thing if you tell him so. I should like an unknown plant from the Conquering Admiral very much. There is a great promotion in all your state, it seems, civil and military and *I approve* of all very much. I like William Hodgrove extremely. We have Mrs Sheriff here rejoicing at her spouse's promotion. When Colonel Close was here he told me of the Banditi's plot to surprise Col Q but seemed to think it would be quiet directly. However a little martial law may not be amiss before we determine what to do. I confess I should like it most particularly when it was quiet to go round by the Coimbatoor country. I will certainly get the portraits of Colonel Close and Purneah. They are expected in a day or two and will ask him about the old *Ranee*. I think at her age you might safely have her picture without much danger of carrying her away from her beauty and she is certainly a very interesting old personage. I cannot say much for Purneah's beauty. He is short, *rather* fat with a large head, but looks clever and good humoured. His son is exactly like him and a giant but in great order and gravity. I dare say he will be like his father.

I am very sorry you were prevented from writing by a headache. Harry's complexion is like an English rose. *Adieu.*

June 28th, Henrietta to Lord Clive

As I did not give the best account of myself in my last letter I write again to tell you that I am better but still not well and easy – and not yet going out with the lion. We have had rain and are not cooler for it, which is extraordinary.

A few days ago a stranger was seen wandering about in a blue coat and nobody could tell who he was or where he came from. At last the commanding officer sent to desire him his name, which he sent in great form, and it turned out to be Dr Buchanan* sent, as he wrote word, by the Governor General in Council. He certainly did not look like a parson and I wonder he had not called here as he knew you and brought seeds to me from Dr Roxburgh to Madras.

The 19th are arrived on their way to Chittledroog. They are waiting for the second division, which comes by Salem. The rest of the family well and in good spirits. We are going to plant out some of the myrtles in the garden. We have not had a newspaper today, which is a great disappointment, particularly as we are anxious about our fortunes *in the lottery*. You have never told me if you wish any more sandalwood trees. I was in hope to have found some good marble or something worth sending, but I find nothing but a coarse grey granite in large pieces, but not good enough for any tables.

Many loves to you.

* Francis Buchanan, MD, *A Journey from Madras through the Countries of Mysore, Canara, and Malabar*, 3 volumes, 1800 written under the orders of the Most Noble the Marquis Wellesley, Governor General of India

June 29th, Henrietta to Lord Clive

I wrote yesterday but as Captain Brown heard of the elephants today I write to tell you that they were four or five days longer in getting to the pass than they ought to have been and had expected to do and that he says you should have both the *sepoy* who was in charge of them and the chief elephant driver punished.

I am better but have not yet got rid of pain and weakness in my back and bones.

We march tomorrow to Chitteldroog. We hear that Dhoondiah has written to Colonel Wellesley to know what business he had to enter his domain and that if he does not immediately retreat he will come and drive him out with 50,000 men. This I suppose is a sign he is alarmed, but chooses to be valiant. Colonel Close says that Colonel Wellesley hopes I like this place because being here has been a great advantage to him in Captain Brown and sending on stores, which my bullocks have assisted, and he compliments him much upon it. It diverts me that we should be of use to the state. There are upward of 1000 (of the old respectable people chiefly) persons come into the *Pettah* since we came here, near a hundred of them are weavers and the streets are really filled with people. They believe they are safe now.

Many loves from the girls.
Very affectionately
H. A. C.

On June 30th regiments come and go from Bangalore to fight Dhoondiah: the first division of the 19th Regiment resumed their march and the 2nd detachment of the 19th Regiment under Major Patterson arrived.

July 3rd, Henrietta to Lord Clive

I intended writing to you yesterday but as Harry was not quite well I though it better to stay till she was better. It was a little bile and a trifling complaint in her bowels, which an emetic yesterday seems to have cured. She is much better today and in good spirits. I am better, too, but not quite as I should be. We have no news except the confirmation of the taking of *Rannee* Bednore (taken by Wellesley by escalade on the 27th June) from Colonel Close which he sent yesterday here. It seems as if Dhoondiah would soon be taken or demolished. Colonel Close has sent great supplies to the army, which he says, will be of the greatest use and enable them to go on directly.

The trees you sent up are doing well. The myrtles are budding. I think I have found some old orange trees that have been much neglected. I am going to try if I can *bud* some and make trees with them and send them bya bye to you. I do not know that I am enough of a gardener to do this well but there is no harm in trying experiments. We have fine rain and are going to sit in the warmest room tonight with the thermometer at 70 at 7 in the evening. Many loves to you. Harry is much better this evening.

Adieu.

July 5th, Henrietta to Lord Clive

It was a little shabby you must allow to send my two letters without saying a word in the cover. I return them to you. One I see you had opened. The other is rather extraordinary and as it is a request to you. I send it likewise.

Harry is not yet well. The bile is the cause of her illness and must be got rid of before she will be well.

Captain Warren of the 33rd who was with Colonel Close came here yesterday and has been upon the trial at Zundredroog. The proceedings are sent to Colonel Wellesley. One of the criminals poisoned himself before his trial.

Captain Warren has given me three very pretty drawings done by himself of the town and other views near Zundredroog which you will like to see.

Charly is quite well. I cannot say I feel myself near so much so as I was before my illness.

Adieu.

The travellers attended the feast of the *Lascars*, called the *Cherut* (cigar) feast on July 5th and observed the gods, some made of sealing-wax, as they were drawn about in carriages. This was followed on July 6th by a Fire-feast where they were told that people would walk through the flames to be purified. Charly observed that 'the fire was not at all hot, having been covered with fresh charcoal, so that there was only a little smoke. The carriage in which the gods were carried by the men, first passed round the fire, then the sealing-wax gods, and then the people covered with yellow, got up for the occasion to make a show, were to walk through the fire. People of all castes, even Pariahs, picked up the ashes, with which they rubbed their foreheads, to clear off the sins of the year. The thermometer from 69 to 79 degrees.'

July 7th, Henrietta to Lord Clive

Harry is much better today and has nothing remaining, I hope and believe, but weakness. A dose yesterday cured her. Charly is in perfect health. I cannot say I feel well. Colonel Close recommended a journey to Colar and a little round, which he marked out which if we are all well I mean to set out upon the end of this week. I think by the time this expedition is accomplished we shall know more about our farther journey or at least when we get to Seringapatam, but I mean to remain here *after* our return from Colar.

If the scheme of going through the Coimbatoor country, you should not think safe, I should like to go the shortest way from Seringapatam to Trichinopoly and Tanjore. I confess I have heard so much of those places that should much wish to see them and by that means we should pass a very small part of the Coimbatoor. Colonel Close knew when he was here (and told me what had happened there) how much I wished it, and he thinks that it may be done in short time with safety as soon as the examples are made and of his own accord has Captain Macleod, as soon as we move toward Seringapatam, to write all sort of information to Captain Brown.

As you will know all things you will be able to decide what we are to do, but if after that anything arrives we shall know it by that means in time. Colonel Close thinks then when these examples are made that with the information of Captain Macleod and Major Macalister's troops being about the country all will be perfectly safe. I suppose it must be several days before the proceedings of the court martial . . . can come to you from Colonel Wellesley.

We had a very fine rainy night last night, which will be of the greatest service to the country. There has not yet been sufficient to fill the tanks at all.

Yesterday a *lascar* arrived with some very fine pineapples for which we are much obliged to you. Only one was spoilt on the journey. We have not heard if the elephants arrived as they might have done at Madras. I suppose Josiah Webbe is soon setting out.

Loves to you from the girls.
Yours very affectionately,
H. A. C.

This is my brother's birthday. God bless him.

July 9th, Henrietta to Lord Clive

Harry is quite well again and we are thinking of going on our little journey in a day or two if the weather is good. I am sure it will do us good, particularly myself. Yesterday Colonel Sheriff came here. I saw him and he gave me an account of the taking of Rannee Bednore, which must have been terrible to see though quite necessary. There was a fort at some miles distant much stronger than Bednore which they were to attack in a day or two, but when they arrived there was not a fort remaining. Everybody had taken alarm. By a letter from Colonel Close to Captain Brown, the army, which I suppose is Mahrattan and was coming to join Colonel Wellesley, has been completely defeated and cut to pieces . . . It is unfortunate Dhoondiah should have any success to encourage him . . .

Everything is beginning to look green. There are some large fields like England near the gates, which are pleasant to see. Many loves to you from the girls.

Adieu.
H. A. C.

July 10th, Henrietta to Lord Clive

At last a long letter arrived from you this morning, which gave me much pleasure and I thank you much for it. I do not feel well and a letter really does me good from you. It is odd but I have never felt well since the short illness I had a month ago. I think the little journey will do me good. Though you did not answer me about my finances at first yet you have so well done it now that you are *quite* excused. Nothing can be more handsome than you have been and indeed more than I expected, and all my hobbyhorses will flourish extremely.

I try to collect any little things I can to show you as manufactories and, my natural history is, I hope, likely to be in a good way. I want to have all that I can of Mysore and have birds *stuffing* and insects *bottled* by Dr Hausman. Dr Hyzer is in hopes of producing some very curious stones from his tour, which are to be given to the Governor and Council, I suppose, and a little heap to me. I am sorry to say that two words from Colonel Close last night confirmed the news of his first letter which I enclose to you. I am sorry Dhoondiah should have any success.

Your account of your gaiety and sorrow in losing Josiah Webbe diverted me. I am sorry the town Majors and the Library secretarys *grieve* so much. It is good for the public affairs that he goes, but I am very sorry on all other accounts. He must be a great loss to you and I thought him always very pleasant.

The Governor of Bangalore (Captain Brown) and I will take care of your plants. Apple trees that have borne you may have by *hundreds literally*, if you please. Peaches are more scarce. There are some very fine layers of Cypress, but it is a doubt if they have not been cut too soon. It will be of use, or well worth while, to make this place a repository for vegetable instead of the Cape. The plants are so fine that any quantity sufficient for you or more might be had of all Europe vegetable without the risk there is of their being spoilt coming from the Cape. We are nursing some nondescript cuttings, one of the sweetest flowers in Asia, which is to travel to you Bya Bye. If any are sent to you pray let the greatest care be taken of them. It is a large tree, but the seeds are not good. There is a sort of honey on the flower, which attracts the ants, and they kill the seed.

We have had two nights violent rain, which is very welcome indeed. I trust you will have a continuance of your showers, otherwise I shall expect you to be scorched well, and burnt as much as the earth at the Red

Hills where I imagine it must be terribly hot in spite of the tank. The girls are quite well. Harry is looking as usual. Charly cannot be better.

God bless you, ever my dear Lord,
your very affectionate
H. A. C.

July 12th, Henrietta to Lord Clive

You will be tired with the sight of my handwriting I am sure. I now send you the stories of Tipu Sultan, which you are to open, and choose one for yourself and the other for Lord Wellesley. The *Munshi*, who Colonel Close sent me, was once Tipu's treasurer as he says and I believe was about his many affairs. He had the direction of writing the stories, and the verses of the *Koran* were chosen by him. I have made him write down exactly what was upon the whole. Round the canopy or umbrella were many sentences of the *Koran* and upon the head of the tyger, which is all expressed in the paper enclosed in Arabic.* I have put in a bit of paper explaining how I got it, as I believe the zeal with which it was destroyed did not give the plundering time to know that there was an inscription on the canopy. Signora Anna desires me to say you should have had them† sooner, but that she had no good place to paint in here and that it is the first thing of the sort she ever did. We have asked many questions of the *Munshi* and it is altered as much as he said was necessary from the model and a slight sketch. He says the face is very like Tipu. I have another copy of the Arabic writing, which he is to give me, and in Persian for you. I know that William Edmonston said what was engraved upon the Tyger's forehead was difficult to explain; therefore I was more particular in getting it in case you chance to send it to Lord Mornington. Pray take great care how it is packed up again.

You say nothing about white roses, but I mean to send you some. They are delightful here. We have had a good deal of rain and therefore did not set out as we intended today but rather the day after tomorrow.

* I did not find this paper among Henrietta's letters.

† In Tonelli's painting, Tipu Sultan is on his throne.

As we do not go the direct road to Colar, perhaps I may not have an opportunity of writing for a day or two. The girls are quite well and send many loves to you.

Adieu.

On July 13th the travellers left Bangalore for a change of scene, and went to Sherzapoor, passing through many villages. Rain filled the tanks causing the artificial wall that formed the dam of one of the tanks to burst, so that it overflowed the road. Henrietta described the area as having 'very little jungle, but much cultivation, and verdure at this period of the year that it put us in mind of England'. The sun was so clouded, that they could walk about till half-past twelve, picking up some curious stones, which though pretty, they feared were only trash. Their encampment was in a mango tope. They walked about the narrow streets of the village of Sherzapoor that contained about one thousand families, many of them occupied as weavers. In her journal Charly gave details of their visit to some tombs built of brick and *chunam*: 'The tombs of the women are flat at the top, and those of the men are round, with a pointed top. Said Padshaw (a holy man), his wife, and a young child were buried together. There was a great building containing a man's tomb whose wife died when he was ten years old; he survived her one hundred years. Her tomb is to the right of his; his nephews, and niece, lay on his left side. He was said to have been so good a man that twelve women who were his slaves, always slept, and ate their rice at his tomb. The building was open on two sides.'

July 13th, Sujapoor, Henrietta to Lord Clive

I received your letter this morning just as we were setting out for this place and Colar and much it pleased me. You are grown very good to answer my letter so immediately, to let us do just what we wish. We are now on our road to Colar and Nundydroog by a way chosen by Colonel Close who very much wishes me to take this tour which he says is through the finest part of the Mysore country. We shall set out from Bangalore as soon as we return after giving time enough for our packing up and resting our animals.

We are diminished in elephants. One is dead from use having gone to Josiah Webbe's and we have three sick. Therefore we are very careful of them. Some of our bullocks are dead too. We are much pleased with the permission to go to Trichinopoly and it is what I wish above all things. Brown says that when we are at Seringapatam it is not much out of our road. I mean not very far round and the gratification is very great. I should have set out sooner on this journey, but my illness and Harry's made it impossible. I do not believe we shall stay long at Seringapatam. I find there is not much to see except the place itself, which a few days will do.

I wrote to Colonel Close about his picture and Purneah's for you. He is going farther off. I am afraid it is out of the question. I asked if I might desire to paint the *Rajah* and his Grandame's portrait and he says they have not religious prejudices about such things and he thinks the request from myself will be very well taken when we go there and he has told the old lady that we were to go there. I had thought of some cows and a gentleman for you and intended to ask Colonel Close and surprise you with a herd. I hear that at Tanjore they are likewise very beautiful.

We have had a most delightful day and came in at half past ten in the *bandy*, quite cool and comfortable. Now at 1 o'clock in my tent the thermometer is at 76. Captain Brown says that he thinks three *bandies*, two *doolies* (which are the best for delicate plants as they shade them from the sun), and about six coolies would take all the trees that we can send you. Unfortunately the cypress layers were too soon cut off and have failed.

It will be very right to send some careful person to return with them and if you could spare anybody to leave at Bangalore it would be a very good thing. The people in the garden are perfectly ignorant. One half belongs to the *havildar* and the plants with all his care that are now preparing for you and any other things worth having in future are not secure at all from being taken away or neglected. Dr Hyzer is not likely to return for two months and we have seen proofs that the people are not to be trusted by the disappearance of fruit and there are your plants and many seeds to be taken care of. I am very sorry there seems so little chance of your seeing this place and our seeing you. But as it is so, we will not lose any time on our return to you, seeing all we can and having a great deal to say when we meet with you again.

I have walked today till 12 with pleasure. We may not have found any onyx or carnelian, but a great deal of limestone. I shall keep this letter open till tomorrow morning in case I have anything more to add. I have not seen any of the sort, yet there is a little odd low stone table or seat supported by elephants of stone that I have a great fancy to bring. It is not belonging to any religion or any *swamy*. It is in the palace and the *havildar* says I may have it. I have at last got some wood (but not what I have heard of) from Tavendroog. And have sent for more sandalwood. The red wood came from the neighborhood of Ryacottah where the goddesses frightened my *lascars* so much that the trees were not brought while we were there. Perhaps I may find some at Seringapatam. Good morning to you.

July 14th, Maloor, Henrietta to Lord Clive

We are just come here after a very pleasant journey through a country of fine cultivation much like large fields in the Vale of Evesham and are now sitting under a mango tope perfectly at our ease. I forgot to mention that one of the *bandies* will bring you three very pretty antelopes and a spotted deer all tame and great favorites. The antelopes are really very beautiful and of the best race. I enclose a note that I desired Brown to send me which is perhaps more exact than what I may have written. I enclosed a note for Thomas Harris to you near a fortnight ago and have not had any answer and Dr Hyzer's painter is unemployed till it comes.

Adieu.

We are all very well and likely
to improve on our journey.
H. A. C.

On July 14th one elephant died from want of sufficient food and the others looked very thin. The late elephants' keepers were strongly suspected of taking their allowance for themselves. On the way to Colar, Henrietta, Harry, Charly and Anna Tonelli had to walk through a thick

Government House and Council Chamber, Madras

View of the Ameer Bagh, Madras

Mohamed Giaffer

Palanquin with bearers, and a message camel

Encampment at Arcot

Ryacottah

Hyder Ali Khan, father of Tipu Sahib

Tipu Sultan, 'The Tyger of Mysore'

Krishna Wodeyar,
the Rajah of Mysore

The Ranee of Mysore,
grandmother of the Rajah

The Rajah of Tanjore

Simon's Bay, Cape of Good Hope

Illustration from the fair copy of Charly's journal, with a key to the diagram

1. Endymion.................King's ship. The Commodore.
2. Star.......................ditto. A brig, sailed about with orders.
3. Sir Edward Hughes......East Indiaman.
4. Prince William Henry...ditto.
5. Castle Eden...............ditto.
6. Earl Spencer..............ditto.
7. Tellicherry................ditto.
8. City of London...........ditto.
9. Walsingham...............ditto.
10. Hawke.....................Extra ship.
11. Harriett....................ditto.
12. Hope........................ditto.
13. Lucy Maria...............Trader.
14. Anna........................ditto.
15. Thetis......................ditto.
16. Surat Castle..............ditto.
17. Marianne..................ditto
18. Herculaneum.............ditto.
19. Denmark..................ditto.
20. Swede......................ditto.
21. Cornwallis................Whaler.
22. Queen......................ditto.
23. Salamander...............ditto.

jungle and finally found it necessary to get into *palanquins*. The hills were covered with large stones. Although Colar had been mostly abandoned during the war, it once again had become a flourishing place.

July 15th, Colar, Henrietta to Lord Clive

I cannot say how I was surprised and delighted with your great packet by express, which arrived here at 12 o'clock today and in return, I send you all my other news, which you have not had. I send you Elizabeth Walpole's letter because there is a great deal about your sister and much new. I am diverted with some of it very much. I think William W's having bleedings at his nose a very good thing and I cannot help thinking events will happen to her which all these symptoms have more or less to do with and that then she will be well. I have much Scotch news of the Dalkeath House (Lady Douglas) with many good wishes to you and for our return.

I send you a list of the roses coming for me. Pray let them remain as they are. If they are opened, I am afraid they will be in sad confusion and spoilt before I come back. Therefore I beg they may remain as they are. The books from Mrs Clive you may open and read . . . My brother's account of the boys is charming. I am very glad he has removed Robert. I have long thought Mr Faithful had too many to take proper care of them with only one other master. Don't you long to see them very much? Pray send me word if the *Queen* will be a safe ship to send letters. I must write heaps, if it is.

You are really excellent to send an express. It has done me more good than anything I have seen since the last letters. You will see that the Shropshire ladies are marrying fast. Mrs Amber has written to announce her marriage. Pray return my letters again that I may answer them.

We are at Colar after a very pleasant journey. This is a delightful country much more like Europe than anything I have seen. It is much cultivated and the people look clean and happy. We are all much pleased. We have discovered, a part, a most iniquitous cheating in the food of the elephants. It is not yet quite clear, but that they starved them. When it is clear you will hear of it.

Pray take care of the roses and seeds. I should like to see a hyacinth once more. They should be planted with a *great deal* of sand and a little mould. I am afraid by my brother's letter that your affairs in England do not go on as prosperously as here.

We are just returned from seeing the burying place of Haidar's family [his body was at a later date moved to Seringapatam]. The multitude of people here is very great. There are about 13,000 or 14,000 inhabitants all looking clean and the women with many ornaments, which is a sign they are not poor. Signora Anna has good news from Italy.

Good night. A heap of pineapples are just arrived, for which we thank you very much. We go upon a hill tomorrow and the next month – *Adieu.* I have not felt so well for a long time as I do today. I have not an ache since the letters came in.

Ever my dear Lord,
your very affectionate
H. A. C.

Don't you think I am much obliged to your mother for not letting Mrs Tyler send me two young ladies.

July 17th, Narsapoor, Henrietta to Lord Clive

We left Colar this morning and came to Narsapoor, a very pretty place surrounded by hills yesterday. We went up one of the high hills near the town, which Dr Hyzer had described as fairyland. I do not think it is quite that but it is very beautiful and not unlike the Cape, but with smaller and more fertile valleys between the hills. This is by far the finest country we have seen. The whole is much unlike the *ghauts* and even much prettier than about Bangalore, but I believe not so productive though there are many considerable tanks which we saw from the top of the hill. Captain Brown is gone to see how all things are going on at Bangalore and meets us again tomorrow.

I forgot to send you your mother's letter which I shall enclose today. Whenever you have done with the newspapers I should be much delighted to have them and will return them to you. The Duchess of Newcastle and Hamilton are going to be married: the first to Colonel

Crawford, the second to Lady Exeter. I should have thought they had both had enough of the holy state. Good Morning to you. Many loves from the girls. Harry desires you to direct the enclosed to Mrs Rothman.

Adieu.

Ever, my dear Lord,
your very affectionate
H. A. C.

The tanks were dry from want of rain, and the *Brahmins* have had a long fast, to propitiate the gods. There is a mud-fort out of repair. The country is pretty, but the day very cold.

July 19th, Henrietta to Lord Clive

We went to Deonelly, the latter part of the way through jungle, the direct road being too bad. The fort was half-built by Tipu, of stone, brick, and *chunam*. It is said, that the public garden situated near the fort, is in a high state of fertility, and abounds in fruit trees.

I thank you much for the heap of letters which I received this morning which though they do not contain much news it is always pleasant to have them. Many of them are recommendations to you of which I offer an abridgement as Dutens letter has a little news and *some scandal*. I send it. It is Governor Johnston's widow that is Mrs Nugent, and it is an old story except her having run away. Mrs Ashton is better. We came here this morning from Ooscotah, which is in a charming country and a very good situation. The whole is perfectly unlike the Carnatic, rich and well cultivated, but fewer topes than we have had for some days. Tomorrow we shall be at Nundydroog, the capital of a large and valuable district built on the summit of a mountain about 1,560 feet in height, three-fourths of its circumference being absolutely inaccessible. The only face on which it can be ascended is protected by strong walls, and an outwork projecting to the right of them which affords a most formidable flanking fire against an enemy.

I suppose you have heard that the *havildar* is hanged and two of his principal agents flogged which will probably make all quiet again. From all the ill behaviour of the Zahir troops and, what is worse, of the English officers in beating and pillaging the country people, the sight of a red coat causes alarm. Even the bodyguard, if they go into a village, spread a degree of fear though they are in perfect good behaviour. What a pity it is. We have not heard yet if Colonel Dallas has tried his *havildar* who was sent down a prisoner by Colonel Close's order for horrible behaviour near Bangalore.

I was quite surprised at the general orders about Colonel Doorten. We had heard of his removal and were anxious to know the cause, which reports made to be bad, but the order explains a great deal. I am quite surprised.

The regulation and increase of pay I understand is in great favour. Your health was drunk at Ryacottah with three times three, and I am indeed happy it is during your time that so many good things have happened. I have not been well these two or three days but the journeys are not long and are of service to me rather than otherwise. The scramble up the hill at Colar was rather too much. I believe there are gusts of wind that are chilling. Sometimes my complaint is in my bowels. Charly has a little cold and Harry is almost as stout as her Mama was some years ago. Many loves to you from the dear girls.

Adieu.

Ever, my dear Lord,

yours very affectionately

H. A. C.

I found two coffee trees much neglected at Ooscotah. One is to be sent to Bangalore. I am afraid the seeds are too old, but I will endeavour to send them to you, at least a few. The *havildar* did not know what they were and it was difficult to explain that they were valuable, as they did not appear very luxuriant. I expect a large Rose or two from Mrs Franks and Lord Hartford . . . Let them be kept in a dry place and not opened. I do not know if they came in these ships or are not yet arrived. Probert will not pay the bill till I have seen the things.

On July 20th the travellers arrived at Nundydroog, a strong and important hill-fort, that commanded the road from Colar to Bangalore, to breakfast with Colonel Cuppage, the commanding officer. Colonel Cuppage had lately discovered a plot by Dhoondiah to surprise the fort, and then place a strong garrison of his followers in it. Letters were intercepted from Dhoondiah to the *havildar*, which proved that he was also raising troops for him. There were also two accomplices who were rich Moormen. One man was hanged, and the two accomplices had 500 lashes each, and were to have the same again, and to be imprisoned as long as Colonel Wellesley pleased. The *havildar* was a man of high caste; he had thirty villages under him.

July 20th, Nundydroog, Henrietta to Lord Clive

I have just had a note from Grant to say that a sister of Mrs Rothman's was arrived and that he would take her into his house. I am sorry she is come while I am absent, but have written to Mrs Baker to help her, which I am sure she will do, and it will be a great comfort to her. Mrs Rothman did not know if she was coming or not.

We are just arrived here it is a most glorious country and beautiful. I am not well and writing in a hurry. It is very odd, but since I was ill at Bangalore I have never felt perfect. The rest are well and merry. We halt tomorrow.

God bless you.
Every blessing, my dear Lord,
yours very affectionately
H. A. C.

On July 21st it rained all day and all night, preventing the travellers from ascending the 'rock'. A fog always rested upon Nundydroog in the morning, sometimes lasting until noon and never lifting before seven or eight. An officer slept in the garrison every night, with a guard of one hundred and seventy men. On July 22nd as they proceeded the twelve miles to Burrah Balapoor, the rain still continued; but after dinner, they were able to visit the village and fort.

July 22nd, Burrah Balapoor, Henrietta to Lord Clive

I intended to have written to you by this day's *tappal* but it was late when we came here and I could not well do it. We were obliged to give up our expedition to the top of Nundydroog as it had a very large cap upon its head the whole time we were in the neighbourhood and it was in vain to expect any fair weather. It rained more or less the whole day and night and we were not sorry to get away with a glass of sweet lime this morning. It must be pleasant in very hot weather, but we were not too warm. The thermometer was at 69 in the middle of the day. We are now at Burrah Balapoor. It is now raining. Tomorrow we proceed to Yella Wanka and from thence to Bangalore.

Captain Brown desired me to tell you that your gardener was arrived when he was there two or three days ago. We are all pretty well. I am much better than I have been for several days in spite of the rain. By a letter from Colonel Close to Captain Brown: Dhoondiah had looked at Colonel Wellesley's army and retreated, but he was preparing to follow him and had taken Hurdgul on the 14th and that he had heard of Colonel Brown's approach and was preparing to make a speedy attack on him. This may all be old news to you, but as it is new to us I send it to you.

On July 23rd the road on the way to Yella Wanka passed through 'thinnish jungle', but some parts were well cultivated, and green; there were no rice-fields, but other grain had been sown in the fields. After breakfast the travellers walked through the village that had several *Choultries* in it. They went to see a *Brahmin* temple, and were only allowed to look in at the door, as it was thought that foreigners would pollute it. They were allowed to enter the mosques. Later they found themselves in a violent rain and wind storm. A small rivulet that was quite dry, became a torrent, and knee deep. When they reached their tents they found that water had come under the mat, which they did not discover until the servants on entering sank into the water; they then cut trenches to drain it off the tents. At no time did rain penetrate the tents.

July 23rd, Yella Wanka, Henrietta to Lord Clive

Here we are in another rainy day. I have this moment received the newspapers for which I thank you much. I have a letter from a man in the India House who was poor Ashton's agent who says in January he cleared from the India House seeds for Hartford and several things for the boys which were given by me to Captain Sampson at his request and he promised to have then delivered directly. The seeds are probably spoilt. I hope you will never give a commission again. There seems little news that we have not heard before.

Captain Brown has a letter from Colonel Wellesley's army. A party on observation narrowly escaped from one of the same sort of Dhoondiah. Colonel Stevenson was nearly taken. His horse fell and was taken. We hear 30,000 rupees are offered for Dhoondiah's head and that all his infantry have deserted from him. *Adieu*. I shall write from Bangalore.

Many loves to you, ever, my dear Lord,
yours very affectionately
H. A. C.

July 25th, Bangalore, Henrietta to Lord Clive

After having a good deal of rain we came back here again yesterday morning, Charly with a bad cold, the rest in good health and not a little pleased with the journey. In five days that is to say on the 30tieth we set out again to Seringapatam where I believe we shall remain about four days and the same at Mysore while your pictures are done and then to Trichinopoly. The route I wish to know exactly from you. Are we to go to Coimbatoor or straight from Seringapatam to Trichinopoly and from thence to Tanjore. I should like much to go to Tranquebar, if we may. I find there are some cabinets of natural history and that it is a place where there are many things to be had in that way, besides plants from thence by the coast to Pondicherry and Caragolly. I should hope you might meet us there at least. Pray send me an answer upon this subject and return me my English letters because I wish to answer some of them by the *Queen*.

We shall have as much baggage as we can space, as our conveyances are much diminished. I shall send some seeds, which I beg you will have soon for me in a day or two in pots. They will some of them do for your terrace, Bya bye. Charly's cold does not hurt her spirits or good looks much.

Adieu. Love from the girls.
Ever, my dear Lord, yours very affectionately
H. A. C.

July 25th, Bangalore, Henrietta to George Herbert

My dearest brother – I had the great pleasure of receiving a letter from you on the 18 July by the long expected fleet and it gave me the greatest satisfaction though you did not mention your own health, but Robert, Wilding and everybody else tells me you are in the most perfect health and spirits which revives me. Lord Clive sent me your letter to him, but has not yet returned mine which I sent him. The account you gave of the dear boy delighted me. I am sincerely glad Edward promises us to be so amiable and have no doubt Robert will be much the better for being removed from William Sackfield. I mentioned so to you last January when he increased his school from thirty to fifty without increasing his masters. It appeared to me that money, not learning was his object and I know Robert requires a great deal of attention. He writes natural pleasant letters and a very excellent hand. Edward, too, is much improved in his writing. In short my letters have made me very happy.

The fleet came unexpected to me. I did not know till the letters came, which Lord Clive had sent by *tappal.* We were on a ramble to Colar and Nundydroog where we have been a little pelted with rain though it is so great a blessing one cannot be sorry for it and the thermometer is seldom above 78, generally below it. The health and spirits of your nieces are much improved. We shall be at Bangalore again tomorrow and soon proceed to Seringapatam and from thence by Trichinopoly, which I am very anxious to see on the late Lord Clive's account. And from there we go through the Coimbatoor country to Madras, if we are allowed to do so by some p*olygars* who are sometimes rebellious and have lately been disposed to assist Dhoondiah, who is again troubling us. Colonel Wellesley is gone with a considerable force against him and has taken all his forts but one against which he is going in a few days according to the last accounts.

Dhoondiah's infantry here have all left him. He has about 4,000 horses such as they are, but as all [of his men] are volunteers (*looties*) and only follow him (at least the greatest part of them) for the hope of plunder; they will of course quit him also. The war may survive prolonged, but must end in his destruction. I hear 30,000 *rupees* are offered for him. He has been able to persuade many of the *polygars* as far as Dindigal to assist him but their prudence has been discovered. Only one hundred men attempted to come up the Pass to join him which could not have been done, but in a balloon, without being destroyed. They are all taken or killed. Another person, who had begun to raise men for Dhoondiah, has been taken, tried, and hanged. Therefore I hope we shall be able to pursue our journey in safety, which I will not do otherwise. At Seringapatam I shall see the new *Rajah* and his grandmother.

I am very glad you have seen Major Allan. He can tell you so much about this country and us. There is not the smallest doubt that Lord Clive's government will be the most honourable and prosperous that has ever yet been. A circumstance has just passed which will raise his name much amongst the army. The black infantry were paid much too little to live with tolerable comfort which he has remedied and their pay is increased to the betterment of these poor people and now the army will insist on better men and go on in a most flourishing manner and they cannot have any temptation to go into any foreign service which used to be the case. All this which is pleasant to hear has happened and Lord Clive is much cheered with its being settled. His affairs are going on tolerably well. At least they were so when we left Madras and though we have a part their increase of expense is scarcely anything. I am *very* rich, too, with £800 here and £200 in England. We are very comfortable in ourselves. In his letter to you I can say that that is the case.

Every now and then I have alarms about my own health but there is no serious reason for it now, but when we return to Madras I am afraid we shall all droop again. The climate is not favourable and it is utterly impossible for us to stand the months of May, June, and July in the Carnatic.

I shall certainly get you a good Japan cabinet for Princess Elizabeth. I will not swear that it will be old but I have had some given to me that are very beautiful. But as I have some strange dark complicated Armenian acquaintances that trade to all the Japan and such strange places, I will find our Princess something very good.

I hear that you are in great form with the Majesties. I should have liked to have seen your fête. Why did not you describe it to me in all its forms? Probert and Wilding both give good accounts of you.

There are, I hear, a great importation of ladies which I escape being at Bangalore. Your nieces desire a great many loves to you and I believe will be very happy to see you again as much as their mother.

God bless you my dearest brother.
Ever your most sincerely affectionate
H. A. C.

July 27th, Bangalore, Henrietta to Lord Clive

My dear Lord Clive – Yesterday Captain Brown had a letter from Major Macleod to say that the road to Trichinopoly was perfectly safe for us which delights us not a little. There were *many tygers* near the pass but the jungle has been destroyed and they have disappeared.

I wrote you word that Charly had a cold. Dr Hausman ordered her feet to be put in hot water for several nights, which I thought too much. Yesterday he gave her some physic and last night there was an unexpected change in her constitution which I had rather had not happened this twelfth month. I shall keep her quiet and take all possible care of her. She is in good spirits and her cold is gone nearly. Harry is quite well and growing strong. Charly is much more so than you have seen her in India. I hope this will not naturally affect her growth, which is now very rapid, indeed. But while she increases in strength, that is only good for her.

We have heavy rain sometimes and a great deal of wind, but it is very pleasant and cool.

We are most anxious to hear something more of Dhoondiah who appears almost hunted down. Pray tell me if the *Queen* will be a good ship for letters and pray return mine that I may begin to answer them and tell me too when the *Queen* is expected from Bengal. Pray direct the enclosed to Mrs Rothman. William Wetheral at Kistnagherry sent me a letter a few days ago from the Duchess of Devonshire desiring I will request you to do something for him in her name. A great deal about him and her wish that you may attend to her recommendation on account of his being grandson to William Andrew Ross once at Madras. Pray give the enclosed. I am grown well again.

Many loves to you ever my dear Lord.
Yours very affectionately
H. A. C.

July 29th, Bangalore, Henrietta to Lord Clive

My dear Lord Clive – Since I wrote last I have seen Warren of the 32nd Engineers who is measuring at Ooscotah. He says that the road by which he rode is, he believes, not passable for *bandies*, consequently not for us. Therefore unless we hear to the contrary we must go by Coimbatoor. Captain Brown has written to Mr Macleod to inquire about these roads which answer I suppose will come to us at Seringapatam.

We hope to set out on Thursday but the *bandy* that came from Madras was so broken that it must be mended before it can move and we cannot spare it. We are obliged to leave a good deal of baggage. Everybody spares something.

Captain Brown has a letter from Wilding and wishes you to tell him what answer he is to give to Butler. He says he came to him and complained of a thousand hardships and ended with saying that with 16 guineas he would be satisfied which from the postscript of Captain Brown's letter to him Wilding refused to do without an order from you. The old coachman has got a very good place but says he will return to you whenever you please. Pray send word because when the *Queen* goes Captain Brown will write to Wilding.

We are all pretty well. Charly, is much as she should be, but weak at present. We hear of Lord Wellesley's pursuing Dhoondiah and being within five days march with a possibility of his being shut up by the River Malperba, which from the want of boats would take up to fifteen days for him to cross and Colonel Wellesley would in that case overtake him or he might meet with Colonel Bowers's detachment on the Nigar side of the River.

Have you received the watercolour from Signora Anna and my Arabic paper? Many loves from the girls.

Adieu.

My dear Lord, ever your very affectionate

H. A. C.

On July 31st the travellers made one final excursion to see a cave, at some distance from Bangalore; it was said to communicate with the fort, but that did not seem very probable, as the distance was too great underground.

July 31st, Bangalore, Henrietta to Lord Clive

I thank you much for the letter I received this morning. We are in the act of packing up. Part of the baggage is gone and we march tomorrow morning. I told Captain Brown what you said about the carriage of our affairs which are pretty numerous. We are obliged to leave the great tent and everything not absolutely necessary. The gardener shall stay and bring your plants and we will hunt for more seeds for you on our journey. I am very glad you mention Dindigal as we must go by Coimbatoor at least so at present . . . We are well and leave this place with regret not expecting to be *cold* again for sometime. I told Signora Anna what you said about the throne. I do not think she intends the engraving at least at present as she cannot work at it upon the road.

Pray let me know when the *Queen* is expected at Madras because we must send in our letters if it will be soon. *Pray return my letters.*

Adieu.

Many loves to you from the girls.

Ever, my dear Lord, yours very affectionately.

H. A. C.

The paper is abominable. Pray remember they must not *dash* water over my bulbs or they will all die.

The travellers left Bangalore on August 1st and went to Beedadee, about nineteen miles on their way to Seringapatam; their baggage had been sent to Ramgherry the day before. The country was wild, covered with thick jungle and infested with tigers. It was much hotter than it had been for some time; the thermometer reached 88 degrees in the middle of the day. Their journey was beautiful but a bit unnerving as there appeared to be many places where tigers might conceal themselves. They visited the tomb of Haidar's *fakeer*, and his family, where they were invited to come in. Strangely, the *fakeer*'s son did not get up to make them a *salaam*, though they went into the room where he was sitting and saw his wives. He made three *salaams* down to the ground to his mother, an old widow, who was sitting down supported by cushions, with her son's daughters, and wives, on each side of her; according to Charly, 'she never moved, for widows never do'. The place was like a *choultry*, with high walls around it, and the attendants were Moorish slaves. Not having an interpreter, the travellers could not make out why they had been invited to enter, but they stayed some time. When they left the building they found Giaffer in a great state of excitement. He immediately questioned them as to what had passed, asked if they had eaten anything, and very seriously insisted that they should never enter any native house without his knowledge. In the evening, Giaffier intercepted a present of dinner sent by the *fakeer*'s son and gave it away to the followers.

August 2nd, Rangherry, Henrietta to Lord Clive

I must write a few words to tell you that we are all well here. We left Bangalore yesterday morning and went to Beedadee. It was a long stage but the road was very pleasant, though very wild. The hills near the villages were so much covered with wood that it put me in mind of those in Berkshire, which I think a great compliment to it. Today the drive has been beautiful the trees were large and small parks cultivated with wild rocks more like *Shelton*, the whole really charming, and not bad for my lion. We see new villages springing up everywhere since Colonel Close and Purneah came here. There is a small one at this place which is, as Saffer informs me, to be called after you. We are all pleased. Tomorrow we proceed to Chinnapatam where we halt a day and from thence Captain Brown goes on to Seringapatam to prepare for us. I imagine we shall be there on Tuesday by a very long march or on Wednesday. Captain Brown has left in charge William Read of the 33rd (who is at *present Governor* of Bangalore) to continue to send you the produce of the garden and the charge of the things we have left there vegetable and moveable. He is adjunct of that Regiment. I think I have no particular news to tell you. We walked about in the evening. I saw a great many of the trees we brought from Vandalore in the jungle, but no *tygers*, which we had heard of. *Adieu*. The girls desire their loves to you.

Ever, my dear Lord,
yours very affectionately
H. A. C.

In the evening of August 4th Henrietta, Charly, Anna and Harry went to see two Hindu temples. In the first temple there was a large figure of Vishnu which was better proportioned than any they had yet seen. There were many small figures in the other temple, but they were not near enough to see them distinctly. The thermometer was as high as 90 degrees in the middle of the day. The travellers received shawls and gold dresses. On August 5th the party encamped two miles beyond Moudean in order to shorten the next day's journey.

August 5th, Moudean, Henrietta to Lord Clive

Here we are within seventeen miles of Seringapatam very hot, but well. I am sorry to see how soon heat affects the looks of my two ladies. I am afraid you will not see any rose till we get to England again. The change of climate since Bangalore is astonishing. In twenty-five miles the thermometer was near 90 degrees and I am afraid it will not be cool till we leave the Mysore, which I shall do as soon as possible. Yesterday at Duddoor, Purneah's son, Narsingrow (dressed in blue satin with a red velvet umbrella held over his head and his horse's bridle studded with silver) and his brother, Bucherow met us. The son is good looking and fat. The brother looks *dull*, the others very lively quick looking old men. This morning they waited near this place and were on horseback till I came to the tents. I never saw more comical figures in my life. I wish I could have put you under my *palanquin*. I think we would have been amused. They looked more like ancient ladies than men. They have gone on and will meet us at the River tomorrow. There it is very high, which I am glad as I hear that when that is the case it is never very hot. Only accounts vary so much that it is difficult to know what to believe. Captain Brown went on yesterday to settle all about our crossing the Cauvary, which does not *sound* pleasant in a basket boat. The country is less beautiful than when I wrote last and will do so all the way, I understand, till we come to bare rocks at Seringapatam. Many loves to you from the girls, who will write to you when we have seen some sights. We heard yesterday that Dummul was taken; therefore Dhoondiah has no force left.

Adieu. My dear Lord
H. A. C.

Seringapatam: August 6th–10th

'I saw Haidar's and Tipu's wives. Some were handsome but still nothing like the beauties in the Arabian Nights nor no pearls like pigeon's eggs.'

Around Seringapatam on August 6th, the travellers found the country appeared barren, except for a paddy field here and there. They crossed the river Cauvery in two canoes tied together containing eighty persons. The other kinds of boats were made of basketwork covered with leather and quite round. The river was not very deep, having fallen seven or eight feet during the last three or four days. The elephants walked through and the bullocks swam: the animals were let loose, and the first in regulated the rest. If he went on well, they did, but if he stopped, the other animals followed his example.

Colonel Wellesley, engaged in the war with Dhoondiah, lent the travellers his house and headquarters in Seringapatam, the Doulat Baugh, which had been Tipu's residence.

August 6th, Henrietta's journal

We came to the side of the Cauvery before eight o'clock. The country is dreary and covered with stones, which increase as you approach the town. The river had sunk considerably and there could not be the least danger or alarm in passing it which was done in five minutes.

I went to the Doulat Baugh and was received there by Colonel Samin, Major Agra and Captain Marriot. It is close to the river, which is very handsome, rapid with large stones and rocks in the centre. There is a high wall before the veranda to the garden and the entrance is by a small door on one side into the little court. There are four rooms besides the halls and in another court several more I believe formerly inhabited by the ladies. The palace is upon the same plan as that of Bangalore but much smaller. The garden is pretty and there are rows of fountains with flowers in a border round them.

In the evening I went to the mausoleum of Haidar. It is a square room with a large door on the top with a veranda supported by black stone pillars from the Cauvery. The Mausoleum contains the bodies of Haidar, Tipu and his mother, all covered with green and silver cloth. Tipu's besides with one of gold with flowers spread on them and perfumes burning at their feet. The room is painted with the spots of the Tyger, Tipu's usual emblems, upon a light brown ground.* There is certainly something very striking in this place. It is kept in high order, a pension being allotted for that purpose and it conveys a great respect to the remains of a dead relation than any European monument can ever do. There is a *mosque* near it which is painted in the same manner and very neat, the steps for the *Iman* of the same black, those which when polished have the appearance of marble.

The Lal Baugh is situated in the middle of a very large garden and though upon the same plan as that at Bangalore is much superior to it in proportion. There are two rooms at each end of the gallery that crosses the end of the great hall, very gay and pleasant that has just been fitted

* Tipu marked his possessions with *bubris*, a pattern of tiger stripes, tigers and tiger-heads.

up by Colonel Close. He lives in the lower part. When I heard of the desolation and destruction of the cypresses which were in every direction by each side of the walls and that it was done by the English,* I could not wonder so much that Tipu disliked the place and never came to it. The change must be very great. I should have preferred very much being there to the Doulat Baugh, which is noisy from being near the roar of the river and not surrounded by the garden. I forgot to mention that on the walls of the Doulat Baugh is a painting of Baillie's defeat, most vilely done in the complete Eastern manner without the least regard to perspective. It is on one side of the door. On the other is Tipu . . . just as he travelled and his old *munshi* by his side on horseback. Above is Haidar . . . All are in the usual way of Eastern figures. Those of Baillie's defeat are very absurd. Some people are without their heads. Others cut in two.

August 7th, Seringapatam, Henrietta to Lord Clive

My dear Lord Clive . . . We are now in the Doulat Baugh, which is pleasantly situated upon the bank of the river. When Colonel Close was at Bangalore it was agreed that as Colonel Wellesley had been so civil about his house it was right to go to that, though I should have preferred the Lal Baugh very much . . . In the evening we went to the Lal Baugh, which really is charming. The garden is not in great order but the situation is very pleasant and the whole being surrounded by walls and garden is more like Chantilly than any place I know.

We went to Haidar's fort and saw the remains of Tipu. The place is kept in high order and is beautiful. It certainly gives one more the idea of respect and attention to the dead than any of our monuments.

This morning I have had a visit from Captain Marriott's [Thomas: later Lieut. Colonel] eight princes. They are fine little boys. The eldest is very like Haidar and Tipu. Afterwards Bucherow made me a visit and I expressed a wish to have the pictures of the *Rajah* and *Rannie* to which he says there will not be any objection. Captain Brown afterwards explained

* Lord Cornwallis's army in 1792

to him that it was impossible for me to receive any present of value from any person and begs he prevent any such thing from being offered. This he has promised to do.

We have just heard of Dhoondiah having escaped with his great guns and that his army had in part been surrounded and the rest dispersed except a part which he had sent to another place on the River. His stores, baggage, elephants are all taken. Many of his people threw themselves in the river meaning to swim and were drowned. The great guns fired upon the troops . . . men and horses killed. I suppose you have heard all this long ago.

Today we breakfast at Colonel Jason's garden where we are to see the breaches that were made and hear the history of the siege.

Loves from the girls, ever my dear Lord,
yours very affectionately
H. A. C.

Charly in her journal entry for August 7th offered a succinct description of the young princes . . . 'The eldest of them is twelve years old, and the youngest between three and four; some of them are good-looking, but they have a little of Tipu's ferocious look, apparent in all.'

Following a visit to Tipu's *zenana*, Charly gave her account of Haidar's and Tipu's wives:

'We saw Haidar's first. There were thirty or forty of them in a verandah altogether; the head-lady sat in the middle, dressed in a white muslin dress, and a white shawl; all the rest had coloured shawls, which are the only coloured things they can wear, as they are widows; they had one pair of gold earrings only.

'One of Haidar's wives could not come out of her room; therefore we went into it. It was, I supposed, at the utmost ten feet long, and six feet broad. The only light it had was from the door. She is a very clever woman, and can read and write Persian, (which not above one in a hundred can). They say she told Tipu, two or three days before the storming of Seringapatam, that she was sure it would be taken and he had better make peace.

'We went to about nine or ten different verandahs to see them all, some of them were of a very light complexion and were very beautiful. In the last was a relation of Chunda Sahib. She was sitting in the middle of the verandah and cried a great deal; they all did a little, out of form, but she really seemed to feel much. They are very quarrelsome, and seldom meet, but they did so this occasion to see us. They each have slaves, and there is only one man allowed to go into the *zenana*, to keep the slaves in order.'

August 7th, Henrietta's journal

I went to the *zenana* where we were received by the chief guard at the door and conducted to Haidar's real wife . . . She has the appearance of having been a very beautiful woman . . . and from thence to Tipu's wives and daughters where I saw also the youngest sons who are still in the *zenana*. Some of the women have fine features and are light brown. His daughters were dressed with jewels and pearls. Their eyes were large and there is a great degree of family likeness between them all. The last we saw was the real wife of Tipu . . . She was old, rather large, and not handsome. She met me on the step of the veranda and cried so much that it was really painful to see her. She was in more state than the rest and had a carpet of scarlet and gold to sit on supported by cushions. I was really glad to quit her. She was really distressed to a great degree. It is not surprising.

The place where they live is large. The court in the middle has trees planted in it and on each side there are verandas where the ladies sit when they meet together. Their private apartments, I did not see, except that which I have mentioned.

We went through the ceremonies of receiving *betel*, limes, and not being perfumed, but poisoned with bad oil of sandalwood, besides a shower of rose water. The bottles of the great *Begum* were filigree. She had more an air of state than the other ladies.

Two or three times a year Tipu visited the *zenana* in form and they were all drawn out round him. He usually spoke to them for a few minutes and went away. There are women of all castes and religions (Hindus and Christians) but he obliged them to change their religion immediately upon arriving there. Many of them are the children of fathers whom he had destroyed. Whenever any person was executed, he seized their effects and the girls were sent into the *zenana*. Sometimes there were two or three sisters of the same family. They pretended some of them to cry but I do not think they all did it sincerely.

The Moor women never wear jewels after the death of their husbands, but they have been allowed to keep all they had at Tipu's death. Tipu had made his father's wives give up all their jewels and fine clothes when Haidar died. After the death of Tipu when Haidar's wives found that they were better treated than they themselves had been, a violent quarrel broke out between the ladies. I hear that it proceeded to very violent language and *blows* as they insisted on dividing the effects of Tipu's ladies.

When the travellers met Purneah's family, Charly found that his wife 'covered with ornaments from head to foot' was decidedly 'not handsome'. Likewise, Henrietta described Purneah's wife in similar terms as 'not a beauty . . . [there was] something less graceful in her appearance than those belonging to Tipu'. Charly concluded her narrative of the day's varied events saying, 'We saw the gate where Tipu was killed; the marks of blood are still to be seen upon the walls. We dined at Colonel Saxon's; his house is the one which Futteh Haidar occupied. Afterwards we saw the arsenal, and the palace of the old Rajah of Mysore; it must have been very beautiful, but it is now in ruins; all the doors had ivory figures in bas-relief, as a border round them. At night the minarets were illuminated, which had a beautiful effect.'

August 7th, Henrietta's journal

I returned home by the gate where Tipu was killed. It was low and there are still many marks of blood on the walls. Bodies were so heaped above and below that all passage was impossible. It is near the palace where he was supposed to have intended to go. I forgot to mention that from the town we came into the great square of the palace where his sons now live. The great room is very fine, supported by two rows of pillars and painted with tygers' stripes of green and yellow upon a scarlet ground. Within is the room in which Tipu slept. It is large and on each window an iron grating and with many locks to the door. Captain Marriot, who has charge of the younger children, lives there.

I dined with Colonel Saxon in a house built by Haidar for Tipu when he was young and afterwards inhabited by Mozes Udeen. It is in the usual form but more airy and large.

In the evening I went to the arsenal. There were 10,000 stands of arms, many made there and found in the palace. They appeared to me very light in the butt but the bayonets were of a formidable shape. There were nine hundred pieces of cannon in the fort. Some were ornamented with two tygers, which had been made here, and some with a tyger tearing a man's head.

August 8th, Seringapatam, Henrietta to Lord Clive

My dear Lord Clive – I intended to have written to you yesterday but I was really so tired I could not. I have seen a great deal, some of which I shall tell you and keep the rest till we meet. On Friday we went to see the *zenana*. There are many that have great remains of beauty, but few are young. The first we saw was the great widow of Haidar and a most beautiful person she must have been. They were in different places and it was right to go to Haidar's family first. The last was Tipu's great widow who interested us in her appearance very much . . .

Afterwards I went to see the ancient palace of the Rajah of Mysore with General Flood. It is built on a larger scale than that of Tipu. The pillars are more lofty and airy. The doors were once carved with ivory, very much worked. Those were all torn off by the soldiers. Mrs Gordon gave me some pieces of it: the carving of the cornices is studded with mother of pearl. As this palace is to be pushed down I desired the Major to secure for you some elephants that are extremely well carved on each side of the door. I do not yet know their size but I think they might do, as you said, for the steps of your new room. The carving is very sharp and good. Their size it is not easy to see as they are much covered with dust, but I believe they are sitting down. I shall have them measured bya bye. I cannot find anything else likely to suit you here . . .

In the evening there was a *ball*, not very numerous but very good. The dancers were Mrs Gordon, the girls, and Signora Anna.

We have so much to see and to do that we are sometimes tired, but we are well. The girls are delighted and in great spirits.

Today we breakfasted at the bungalow at the Lal Baugh. It is upon the point of the island were the rivers join and very pleasant. I am sure if you were to see this place you would be delighted. It is both magnificent and pretty and comfortable. We again went to Haidar's and Tipu's tomb and here we are again having been to a church where the sermon was very short. Mrs Clark prayed where Tipu used to sit in the front of his palace.

Tomorrow we proceed to Mysore and see the antelopes hunted by *chitas* on our road. I think it will make a good Eastern story. We shall go on elephants to the chase. I shall write again from Mysore.

The accounts last night were that Colonel Stevenson and Colonel Gower had met and that the force was divided and intended to surround Dhoondiah who was . . . with 5 or 6000 horse, but had disbanded all his infantry. A director came across from Scindia's Army, which he said was five marches from Colonel Wellesley's with friendly intentions towards the English, which was supposed to be from fear.

Pray will you be so gracious as to send up a few of the roots from England to Mrs Gordon. I have promised to let her have some to try here. We have sent all the baggage on down the pass which is I understand very difficult and have tents from hence which means we shall not have occasion to wait at all there.

I am very glad to find by the letters I received yesterday enclosed by you that Mrs Rothman has a son and is in perfect health. I confess I was growing a little anxious about her. You might have said something yourself. I wish much to know about Tranquebar as we shall go on as straight as we can and I wish to form all my plans. I trust I shall hear from you soon. We know as little of Madras as if we were at Japan. Loves from the girls. *Adieu.* I am in a hurry as we are going to dine with an odd old Colonel Meadwitte, who is not very amusing.

Ever my dear Lord, yours affectionately

H. A. C.

August 9th, Henrietta's journal

We went round the fort with General Ross who explained all the affair and I think I understand the proceedings of the siege very tolerably. We saw the breach more built up. It is three miles round with a double ditch and fortification. It has cost, since the siege by Lord Cornwallis, 60 *lacs* of *rupees*. The inner ditch is not filled with water, which was not at first intended.

Tipu had a dream one night on the subject and ordered it to be filled with water directly. He left a book in which he wrote all his dreams and was very much directed by them. He had a talisman on his arm which while he wore it no harm could befall him. I hear that it was opened after his death and was really broken. There is some doubt if it had ever been complete. After breakfast I went up the minarets of the great *Mosque*. It is kept in great order. There is an extensive view, but over a very dreary country. The steps were not high, but the passage became narrow near the top round. The dome is a little rail and sufficient room to pass.

On August 9th Charly recorded her final impression of Seringapatam: 'We went round the fort, and saw the *choultry* under the ramparts that Tipu lived in during the last fortnight of the siege. We afterwards ascended the minarets. They are high narrow edifices, one on each side of the *mosque*; they are lighted up on the great feast days. This is the *mosque* that Tipu always went to; the place in which he sat had a high wall round it, and was so formed, that a musket-shot fired from below, could not touch him as he was much higher than the floor of the *mosque*.'

August 10th, Henrietta's journal

We went to the palace to hear prayers read by Mrs Clark to the English troops. It did not last many minutes after which I went to breakfast in the bungalow at the Lal Baugh and again to see that beautiful palace, though painted white and nearly covered with gilding is not glaring or disagreeable. Afterwards I went once more to see Haidar's tomb and the mosque where Tipu to the last had a private door that he could go in and out without being seen by those within it.

I dined with Colonel Mandeville in a house once belonging to Abdul Kalich and afterwards went to see Major Grant's house and his garden. I forgot to mention that last night we drank tea with General Ross and went to see the illumination of the Minaret, but the place did not answer for it and the wind was so high the lights were extinguished very soon.

Mysore: August 11th–14th

'In the banquet of life, drink a cup or two and depart.
That is to say entertain not a wish for perpetual enjoyment.'

Hafiz, translated by Lady Henrietta Clive

On August 11th Henrietta, Anna, Harry and Charly rode on elephants and observed tigers hunting antelopes as they made their way to Mysore, the Rajah's capital city and nine miles from Seringapatam. All their tents, and baggage, went on to the Guzelhutty Pass. The *bandies* had to be pulled to pieces and carried, as well as the baggage, piecemeal, on men's heads. Captain Grant and Mrs Gordon lent them their tents, until they could regain their own.

August 11th, Henrietta's journal

... Six tygers are placed each on a sort of bed in a cart, tied down loosely with leather hoodwinks over their eyes. The carriages move on slowly and when they approach a herd of antelopes, a tyger is released. At first he moved very gently, stopping often for some minutes. By degrees he increased his pace to the greatest velocity and sprang after the antelope whose blood he sucked. It was a few minutes before he quitted his hold. The keeper again blinded him and replaced him again in the cart giving him the leg of the animal as a reward. Soon afterwards three tygers were released at the same time, but as they crossed each other and entangled the chain neither of them caught their game. It is a most horrid sport I think and very well to see once as a curiosity.

August 12th, Mysore, Henrietta to Lord Clive

We came here yesterday and in our road hunted antelopes with tygers. It is much like coursing in England . . . The country improves as you approach Mysore, which is situated in a little hollow with much cultivation near it and several tanks. This place is far superior to Seringapatam. It is cultivated and in a pretty little valley and infinitely cooler. I really think the Doulat Baugh almost as hot as it is at Madras. The fort built by Tipu is now falling down. He gave it up after having discovered that it was impossible to have any water. The stores, which he removed from the old fort, are now returning to rebuild it for the Rajah. There were three elephants, one called a white one which I did not discover till I was told of it. He is really little known and a little different from the common elephants.

In the evening I went through the *pettah*. The first street seems entirely inhabited by *Brahmins*. It is clean and the people seem comfortable considering that at the siege of Seringapatam there was not an inhabitant. It is now well peopled.

The tents are placed near a tank near the gate of the fort. The difference in the climate between this place and Seringapatam is very great. We had a fine shower and it was cool and pleasant like Bangalore.

We are going this morning at 10 o'clock to the *Rajah* and the *Ranee*. Colonel Close told me what might be done concerning presents from me and said that the *Rajah* would do as he directed but was afraid the *Ranee* wished to be too magnificent. When I saw Bucherow I thought it better to mention the pictures as the most valuable things we could receive and Captain Brown explained to him afterwards the impossibility of my receiving anything which I desired . . . As I understood there were diamonds and all sorts of things prepared. It is so settled and I go with my shawls and my dresses today, which I believe they are to give in their turn. This, Colonel Close said, was what would be right and I shall have my conscience quite clear of all bribery.

I have expected to hear from you every day and that you would send me my letters again.

We stay tomorrow and shall be in three days at Guzelhutty Pass. That is on the 17th. Whenever you do write it had better now be by the Trichinopoly post or by Salem. The town Mayor . . . goes with us to the pass where we meet Major Macleod.

We are all well. There was a violent storm of rain while we were on our visit, which they say is a very *lucky* event. The girls desire their loves to you and intend writing. Pray return all my letters.

Adieu, my dear lord,
ever your very affectionate
H. A. C.

The travellers went on August 12th to see the young Hindu Prince, Rajah Krishna Wodeyar. His grandmother was also present wrapped up in a yellow shawl with only her head to be seen – not even a hand or arm – while every now and then one of her slaves put a bit of *betel* in her mouth. She had a pair of earrings of red leather in the holes of her ears.

Tipu always left one of the offspring of the Mysore *Rajah*'s family alive, as a hold on the country; but when successors were born, only one was allowed to survive. The present prince was not known about by the English government, until during the siege of Seringapatam. He was found in a wretched damp stable in the care of his old grandmother, and a brother of his deceased mother.

August 12th, Henrietta's journal

This morning for my visit to the *Rajah* and *Ranee*, I set out in great form at 10 o'clock. The street from the entrance of the fort was lined with matchlock men and *sepoys* not very miltary in their dress, but stout looking men. There was a convivial mix of red jackets faced with red (like lancers) and blue Hindu turbans. At the first building I was met by Bucherow and opposite the palace were drawn up the *sepoy* guardsmen commanded by English officers. They saluted in great form and I was carried up the first flight of steps and getting out of my *palanquin* went through another hall or colonnade into that where the *Rajah* was sitting. It is built exactly as the old Mysore palace at Seringapatam and not yet finished. The doors are ornaments with carved ivory like that palace.

The *Rajah* was sitting on an ivory throne that belonged to the ancient *Rajahs* and is seven hundred years old. It is carved in strange shapes and painted with small flowers. The *Rajah* is a fine boy, six years old. He was dressed very magnificently in a silver dress with many ornaments, some very fine and diamonds and fine pearls hanging to the ornament on his neck with several hanging on his shoulders. He had the usual Hindu earrings and above them the pearl drops fastened in a small gold ring through the upper part of the ear. He asked several questions and seemed very much inclined to be merry if his dignity would have allowed him after the usual ceremonies of *betel* and rose water and my presenting shawls and a dress, which he returned.

All the men were sent away in order that the *Ranee* might come in. There was a party of dancing girls and singers performing while I sat there and a great many spectators. He has a few *Sepoy* boys kept there who placed a sort of couch consisting of a large cushion of scarlet and gold embroidered with a back like an old fashioned chair where the *Ranee* was to sit and a chair covered with an embroidered cloth for me. The *Ranee* came in with many attendants and is one of the fattest and most battered women I almost ever saw. She has a very sensible countenance, a good deal of animation. The widows of his kin were seated opposite to me. Some of them were very handsome and not very dark and all appear to be young. I asked to have the *Ranee*'s picture and she consented and it is all settled. Signora A is to go tomorrow morning. I went through the same ceremony of *betel* and shawls and then my visit ended.

While I was there a violent storm of rain came on, which they said would be supposed to be very fortunate. It was impossible not to see with pleasure an unfortunate family restored to the life of which they had been cruelly deprived. During the life of Haidar, the *Rajah* was once or twice a year brought before the people. Tipu discontinued that . . . The *Rajah* was thin and with the appearance of being starved when he was first restored. He is now well and looks very healthy.

The whole of my visit lasted two hours and I was much amused by it never having seen anything of that sort before.

In the evening went to see the fort began by Tipu. It is of considerable extent. There is an inner fort, which it is supposed was intended for his palace. It is now in ruins. When the present *Rajah* was first seated on the throne, he lived in a mud building in this place, which has not now the appearance of having ever been a royal residence.

August 13th, Henrietta to Lord Clive

This morning Purneah's brother came to take leave of me and passed through the usual ceremonies of *betel* and shawls. I found that the *Ranee* had expressed a wish to see me when Signora Anna went to draw her picture and that of the *Rajah*. Therefore I sent a message offering to go there this evening, which was accepted. We came into the same hall where I had seen the *Rajah*. She came in soon after and sat down as she had done the day before. One of the dancing girls was called to interpret between us. She expressed much happiness that the war was over and the power and care of the English and hoped that they would always be friends. She wished much to see Lord Clive, but as that was impossible was very glad to have seen me. She said she had suffered a great deal from Tipu but was in hopes that all her miseries were now over. I showed her the pictures of my children [oval pastels by Anna Tonelli] with which she seemed much pleased.

The *Rajah* came in and sat down by her. After sometime she went away and the *Rajah* was carried to his throne which was not the same I had seen the day before but of red velvet with a very handsome gold lace and with cushions given to him by Colonel Wellesley but originally by the King of France to Tipu. The dancing girls performed and in about half an hour I came away. The *Rajah* sits every evening in this way and all the principal people come and make their *salaam* to him. We sat as we had done before on one side and Bucherow opposite. Each time that I was with the *Rajah*, there was a violent storm of rain, which they say will give people a great idea of my good luck and the good that is to happen to the country.

Travelling through the Guzelhutty Pass into Coimbatoor Country: August 14th to September 8th

'We heard many peacocks in the wood but saw neither elephants nor any wild beasts except the real inhabitants who are as near savages and some of Captain Cook's drawings than anything I ever saw.'

August 14th, Nunjengood, Henrietta to Lord Clive

Left Mysore at 6 in the morning and passed through the most beautiful and fertile country that I have seen in Asia. There are woods, many tanks and the whole surrounded by distant hills. I have never been so much pleased as with this morning's drive. I came to a pretty village near the River Kaprone and presently after to the bridge. It consists of fifty-four narrow gothic arches. The supports are about six feet thick . . . The river is very rapid. It is paved and shaped, as our best English roads are made, covered with drains on each side to carry off the rainwater. From the centre of it the view is very charming. Below there is a view of a large *pagoda* rimmed with trees and the river winding near it. The other side is a pretty view up to a small hill not unlike an English common. The tents were placed at some distance from the bank but we removed them and it was one of the most beautiful and cheerful scenes I have met with. There is a small island between the encampment and the rivers joined near where my tent was placed.

After raving at you for a long time, your letter has arrived this very moment, but too late for me to say all your civilities to the *Ranee* as we are thirteen miles from Mysore. I was very glad that I said a good many things last night like what you say. In the morning Signora A went to do the pictures, which are very like. The *Ranee* asked about me and said she was in hopes to have seen you too and asked about my boys and many other questions. I offered to go without form in the evening if she wished it, which she accepted. She said that she had brought up the *Rajah*, but that he was now your son and she hoped you would take care of him. That she had suffered much from Tipu, but that now she hoped all her sufferings were over and that as the country was in the hands of the English she did not fear anything. I had asked for her picture for myself. She seemed much pleased with those of the boys and the girls and asked if I had one of you, which I am sorry I had not. We stayed there sometime. The little *Rajah* was put in his throne. The men all called in again and after a little dancing and singing we were dispatched and I believe she was pleased with this second visit.

Bucherow goes with us to the pass as well as Mrs Gordon and Allen Grant who are both most certainly civil, good humoured and obliging. Mrs Gordon is well and nursing a little girl.

I send you a letter from Mrs Rothman. She is quite well and Lord Wellesley has offered to be godfather therefore they have desired me to be godmother which I shall perform.

We leave for the Annamallee woods and Coimbatoor with great pleasure I assure you. It is altogether a long journey. Therefore we go on as quickly as we can and will do all you desire about the trees and get you the redwood if possible. You will have a great many sandalwood trees given me by Purneah's order. I answer writing by the side of a most beautiful river, more like Europe than any I have ever seen. You have nothing like it in the Carnatic. There are the ruins of a magnificent old *pagoda*. It is beautiful and much the most so of any place I have seen. It is very odd nobody ever mentioned it as a beautiful place.

Major Macleod meets us at the pass and goes with us to Coimbatoor. All is perfectly safe. When your picture of the *Rajah* is done, I must send a copy of it to the *Ranee*. I desired Signora Anna to do it sitting on his throne as we saw him. *Adieu*. It is late. I shall probably write from the top of the pass again. Many loves to you. I have performed what you desired and given them the kiss on their cheeks, which are still very blooming. *Adieu*. I am really glad to have had a letter from you, which I have been long expecting.

Ever my dear lord, yours very affec

H. A. C.

August 15th, Henrietta's journal

I had a letter from Lord Clive today with many messages and things for me to say to the *Ranee*, which I am very sorry, came too late for me to do it in person. But as Bucherow came with me I took an opportunity in the evening of desiring Captain Marriot to tell the passages to him with which he seemed much pleased. I showed him the portrait of the *Rajah*, which he thought very like. We showed him the *Ranee*'s, but he turned his head away and said it was not to be seen, but however that it was very like her. I went to see a large *pagoda* in the evening surrounded by a very extensive *choultry* on each side and ornamented over each arch. It is repaired and is one of the great places of religious worship of the Brahmins but had nothing remarkable in it.

Charly's journal of August 16th noted that on their road to Boosepoor the party passed through 'a very tygerish looking jungle all the way. At a dry river which separated the *Rajah*'s dominions from ours, a *Lascar* belonging to Captain Grant, was carried off by a tyger, at twelve o'clock at night; the man was lagging a little behind, and was going with our tents, for the next day's halt. Accidents continually happened in this *nullah*. Captain Brown heard a tyger growl. The village people told us, that a few days ago a man was carried off by a tyger, from amongst thirty people, and they found his body almost entirely eaten up. We passed many piles of stones where a man had been killed, and each person who passes in safety, adds one to the heap.'

August 16th, Henrietta's journal

Left Nunjengood very early. Before we had gone a mile we overtook the baggage *bandy* of the bodyguard in a very deep slough, which alarmed me for my little horse and myself. I got into one of the *doolies* and was carried over the bad places. Afterwards the road was extremely good as far as I drove. The country is fine and we passed a very large tank in a fine open place. I had been informed this stage was seventeen miles but it is certainly much above twenty. I was five hours in performing it and the baggage was not all arrived till near 3 o'clock. I saw today several of the *gloriosa superba* (Creeper Flame Lily) growing by the roadside and the red blooming *aloe*.

We came through a thick jungle to Boosepoor which separates Mysore from the Coimbatoor country. There is a tope and near it supposed to be a tygress and two young ones. As Captain Brown rode on rather before the *palanquins* he heard a noise like that of an elephant twice, but he did not see anything. Yet he is satisfied it was the tygress. When the *doolies* passed the maids, the bearers saw a very large royal tyger pass. The consternation was as you may suppose beyond all things.

I was certainly hot today. The country is pretty and the distant *ghauts* put me in mind of Wales and Scotland.

August 17th Came to Tumallah, about 12 miles. The road was too rough for the *bandy* and it was like what we passed yesterday: jungle with large trees very flourishing after the first five miles. Till that distance they are poor and withered for want of rain. After breakfast I took a pleasant walk in this wild place. I hear it will be much more wild tomorrow. Captain Macleod, the collector of the Coimbatoor country came to meet us here. He gives a good account of the road from Dannikencotah to Coimbatoor, but we shall be longer than expected on the journey.

August 18th, Guzelhutty Pass, Henrietta to Lord Clive

My dear Lord Clive – I wrote in a great hurry two days ago and had not time to say all I intended. We parted with Bucherow* yesterday at Boosepoor. We will take notice of all the teak and other trees and all that you desire about their removal by water which, Captain Brown, from what he recollects, there is a river in the neighbourhood which we will enquire and let you know all that is to be known. I am glad you like the redwood tree. I will endeavour to get more or anything I can meet with in that way.

Yesterday we came through in thick jungle and had reason to be alarmed from tygers. The truth is that there is a tygress and two young ones near the road that attack people. Bucherow has promised to have these killed and to have their skins sent to me – and my children. This day

* Purneah's son

we have passed a great deal of jungle and we hear the road is still much more wild which we are to go tomorrow. We have a journey of fourteen miles. We have heard of one of the wives of the elephant drivers being carried away at the same place on their march.

Captain Macleod is just arrived. He speaks Scotch tolerably broad but gives a good account of the road beyond Danikencotah to Coimbatoor.

Today the *bandys* were of little use. This place gives more the idea of approaching a pass than I had at Padinaig Durgan. There is a great chain of mountains on each side and very wild too. We are all well, though it is hot in the middle of the day. The evenings are very pleasant. You will receive bya bye a great many sandalwood trees a present to me from Purneah and a bed made for Tipu Sultan of the same. [The letter ends abruptly.]

Since the road had become steep and rough, on August 17th Henrietta, Anna, Harry and Charly had to be conveyed in *palanquins* during their steep ascent of the Guzelhutty Pass. En route Charly observed a memorial of 'some bells hanging upon a frame of wood, which had been put up by persons who had escaped the tigers'. On August 18th on their descent to the bottom of the pass, some seven miles in length, they walked the greatest part of the way. Charly described it as 'very wild and difficult'. They then proceeded to Boodicoop and found their tents pitched near the River Mya. The thermometer was 94 degrees.

August 18th, Henrietta's journal

Set out at daybreak and was an hour and a half descending the pass. In some places it very rugged and steep and the country certainly wild. A small river . . . runs at the bottom of the pass through a valley to the right between a chain of mountains to the right towards Calicut. These are inhabited and cultivated with barley and different sorts of dry grain. The road is bad from the foot of the pass to Guzelhutty the true name of this little village and the heat was intense. The first view into the Coimbatoor country is very fine. I am afraid we shall be a little disappointed in the beauty and cultivation of the country. It is I hear thinly inhabited, of course, but cultivated. Major Macleod told me he had had some dust brought to him said to be gold and that he believes there were mines at some distance to the right. He had written to government upon the subject. He said, too, that there is some marble near where he usually resides of which he has promised to send me specimens, as well as of the common stone. I met with a great deal of iron and limestone and some few pieces of touchstone. The lime has become hardened and in many places it has affixed itself to pebbles and become complete and hard, but very coarse.

In the evening I walked by the riverside. It is very rapid and deep in some places. In others it is forded with ease. A little distance from the camp was a place that pleased me much as it was much resembling a spot at Oakly Park. Above the river is very rapid and passes over a little fall and over stones and each side is covered to the waters edge with trees, one that I had never before seen and of a large size. The heat was very great and the thermometer at 94. In the evening there was a storm at a distance with thunder etc., and a great deal of wind. I saw several fires upon the sides of the hills occasioned as they say by the friction of the trees in the dry season. The soil is composed of iron lime and a great deal of saltpeter of which there is a considerable work at Saltemungalum.

August 19th Set out from Boodicoop at daybreak and passed the Mya River in a basket boat which I had never done before. It is quite sound and composed of bamboos like a wicker basket. The outside is covered with leather. They are perfectly safe, but not very pleasant. Yet I prefer them to the little canoe. The road was very rough and disagreeable for the little carriage.

We came to Nellakota and crossed a broader river but not so rapid as what we passed in the morning and in the same sort of conveyance. By a mistake of the *Soubadar* instead of encamping here he had gone on to Shremoogur ten miles farther. The road was rough. I quitted the carriage after crossing the river and came on in the *palanquin*. It was eighteen miles, a long stage for the followers after the rough journey yesterday. We were encamped on the bank of the Bhavanee. The temp at 1 o'clock at 93. Suddenly a violent storm came on at 2 o'clock and as we were upon a hard road, and they had not made trenches round the tents, in ten minutes we were under water. The mat floated. There was much thunder and lightning. In an hour it was quite dry again. In the evening we walked but there was not anything worth observation.

August 19th, Shremoogur, Henrietta to Lord Clive

Here we are once more expiring with heat below the *ghauts*. We descended yesterday. It is really a *pass* and as wild as anything in Scotland or Wales. In some places we were obliged to walk and in the whole were about an hour and a half coming down. The country is dreary and wild and we were encamped yesterday by the River Mya, very rapid in some places. We are as hot as possible. I am quite persuaded it is better to be Queen of Mysore, though her palace is not yet very magnificent, than anything in the Carnartic. There were twelve degrees difference between yesterday morning and this at daybreak. We are to be cooler at Coimbatoor. Major Macleod is I think a sensible man speaking broad Scotch with a good deal of William Byres's accent and not very unlike him. We are four out of seven white females he has seen in twelve years. At Coimbatoor, Mr Hurdis meets us. He has sent a variety of routes, which I shall leave undecided, till I see him. He proposes Madura but I think it is much too far and I even doubt about Dindigal. I understand it is very barren and not good roads from thence to Trichinopoly. The country is, I believe, every where less inhabited than in former times. At present the country is so wild that one cannot expect much cultivation.

This country is covered with ironstone, lime and saltpeter. We are all well as we can be, panting for cool air and the high trees in the Annamallee woods. Having escaped tygers, we are not afraid of wild elephants. My next epistle will be from Coimbatoor where we are to be on Thursday. Major Macleod had collected a variety of animals and plants for me. Amongst the rest, three beautiful *owls* and some fine barley, which made me think of England. It came from a high hill on one side of the pass.

Adieu. Many loves from the girls.

Ever, my dear Lord, you very affectionate

H. A. C.

After all possible enquiries, there is no marble at Seringapatam. All the best was brought from Poonah and Hyderabad where it is likely to be met with again. Colonel Pater has some very good marble they say, if it is to be had. I shall send the dimension of the elephants when I get them. You may have four.

August 20th, Henrietta's journal

Left Shremoogur very early. The road was better than it was yesterday except some passes or ravines rough and troublesome. The air was much cooler and the thermometer did not rise above 90. Some miles from Coorloor some troopers of Colonel Macalister's Regiment met us and attended me to the encampment. In the evening I walked out and found some stone, which Major Macleod informs me, sufficiently hard to cut glass as a diamond. He is to send me some large specimens of it. I found a good deal of crystal and much quartz and tali in a harder sort of stone. I showed him the coins I had received from Mrs Gordon. He says several are extremely curious, particularly one in a concave shape which is worshipped by the Brahmins and of great antiquity. The rest are of a modern work and some misnamed which he undertook to have rectified at Coimbatoor. The country is not yet cultivated for want of rain in September and October is the time when it is in its greatest beauty.

August 21st Left Coorloor early as usual and arrived at Coimbatoor, ten miles. The road was perfectly good except in passing some deep and rugged ravines. It is the best soil for cotton with which it is planted at the proper season. Near the town Colonel Macalister met me and I went to the palace. It was built by a Hindu and is much in the same manner as the *Rajah*'s palace at Mysore. It is two stories high. There is a sort of hall of audience surrounded on three sides by pillars on the fourth side it is raised three steps and with a double row of columns. There were other rooms appropriated for me, and a large hall with a small veranda in front. The other side consists of what was the *zenana* and the private apartments now converted. Major Macalister's district produces paper, clear to government of which he is allowed to make one and a half percent. He is a very sensitive well-informed man and was extremely attentive to me.

William Hurdis, the collector, came after breakfast. I consulted him what was the best road for me to take. He had never been at Tellicherry* and believed there was little worth seeing and that the road from thence to Annamalleecottah was impassable for carriages of any sort, being entirely paddy fields and that there were three roads, none of which he could recommend. The first was likewise unsafe from the depredations of the *Sayres*† who come down in considerable number and that the road is never travelled by merchants. The second is only passable by having guards and armed persons placed at certain distances and as in any case I must encamp from the length of the journey it was unsafe from the damps and fogs to risk sleeping in the jungle. From Pollachee he said the road was good and safe and that that being a high situation is perfectly healthy and good. I therefore gave up all thought of Tellicherry and shall content myself with being established a day or two at Pollachee and going to pass some hours in the woods where it is safe.

William Hurdis did not advise my going to Dinigal from Pylney, a place well worth seeing. It is necessary to go around by Darapooram, an increase of twenty-four miles to the distance. But as the *polygar* of the former place is now in complete enmity to government he did not think it right that I should in any case go through his country. He had been in correspondence with Dhoondiah and had engaged to bring all the other *polygars* to assist him. About two months ago one hundred men set out to meet him, but intelligence being sent to Major Macleod and Colonel Macalister they were followed and overtaken at a *choultry* in a small pass above the *ghauts* while sleeping. They had gone up an unfrequented road. Twenty-five were taken and as many killed. Twenty-three escaped and the rest were seized by the farmers and brought as prisoners. I do not think it worth visiting any dungeon. William Hurdis says there is little to see at Dinigal and I believe there is more to be met with worth attention by Darapooram and Caroor. William Hurdis's district, he told me, contains 1,200 square miles.

* A French outpost on the west coast of India

† A tax levied by *zemindars* on goods in transit through their estate, therefore perhaps by extension the tax officers

In the evening I went a little way near the fort. It is destroyed as all these are belonging once to Tipu and afterwards taken by the English and restored to him.

August 21st, Coimbatoor, Henrietta to Lord Clive

My dear Lord Clive – I have only a little minute to write because the post is going out. We are just arrived well and comfortably. The great heat decreased and of course we are revived by it. Col Macalister met me on the road and set troopers in all form. We are very well lodged in the palace with airy rooms to live in. Here I mean to halt one or two days as I see good for my company, particularly Charlotte who regains with a little sure rest now and then. Harry is very stout and strong. They are in high spirits. Major Macleod leaves us tomorrow. I like him much. Mr Hurdis is just arrived and we are to settle our farther route bya bye.

Colonel Macalister says that when his regiment heard of our coming they came in a body to him (the black officers I mean) and desired, he said, to express to me and desired me to communicate to you the thanks and gratitude they feel for the increase of pay from you. They are to come to me in form to be presented tomorrow morning. Major Macleod told me that two or three black officers from Errode came with him a few days before he met us and asked him by what means the increase had been made and by whose order. He said it was from the Government order. The *Soubadar* immediately answered with the greatest feeling in Moors, 'May Almighty God bless him'. It is very pleasant to hear these things.

I hear we have only one difficult pass to Poligaunteherry and a few tygers to meet with besides wild elephants, but I do not feel afraid of them. The road and country are much improved since we left the *ghauts*. It is now in its worst state being without rain. There is nothing soon they expect, and in October they say this country is like paradise. It is very flat except ridges of hills at a distance in a chain from the pass. *Adieu.* The girls send many loves to you. You are to receive letters soon, but constant travelling is an enemy to writing and we have had some long journeys.

Ever, my dear Lord, yours very affectionately

H. A. C.

We have been here two years today. In two more I hope we shall all be gambling at Walcot –

August 22nd, Henrietta's journal
I was to have seen the regiment Col Macalister's unit (the 4th Regiment of Cavalry) but unfortunately we slept so well that it was too late when I was up for it.

After breakfast the black officers came to *salaam* in form and desire me to say to Lord Clive that there had been many governors but none had thought of the real comfort and happiness of the people but himself, that now the army could live at ease and be certain of a provision if any accident befell them in service that they desired me to assure Lord Clive to their gratitude and thanks and that it was not merely the sentiments of that regiment but of the whole army. They then all *salaamed* again and went away.

Major Macleod had assembled a great many *shrofs* to come and give the history of the coins given me by Mrs Gordon. The most ancient one of the God Ram struck by an expedition to Ceylon, which I shall add in another paper as it is too long for this book and many of them were named and the places where coined but a few were unknown to them. The coin represents Ram, his wife, his brothers and two generals who were of great service to him in his wars as well as Hanuman, the Monkey god. There are seven figures: the figure of the latter is on the reverse.

In the evening I went into the barracks, which are clean and airy, and the arms in great order to the lines. The horses do not appear to me near so good as those of the body guard. Afterwards to Colonel Macalister's new house. It is a very airy place. Just above his tope a violent shower came on and obliged us to go home.

August 23rd This morning the 5th Regiment was drawn up on foot and marched by in form. They are all young and good-looking men and, considering that they have only been raised four months, in good order.

A *Brahmin* desired to show some tricks and incongruities. He was an old man I should think of sixty years of age. First he placed the bamboo of a black man's *palanquin* and raised it by degrees like it rested entirely on his chin. He walked in this astonishing manner. He afterwards tried the same with a straight bamboo, thirty-seven feet long and placed it upon a spike he held in his mouth. The wind had so much effect upon the top of the bamboo, which was as high as the roof of the house, that it over powered him. He did several other strange things: rubbing his arm with oil and scraping it off with a red hot bar.

Mr Hurdis, speaking of the natives this morning, told me that those upon the hills, so far from being wild and savage as we imagine, are really the best of people in regard to payment of their rent. He was saying that he always gives them a written paper promising not to extort more than is just from them and requiring payment should be made on or before a particular day. He never receives any agreement from them and yet he never knew them a day beyond the time and almost always the money arrived before the day mentioned. He said the natives are tormented by the *Nawab*'s *havildars*. But he has never sent to them requiring money or pearls (which they had taken from merchants travelling from Manar) that they did not immediately restore them and even cash that had been stolen seven years ago is returned. He said if the Madura district belonged to us instead of the *Nawab*, all would be well.

August 23rd, Coimbatoor, Henrietta to Lord Clive

After much consultation with Mr Hurdis it is settled not to go to Paligautherry. There is little to be seen of any consequence other than jungle. The roads from thence to Annamalleecottah are there; one never travelled since Colonel Fullarton and all paddy ground. The second in the same way with the addition of *Nayres* who come down in troops and rob. The third is guarded for the preservation of travellers, but bad. Each road the damps are so great that Mr Hurdis says his people that have been obliged to stay have always returned ill. This being the case we go to Pollachee twenty-seven miles from hence and make that headquarters.

From thence we shall go to Annamalecottah for the day and afterwards begin expeditions to any parts of the jungle. I hope to be able to collect both timber and seeds for you of the best black and red wood. He says that he is certain there is a variety of new and fine trees and plants in the jungle, but that he does not know anything. On that matter *Brahmins* assured Major Macleod yesterday.

Adieu, my dear Lord,
ever yours very affec
H. A. C.

On August 24th the travellers continued twelve miles to Canatacadavoo. There they found a *pagoda*, dedicated to Soobramanee (Soubrahmanya, a twelve-armed six-headed god of war, born in order to rid the world of the demon Taraka). The jungle was very thick and the thermometer was eighty degrees. Colonel Macalister gave them a cavalry escort for a few days as he felt rather suspicious of the intentions of some *polygars*, who might be tempted to make a descent and seize the travellers as hostages.

August 24th, Henrietta's journal

Left Coimbatoor. About three miles from that place I crossed the Morel, a small river which separates the districts to Major Macleod and Mr Hurdis. The country improves considerably. There are mostly enclosures round each field and an appearance of verdure I have not seen before. The road is tolerably good and the journey was very pleasant. It is twelve miles to Canatacadavoo, a word meaning the skirts of the woods. It is at the beginning of the jungle and there are many tygers, bears and wild elephants.

The village was destroyed by Tipu and Mr Hurdis despairs of its reviving from the neighbourhood of these beasts. It was market day. The people came ten or twelve miles from the different villages to buy and sell their goods.There is a *pagoda* upon a fine rock and some small *choultries*. After dinner, though it rained a little, I went to see it. It is belonging to Soubramanee who was there with a spear in his hand and a wife on each side. It was prettily lighted up . . . The *pagoda* is of the same gold as that at Pylney. We had several new creepers brought, mostly unknown. The *havildar* is to get some of the seeds for me.

August 25th Came through a beautiful country to Pollachee. It very much resembles England. The fields are enclosed with hedges and crop in its early state is much like green wheat or barley. They fold the sheep and cattle with hurdles composed of straight boughs fitted together and I saw some strange inventions for the shepherd: to sleep in was a frame raised about a foot from the ground and covered with bamboos close together; for the sleeping place and over it a close arch of boughs, apparently well fixed together and able to resist the weather.

The village is pleasantly situated. We are encamped in a cocoanut tope. In the morning the neighbouring *polygars* came to be presented to me. The first had the most horrible countenance I ever saw, though they were not any of them in actual friendship with Dhoondiah, they had all received from him and would probably have joined him. He wore his sword on the right side and had a dagger besides. The others were not so well dressed. They were four: two of not the best description; the others without swords or arms and better people.

August 26th Went to Annamalecottah. The road is extremely beautiful and enclosed like England. The country all round gave the neatest prospect I have seen for a long time. The soil reddish and they plow deeper furrows that what I have hereto observed. At seven miles from Pollachee I crossed the river, which takes its rise from the mountains opposite. There are two cascades at a great distance but which form a part of the river. We crossed in basket boats. The river had risen considerably and I am afraid will prevent us from seeing the teak trees I so much wish to see. The rest of the way we went in *palanquins* and soon came to the jungle, which is perfectly delightful. The trees were bright green and the rain last night had made it perfectly cool and the continual moisture gives a verdure unknown in other places. The largest trees were either tamarind or banyan trees . . . but most of these I have seen about the *ghauts*.

Annamalecottah is a small fort in ruins. After breakfast I went through a continuation of jungle to the rock of Tecknelodroogham. It is extremely difficult to ascend, the greatest part being of solid rock but not perfectly smooth. From the top, the view was really delightful. The thick wood reaches to the foot of the mountains and in two places there were small cascades near their top which form a part of the river crossed this morning. On the other side the country is perfectly cultivated with hedgerows and everything like Europe. Some paddy fields erupted which were green. The extent of view is very great. Paligautherry was to be seen beyond the jungle, but it is evident the place would not do to be inhabited by us.

In returning I saw a tree with a new flower which Captain Brown brought me and which is said to be a parasitical plant. The flower is like a honeysuckle but tipped with green. It generally, if not always, is found on the tamarind trees. There are several other plants entirely new, which I brought home and Mr Hurdis has obtained their names and history with seeds, which are to be sent to me when we descend to the bottom of the hill.

I omitted to mention that there were three men, perfectly savage in their appearance. The principal person had a cloth wrapt round his waist and a gold or brass necklace. His hair was long and his features much like the *caffers* at the Cape. Another old man came to *salaam* that was misery and wildness itself. There were two or three boys wrapt in *lunghis*, all looking equally savage. Mr Hurdis told me that they live entirely upon seeds and fruits with a buffalo, which they steal and kill now and then. They are dreaded thieves and generally rob and murder. Twenty-three of them a few months ago murdered six women and children. They waylay travellers of which I believe there are now very few and plunder them. Between this place and the camp I saw some more of these natives and their wives and children. The women had only a cloth round their waist like the men, but no other garment.

The river had risen considerably since we set out. There was a view near the fort of the river with trees to its edge that put me in mind of Oakly Park and indeed the view is generally like what I have seen there from the top.

August 27th I walked out in the morning. It was to be a quiet halting day, which we much wanted. It was hot and there was little to see about the place.

27 August, Pollachee, Henrietta to Lord Clive

I have been longer than usual without writing to you because I wished to tell you something of the teak trees which I was in hopes to have seen yesterday. We were the whole day at and near Annamalecottah but were unable to go towards the part among those trees. There is a severed arm of a rapid river we crossed yesterday and several ravines now filled with water which are such as William Hurdis says should unlikely prevent our getting on. I am very sorry for it. Yesterday we were in a jungle usually inhabited by wild elephants. Part of the road was made by Col Fullarton and though there were no large trees but the tamarind and Banyan yet they were very large and the journey for two or three miles was delightful with several small trees and shrubs that I have never seen. I have got boughs of them and the *havildar* is to get the seed of each of them for me.

In regard to the conveyance of timber the only way William Hurdis says is from the spot by country conveyances to carry them to Darapooram and Amoor from thence they may be floated to the mouth of the Cauvery. He has had some carried to Darapooram for his own use, but he says that though the rivers are rapid in this country yet their rise and fall is so sudden that it would be impossible to send any rafts or timber down them. They are deep in some places and very rocky in others but in general shallow and rise and fall in the course of eight or ten hours which would not allow time enough for timber to get down. The many rocks would risk the timber ever arriving. The only time in which the Cauvery is sufficiently high is in the month of June and the timber should be ready at Caroor by that time. He will get the sizes of the trees as accurately as he can. He has no doubt, indeed knows, that there are a great variety of timber in these woods but their exact sort he does not yet know.

From Annamalecottah we went to a small rock in appearance, Sanikulrogdroog, which has been fortified, but is not a very *frequented* place. The river is like glass and the other side a well-cultivated valley. We passed through the day before with hedges and such an appearance of plenty as was really delightful. The rock was so rough and steep that I persuaded the girls not to go to the top and I believe we had all as much as we could do to ascend and descend but we were not very much fatigued in the evening.

I cannot say the pleasure I have had in seeing this country. It is fresh and luxuriant. The trees are beautiful. We heard many peacocks in the wood but saw neither elephants nor any wild beasts except the real inhabitants who are as near savages and some of Captain Cook's* drawings than anything I ever saw. I never saw such a set of people in my life.

The day before yesterday the *polygars* in the neighbourhood came to make their *salaam* to me. One of them was the most horrible looking old monster and William Hurdis says is not much better than he looks. There were five altogether: two of the young *polygars* whose uncles came as their representatives came here today. They are fine looking boys. Tomorrow we go to Pylney, where we halt a day, and from thence to Darapooram. I hope to have, while we are hereabouts, some specimens of the cardamom, pepper and cinnamon trees growing on the hills. I should like to see the wood of the first. We are all well and much pleased with this part of the journey. The Coimbatoor disappointed me till we quitted the capital and it will again grow dismal in a day or two. It is not hot. We have had a good deal of rain, which occasioned the river to swell considerably between our passing and returning yesterday.

Adieu. The girls are well and very busy
writing to England, which I ought to be, too.
Ever, my dear Lord, yours affectionately
H. A. C.

I have sent, at least I believe it will go, some cuttings of a very curious sort of mistletoe with a beautiful flower. Pray have it grafted directly upon a tamarind tree. It *will not grow* in the ground and is really well worth preserving. I shall endeavour to get more but I doubt my success. Pray let it be done *the moment you receive it.*

August 28th, Henrietta's journal

Left Pollachee and its trees and cool breezes and came to Oudmalcottah, a dreary sandy place without a tree. The road was tedious and ugly. The Queen of Delhi, a *polygaress* of the neighbourhood came with others. She is

* Captain James Cook (1728–1779) English explorer and navigator

about sixty years of age. Mr Hurdis told me a very active, positive old woman who keeps her district in great subjection, but does not exactly pay her rent. She is supposed to be rather well disposed to the *polygar* of Verapache who was raising and did send the detachment to join Dhoondiah, which was discovered by Major Macleod. Several other *polygars* came also. They are all of low caste and wear earrings in the upper part of one ear, a proof of their having been menial servants at least their forefathers to the Kings of Madura. The Queen is of the lowest caste of the Connanies.

On August 28th some *polygars* and the Queen of Delhi (a village so called) strewed the travellers' feet with little bits of gold and silver paper as a token of respect. Charly's journal relates an account of a *polygar* having given her a beautiful young gazelle that was quite tame. It became attached to her, travelling in her *palanquin* and sleeping by her bedside. Returning from an early morning outing after being back in Madras, Charly found the gazelle lying dead in front of the house. Unattended it had lept from a verandah at the top of the house to the grass below. Charly grieved the loss of the gazelle.

August 28th, Henrietta's journal

The Verapachy *polygar* having behaved ill and being the person who raised soldiers for Dhoondiah and all correspondence having ceased between him and Mr Hurdis, it was not thought prudent for me to pass through his country to Dindigal. From some reports when we were at Pylney we heard that he had increased his number of troops and peons and was cleaning his roads; whether to receive me was a doubt. The nights I was at Pylney it was for several reasons thought right to double the guard round the tents and to have everything ready in case he should come. However, I heard nothing more of him.

August 29th, Henrietta to Lord Clive

We left all our pretty country and our trees behind us yesterday and have had two dreary marches with much dust and wind. No more rain but a good deal of heat. We have calculated the probable progress of our journey which at the shortest and without more than the necessary halting days. By all accounts we shall be at Madras not before the 11th October. It is a long while to fix, but it is really as soon as it can be done. We are all well.

Tomorrow we halt or rather the day after at Pylney and then go directly to Darapooram. It is sad to see the difference of the country and the weather in these few miles and we are still near hills. I hear we are not to be much more amused with prospects as we approach the Cauvery. William Hurdis will try to float some timber down to see what can be done about your teak trees and let you know the event. I have several specimens of trees whose appearance are quite unknown to me and I am to have the seeds.

The girls will I am afraid lose their bloom before you see them and be quite brown. I shall be *black*, much more so than any of the *Herberts* at *Powis Castle.*

Adieu.

Many loves to you.

Ever, my dear Lord, yours very affectionately

H. A. C.

August 30th, Henrietta's journal

Came to Pylney. It is a pretty place and cultivated with a considerable river passing near it. There are two hills near. On one of which there is a famous *pagoda* dedicated to Soobramanee concerning which there are many stories told and too long for me to insert here. I passed the day in a bungalow built by Colonel Oliver. It was very hot and the glare very disagreeable.

In the evening I went through the village to see a *pagoda* dedicated to Soobramanee It was very large; the ornaments better carved than these places usually are. There was a long passage or hall supported by pillars and covered with stone across which were hung garlands of flowers and a variety of lamps on each side leading to the holy place where the god was placed. Flowers were offered to him by being put on the altar at his feet and lights (I suppose fifteen in a pyramidal form) were waved before him.

Then a lesser light, one in a glass dish, after which a bell was rung and some prayers recited and then flowers were brought and put round my neck. It is remarkably pretty altogether and I was much pleased with it. I believe it was the god Soobramanee as there are many offerings of slippers on the roof of the entrance.

August 30th, Pylney, Henrietta to Lord Clive

This morning to my great joy and surprise I received the enclosed letters, which I send to you directly. I wish my brother had not occasion for Harrogate though I have no doubt it will do him good. General St John with his wife are good people. She is one of Lord Craven's sisters and a very good little woman. I shall be glad to see him and hear how my dear boys look, shall not you? Captain Brown has a long account of your old regiment, which he seems charmed with. I have not had time to hear it yet. We are in a more Christian-like place than for these two days, but it is hot and sitting in a bungalow built by Colonel Oliver. All well and merry.

You will be sorry to hear by your uncle's letter of the death of poor old Sophie. I hope she is the only friend I shall lose by my absence and am very sorry for it.

We halt tomorrow. The roads are heavy for the animals and we have five days march afterwards before the next halting day. God bless you. I am glad to find that Edward grows and Robert improves. I hope we shall see those good souls. Have you ever written to them? Some very fine mountain limes are just brought. I have desired some trees for you. They are larger than any lemons I have seen except in Italy.

Adieu. Many loves to you.
Ever my dear lord, yours very affectionately
H. A. C.

The letter from Edward to you came with the others enclosed by General St John.

August 31st, Henrietta's journal

I went to the top of the hill to the most distant *pagoda*. The ascent is tolerable easy having steps cut in the rock. There are some little *choultries* on the way and some lesser *pagodas.* One *pagoda* is to the giant who watches Soobramanee where there are slippers brought as offerings. The *pagoda* itself is not near so large as that I had seen last night. They brought me flowers and a filthy mixture composed of oil and jasmine with which the people rub their throats.

There is at the door of the most holy place a guard or champion in a sort of armour and with horsehair in a bunch on his head. Behind his girdle is a large piece of brass with two heads of the same hanging down before him, a sword drawn and a cloth thrown round him. If the holy place should ever be in danger of being taken, it is to be put in a bag and thrown down from it. On the way down I saw several *fakeers* with their hair matted and of a great length twisted round on the top of their heads and thought it was some ornament. They were dirty figures. There was an old man who had elephantiasis, the first I ever saw. It is a most shocking disorder.

In the evening I went round the tank. It is considerably raised and deepened and is now fourteen feet in the deepest part and being a good deal above the land on the other side. It is convenient for watering it and generally produces *three* crops. I went afterwards to a *pagoda,* but it was not so handsome as that on the preceding night. The road to that on the hill was illuminated and the *pagoda* itself, which had a very pretty effect, the lamps being placed on each side of the way or rather there are holes made in the rock in which the oil is put.

August 31st, Pylney, Henrietta to Lady Douglas

My dear Lady Douglas – I have had at last the pleasure of receiving two packets of letters from England and that doubly by having letters from every soul I have particularly wished to hear. You are a delightful person to write to me wherever there is an opportunity and I have letters from all Dalkeith house, which makes me quite happy. I assure you that sort of comfortable correspondence is, I really think, the great luxury in the East. I like to know how every body is going on and how the world is peopled by your nephews and nieces . . . To the greatest degree I can perfectly enter into all your lives. I think very often of you and all your offspring. It is now two years since I landed upon this sandy shore. In two more I trust

I shall be in a better place but I do not yet know any time when I am likely to be so happy. I wrote to you in April from Ryacottah where I had travelled, not with seven leagued boots but with elephants and camels like an Eastern Damsel with all possible dignity.

From thence I proceeded to Bangalore, which is the only place upon this Eastern Earth worthy to be called a country. The air is so wholesome and delightful that I felt it *cold* and shut the doors. It was not like a cold fog, which prevails in the Carnatic, but like an autumn day in England. When I lived in Tipu's palace near three months and rejoiced that I was not one of his wives who had only two rooms, one within the other with a very small window in one and without any in the other. They sat and ate *betel* in miserable confinement with the happy prospect of being sent for by him and perhaps to have their necks dislocated if such was his pleasure. These fair ladies were never allowed to speak to him unless he asked them a question or began the conversation. They were reminded when they went into his apartment by the old women who attended them that they must *be silent.* Some they say had ventured to speak and that without hesitation he has had them *instantly destroyed.* Think of the blessing of being the wife to that great Potentate on such terms. He was not magnificent even in regard to their dress. He gave them very small jewels of little value and if not great occasions they were not to be dressed. The jewels were always returned *again to him.* He had ordered the inhabitants to quit Bangalore after it was taken by Lord Cornwallis and that the fort should be destroyed which were nearly done. I had an excellent garden with alleys of cypress trees and the only sweet roses in India.

From thence I proceeded to Seringapatam and saw all the marks of horror of the siege and storm, which has given me a *pretty idea of fortification*, a new accomplishment. I am sure it must be my own fault if this is not the case as it was most learnedly explained to me. I saw Haidar's and Tipu's widows. Some were handsome but still nothing like the beauties in the *Arabian Nights* nor no pearls like pigeon's eggs. Some of them thought it necessary to cry, but I did not see many real tears except in the true wife who was neither young nor handsome, but she really seemed to feel concern. Yet in fact, except the pleasure of seeing him and the chance of being *hung* and destroyed, their situation is exactly as it was in his lifetime. They have more certain provision and all their little wishes gratified. It is really more like a convent than anything I ever saw. The *real* wife is the head and chief. They are all married but those only are called the real wives on whose marriage there was great rejoicing and ceremonies, which cost one or two hundred thousand *pagodas.* Therefore it is not convenient to have many of these ladies. His daughters are fine little girls and very like the pictures of Tipu.

After all these affairs I went to Mysore. The little *Rajah* is six years old and a nice little boy with a most sensible interesting countenance. His grandmother is as short and as fat as any human creature can be that is to move upon the face of the earth. She looks very well for her age – sixty years – and has the appearance of much sense. These people are really interesting and it is wonderful that after being confined between thirty and forty years she should be restored and that, through Tipu, who wished to annihilate the throne and name of Mysore, this little boy should live and that he should now sit upon the *ivory throne* on which his ancestors and predecessors *sat 700* years ago. It is impossible not to moralise upon the decrees of providence on such an occasion and on the uncertainty of all human affairs. I shall always think of the two days I passed at Mysore with interest and shall care more about the affairs of India than I ever did from having beheld these two persons.

Since that I have descended the Guzelhutty Pass which is something like a Scotch or Welsh mountain, a very great compliment to it I assure you. One of the people attending my baggage was carried *off by a tyger* the evening before I arrived. Some of my belongings heard *it growl* and Charlotte is quite persuaded she saw *its tail.* I assure you the consternation was extreme. Everybody had a horrible tale to tell. But the poor man was really devoured and two other bodies were found half eaten just by the side of the road. This was really travelling in the East.

I have been at Coimbatoor and in unfrequented woods in search of teak and other strange trees. Many I have discovered that are quite *new descriptions.* I shall have some seeds. When I return to Madras I think I shall be able to send you some pretty creepers for the little hot house. When I meet with a beauty, the Collector or somebody promises to get the seeds. I have really found one or two plants that are very sweet and not known. I sincerely hope that your journeys may all do as much good to your family as mine has done to my girls. They grow tall and not too thin. I think of England very often and with what pleasure I shall see it again.

Thanks to you for the *Darbish muslin* from Mrs Fleming at Glasgow. I have not yet seen it, but I hear it is at the capital where I cannot arrive before the 18th or 20th October as I go to Trichinopoly and Tranquebar. I believe I am thought a strange restless animal. A black woman never moves and the white ones in this country are not much more active. Besides I descend from my dignity and walk upon my own feet at every place where I take up my abode.

This was written in a breath and having reposed and read your last letters once more I shall begin again and having finished the East talk a little more of the North and some of its good productions for instance the person you certainly do not love a little who I must call as you do 'Car'. I am charmed to hear she delights in drawing and composing. It is what my perfect old Mrs Byres always said the most lasting and the most gratifying of the arts that if you sung or played like Orpheus it soon passed, but that a drawing was a lasting amusement to yourself and your friends. It is what I should have like to have done if I had ever been able and I am sorry that at present I see very little disposition in either of my girls to draw at all either man or beast – It was once my great hobby horse. Here I have not power to do such things . . .

How I should like to be put down this minute and hear the readings and see the drawing in your sitting room and all the comforts thereunto belonging, as the greatest part of my life is passed in thinking how to keep my two blessed girls in health and to do as much as I can for their improvement. I feel how much pleasure you must have in seeing yours of more different ages prosper before you. I should like to see them again. The little plaything cannot know me but the more ancient I think will remember me whenever I am so happy as to return to my own country.

The account of yourself and proceedings delights me. There is nothing more pleasant to me than to follow any person for whom I am interested. I have seen you in my mind's eye through your journey and only wish I could do it with my real eye as well as my mental.The story you tell me of your neighbour's infatuation diverts me much. There seems a great deal of that sort of infatuation in London and nothing but ladies leaving their spouses. Don't you think the world is not so good as they were in the days of your and of our youth and that instead of mending they grow worse? Without any vanity I do really believe that your daughters and mine are and will be the most innocent that have been or will be in the world to which I do as really believe that many people do not attend sufficiently to that essential part of education that accomplishments have been usually more attended to than more spiritual things.

Pray remember that every relation of your movements and of your doings is delightful to me that I see you all merry at Bothwell and Dalkeith . . . and that there is nothing I wish for much more than to remain in all your remembrances. May all good attend you.

Most sincere wishes.

Yours

H. A. Clive

Pylney, where I have been to see a famous *pagoda* and caught cold from garlands of wettish flowers that the priests put round my neck after they had been offered to *God Soobramanee*. The stories of the *pagodas* are really very entertaining.

September 1st, Henrietta's journal

Came to Darapooram. It is in a very sandy dusty situation and very hot. Mr Hurdis is building a house, which will be very uncomfortable in a short time. He showed me some coins late found about thirty miles from hence, most undoubtedly Roman and gave me several of them. In the evening I walked to his new *Brahmin*'s village and saw some timber from the Annamallee Woods, forty feet long and two feet square brought by bullocks at the expense of sixty rupees each.

September 1st, Darapooram, Henrietta to Lord Clive

You will receive in about eight or ten days some lime and lemon trees which as the fruit was uncommonly fine I desired William Hurdis to send you and by the *tappal*. You will receive the fruit itself as a specimen. I have just seen some boughs of the cinnamon trees from the hills: wild. The leaves are very large and strong and the cinnamon taken off by the country people without knowing how or when it ought to be done. It is not so strong as the best from Ceylon. There were some fine pepper vines and some other boughs of which the fruit will be sent to you as it is new to me: medicinal and used in dyeing. I have some specimens – two – of a sort of redwood but not near so beautiful as that I sent you from Ryacottah. There is sandalwood, but not so fine as some you will have from Seringapatam nor near so large.

We had a long march today of seventeen miles. It is very hot but we are well. I hear you are very gay and giving balls, but you do not trouble yourself with writing. Your *last* letter was dated the 10th August. Did I tell you I have had a letter from Captain Malcolm before he arrived at Sheraz? I keep it till we meet. This is an ugly dreary place with little cultivation or trees and a hot wind blowing the dust – *Adieu.* We hear from William Thomas that the ships do not sail till October. Is it true? And is there any October fleet? *Besides pray let me know* because of my letters. I see Lord Wellesley has £200,000 from the Company. Is it true? Are any other governors to have anything? I think they ought.

Adieu. Ever, my dear Lord,
yours very affectionately
H. A. C.

September 3rd, Chinna Darapooram, Henrietta to Lord Clive

We are just come here and the change of weather has been very great within these two days. Yesterday the thermometer was at 94. Much hotter than you are at Madras. I trust that we shall soon get into a cooler climate. I have three times passed the river by which your timber must be floated if it goes in that way. It is now only knee deep . . . I have not desired any trees of the other woods till I show them to you. The heat has not oppressed us much. As you may suppose my next letter will be from Caroor where we shall halt a day. William Hurdis says that some fine timber used to come down the Godavery and Kistrah to Madras. Teak particularly.

Adieu. Many loves to you.

Ever, my dear Lord. yours very affectionately

H. A. C.

September 4th, Pallipalum, Henrietta's journal

It was pleasanter than it had been for some days. I took a long walk in search of stones and found many crystals with which the country abounds. They say that they increase the fertility, which may be on the same reason that stones are put round greenhouse plants to present the cooperation of the moisture in the ground. The appearance was improved though the country was not pretty but rocky and wild. There is a rapid though narrow river close by the tents, which contributed to make them comfortable.

September 5th, Henrietta's journal

Came to Caroor. It is a deserted place and Mr Hurdis has little hopes of its improving from going out of the great roads. I went to some rooms built over a *choultry* . . . It was extremely hot and oppressive. Several *polygars* came to make their *salaam* and two widows of that of Rangherry, about which there is a disputed suspicion. There has been much iniquity, bribery, and treachery respecting their poor people. The sons or I believe the nephews of the late *polygar* and real heirs were not arrived. The ladies suffered much for a long time, but Mr Hurdis refused to let the boys come as *polygars* in that would have been organising to their claim, which he did not then know, would be proved to the government.

In the evening I went round the fort. There was a magnificent *choultry* round the *pagoda* dedicated to the destroying power. But, it was destroyed by Major Birsema when he was with Col Fullarton and I understand very unnecessarily. It is a very great pity. It was built of granite and much better done than the figures in *pagodas* are usually. I slept in the tent and breakfasted the next morning in the fort.

September 5th, Caroor, Henrietta to Lord Clive

We came to Caroor this morning and are established in a house built by Mrs Wynach when she was here. I am surprised that you do not write to me when I have written such long stories of Seringapatam. I hear you are very well and very gay but I am afraid you are too much in your garden and are planting there instead of writing to me which is uncomfortable. We hear the ships sail on the 20th. Is that true?

It is very hot and for these last three days Charlotte's nose has bled again which it had long left off. The heat affects her almost immediately. Every day I trust it will grow cooler.

I do not know if you have received plants and cuttings without end that have been sent and they have never been acknowledged. I have some seeds of the mountain lemon, which I shall bring myself and you will have some sheep bya bye, that have wool and are *like sheep* and very good mutton for your farmyard and a bull of great beauty as I hear, as I have not seen him. This is a dreary country in general, but cultivated round Canoor and less hot than I expected. I long for the sea breeze –

The girls desire their love to you. I am afraid their good looks will not reach Madras. It is Harry's birthday today and she is certainly as stout as is necessary at her age. *Adieu.* Pray write because it is really uncomfortable to be *near a month* without hearing from you.

Ever my dear Lord.
Yours very affectionately
H. A. C.

September 6th, Henrietta's journal

It was hot. The thermometer at 94, yet not near so oppressive as it had been the preceding day at 89 in the fort. In the evening I went through the *pettah* to the river and had a pleasant walk. It is an inconsiderable place. On returning this evening I was surprised by a great many women setting up a most extraordinary shrill shriek. It is the way of expressing great pleasure among that caste and it is always done at marriages and funerals. It was one of the most extraordinary civilities I ever met with.

September 7th Left Caroor and went to a sugar manufactory established by Mr Campbell. He has just built a pleasant bungalow and has begun his garden. But there is much doubt if it will answer to him. The soil there will not bear the sugar cane another year. Therefore the crop must be considerably diminished and there is not any wood within his reach, which is absolutely necessary for the sugar. I proceeded to where one of the *Nawab*'s people met me with the usual ceremonies of fruit and flowers. Mr Hurdis quitted us this evening after having conducted me through his country or district.

I omitted to mention some very extraordinary hills of sand, which we passed this evening. They are said to have covered one village and I believe it is true from the appearance of the cocoanut trees on the upper part of the hill, which are evidently many feet deep in the sand.

September 8th Came to Peomony. The heat was very great and the thermometer at 95. A pretty *pandal* had been created by the *Nawab*'s people. It rained in the evening, which prevented me from going out, and as the march had been unexpectedly long this morning, I was not sorry to remain quiet.

Trichinopoly: September 9th–16th

'I feel the unpleasantness of absence very much.'

September 9th, Allitoree, Henrietta to Lord Clive

We are arrived after a long march and are once more in his highness the *Nawab*'s country which is better cultivated and better looking than his is usually. The day after tomorrow we shall be at Trichinopoly where I hear it is less hot than it is here. I am much disappointed in not having heard from you for near a month and I wish it much. I hear you are well. Mrs St John wrote me word you were giving balls and were very gay and I hear of a breakfast to the *Nawab*, which Thomas sent to Captain Brown, but it would really give me pleasure to hear *from* you. I have written without end to you and have told you all I have done which I should like much to know if it is right or not.

It is very uncomfortable not to hear something and with fatigue and considerable anxiety about the girls I feel the unpleasantness of absence very much. They are well now and indeed Harry is generally so; Charlotte's nose has been quiet these two last days. Pray come in from the garden a little sooner and take a pen and write to me. I sent you my last English letters and should be glad to have them again. I have got some fine nutmegs from the hills, some cardamons and a plant of wild – not unlike – satin wood which I shall bring with me. The nutmegs are scarcely ripe but are curios to us who have never seen them growing. The leaves are very large. All these things come from beyond Dindigal and you may have any quantity of the timber if it can be transported but I did not desire to have any till you have seen it.

General Bridges gives me his house on the plain but I really think we sleep nowhere so well as in tents. *Adieu*. The girls desire their love to you. They are as busy as the weather will permit with their English letters.

Ever my dear Lord, yours very affectionately

H. A. C.

I am afraid I have lost a box of millinery, which ought to have been here many months ago. I never heard by what ship it was sent, but a bill has been sent to me by Wilding. I am afraid it is owing to W Strachey. It is not amongst those sent by Wilding and it is between William S and William Franks. He is a sad person to send commissions and kept the box, I know, for months in his house. I am afraid Major Allan has not delivered his commission any more than Captain Sampson. I sent some seeds to Lady Douglas, which she had not received.

September 10th, Trichinopoly, Henrietta's journal
Charlotte being much fatigued and weak I did not go out today at all. I was a little disappointed at the appearance of the Rock. It is not high, at least not so much so as I expected.
September 11th I stayed at home till the evening and went out for a little while till the rain came on.
September 12th I went out in the morning to the Golden Rock (near Trichinopoly) upon which a *fakeer* now lives. It is low and rugged without anything remarkable. In the evening I went to Mrs Dache's garden. It is kept in high order and there are several small buildings scattered about. It is extremely cool and pleasant particularly one in which under a tent there is a bath. After my return home there fell a most violent storm of rain with the most violent lightning I ever saw.
September 13th Drove out in the morning to see Sugarloaf and French Rocks (in the plain of Trichinopoly). The road was rough and the Rocks completely barren. I saw some of the trees called the true cedars of Lebanon. They are pretty of quick growth and perfectly new to me. In the evening went to the side of the river, which is broad and very handsome on the Island of Seringham. There is a great appearance of cultivation and verdure from the paddy fields.

I forgot to say I had been in the evening to the house of the *Nawab*, a pretty place but quite in ruin. The garden is very large and by the side of a broad *nullah*. It might be made a charming place and is perfectly located. He will not allow any European to live in it. He says if any officer was there he should never get rid of him again.

September 13th, Trichinopoly, Henrietta to Lord Clive

We are still at Trichinopoly. I found Charlotte much in want of rest and therefore have stayed from day to day that she may recover. There are reasons to explain which make her so very delicate and weak that she is incapable of exertion. I trust one day more will enable us to proceed. I have only as yet seen the French Rocks and the different remarkable spots. The day after tomorrow I hope to go to the fort and Rock and the next day to Samiaveram and from thence on that side of the River to Tanjore, which saves our returning here and crossing the rivers again.

I shall get some seeds for you of the *real* Cedar of Lebanon as it is said. It is pretty but quite unlike our cedars and a China shrub which I saw in a garden of William Dake's (Mrs Floyd's father) last night. I have not seen a place so neat for a long time and most flourishing.

The height of the Rock (236 feet), as I have seen it, disappoints me. The heat has been very great and we feel the advantage of a house during the day. We have had rain every evening and last night a most violent storm of thunder, lightning and rain. I never saw the lightning more violent. It will cool the air and do us good. We are all well except Charlotte from the heat. Harriet, I think, I shall bring back looking very well and hope Charlotte will revive again. At present she is not what she was a month ago. We shall not be at Tanjore as soon as I expected but that cannot really be helped. General Bridges is extremely civil and gives up the house completely, which is very comfortable. Mrs Dye is here but looking very ill and very unlike what she was at Madras.

We are bringing stones and a variety of treasures from this place. I have yet no letter from you. *Adieu.* My Dear Lord we shall be glad to behold you again. The girls desire their love. They are pleasant animals and I believe you will think them a little grown.

Adieu.

Ever your very affectionate

H. A. C.

September 14th, Henrietta's journal
Went to church in the Fort. The clergyman unfortunately speaks very unpleasantly with a strong accent. The sermon was preached by Mr Ball. I liked the manner in which the boys stand and answered the responses infinitely better than those at Madras. Afterwards I went to Colonel Brown's house, which is really the main guard. It is very cool and there is a fine view from the top of it. When I returned home, two Malabar priests came with a petition and an old man, Modeen Sahib, who was with the late Lord Clive at Samiaveram and was wounded with him. He is a venerable old figure. He has given me a short account of that day and is to go with me to that place and describe every part of it to me. In the evening we drove out as usual.

September 15th Went up the Rock at Trichinopoly, the greatest part of the way is under a covered way with stone steps which continue to a small *choultry* from which there is a fine view. Afterwards the way is over the rock but neither slippery nor steep. In short I was much surprised at the ease with which we ascended, as Charlotte had not been well. She was carried in a chair.

After coming down I went to the *Nawab*'s house where there are some pictures belonging once to Mrs Dupleen and brought from Pondicherry of the King and Queen of France and other private persons whose names were not known. There was besides Stubbs* original picture of the horse and tyger and one of a tyger fighting with a lion. It was a very shabby dirty place and not the least remains of splendour. The garden had nothing in it but a large royal tyger worth remarking.

The *pettah* within the Fort is much crowded and has many inhabitants. There are some without the walls where there are barracks and where most of the horses of officers etc. are. After my return, the nephew and future son in law of Tondiman came and made his *salaam* to me. He has the appearance of a true *polygar* with an immense scarlet and gold turban and a large pair of whiskers. He brought a silver cup and some pearls which

* George Stubbs (1725–1806), painter whose images of lions and tigers came to be symbolic of the British/Indian conflict.

General Bridges undertook to return to him, but fruit and flowers I accepted. In the evening the *Nawab*'s relation came to take leave of me. We had had almost every evening violent rain, but it did not cool the air.

September 15th, Trichinopoly, Henrietta to Lord Clive

After expecting to hear from you with great anxiety at last I have had that pleasure for such I assure you it is to me. You do not mention your own health by which I trust it is good. We are all pretty well; Charlotte reviving. We met your letter at the bottom of the Rock of Trichinopoly from which we had just descended. Charlotte was carried in a chair therefore had not fatigue and was pleased. The ascent is by no means difficult or fatiguing. We scarcely feel it . . .

Tomorrow we go to Samiaverum with the fine old Moorman, who was with your Father. He is to tell me the whole story and show the spots and places that are so remarkable.

I am in hopes that instead of the *Nawab* you will come to meet us somewhere. At present I do not see any reason to suppose we shall prolong our journey more than I told you. Much depends on Charlotte. I wish to bring her stout and well if possible. I am sorry you have been disappointed of timber for the new part of the house and have little chance of getting any from the Annamallee Woods till next year. I shall certainly say all to the *Rajah* you desire and get a sketch of him.

Mr Torin was here yesterday and is gone to prepare for me. We end the baggage on this side of the river and go a bad and beautiful road in the *palanquins*. No horses can go therefore the bodyguard will march upon their own feet much to the surprise of the *havildar*.

We go to Tranquebar by the river. Not to Nijapatam. If you have not received *heaps* of cuttings, either they have been neglected to be given to you or omitted by the *tappal*. Some *rare* plants from Pendangdroog went at least once or twice a week for sometime. Some were from Ryacottah and some from Pollachee. All of these were rare . . .

I should be much diverted to see the *Nawab* and Mr Webbe with his *three wives*. I hope he will allow me to see the mistresses. Webbe's having seen only Mohamatan ladies I should like to see a Persian and Hindoo.

We have had little rain till these last few days. We are supposed to be very *lucky* to bring it to every place. I will finish my letters as soon as I can and send them. I have begun to your Mother, Uncle and Aunt in answer to theirs and shall to Mrs Walpole. Thank you for writing to my Brother. I think he should have been much disappointed if he had not heard and a letter from you besides is always pleasant to him. *Adieu*. The girls send their loves and will write when their English letters are gone. It is late and I must dispatch my letter. I shall write when I can of the road to Tanjore.

Adieu, my dear Lord.
Ever yours very affectionately
H. A. C.

September 16th, Samiaveram, Henrietta's journal

Left Trichinopoly and crossed the Cauvery at daybreak in a large boat which admitted of the *palanquins* crossing abreast in it. It was slow on its passage but the view of the river and island of Seringham on one side and the Rock on the other was beautiful. The Coleroon is wider than the Cauvery, but more easily passed. The road was very bad chiefly through paddy fields and there were several deep *nullahs* to be crossed. The journey was long and we did not arrive at Samiaveram till past 9 o'clock. There was a pretty *pandal* erected at the *choultry* which is called Clive's but Modeen Sahib who I took with me assured me it was not in that which Lord Clive slept. He showed the spot to Captain Brown where he said it had been. There was not a vestige remaining but a *pandal* was placed there for me. Upon examining this spot with Orme's book it exactly answered in every respect to the distance from the lesser and greater *pagoda*. In the evening I went to the place and have not the least doubt it was right. Modeen Sahib described the Line to be down the road and that Lord Clive's tent was pitched near the then *choultry*. He was wounded in the arm on that day and remained afterwards sometime with Lord Clive. The large *pagoda* is in ruins and much neglected. The people call all the *choultries* General Clive's. The heat this day had been terrible. The thermometer in my tent was at 96. In the others less high and in the evening there was a most violent storm of rain, thunder and lightning.

September 17th, Henrietta to Lord Clive

I quite forgot to send yesterday the letter from Captain Macleod and indeed it was packed up so here it is. We are at Samiaveram. There are several *choultries*. I have not yet ascertained which it is exactly. I have Robert Orme and the old Moorman I mentioned to you yesterday. Therefore in the evening I shall be quite sure. We are pretty well. Charlotte delicate but bearing a long journey tolerably well and recovering her looks gradually.

General Bridges came here with us. He has been extremely civil and good indeed and insisted on coming so far on our road. Mr Harris has sent a route from Tanjore to Captain Brown today. I think if nothing particular arises we shall be at Madras by this day month.

This morning as I was getting into the *palanquin* your letter of the 13th arrived with my Brother's. It is a very old letter but it is satisfactory about the boys. Lord G Barnard's is entertaining. I have written two letters to her [Lady Anne Barnard at the Cape of Good Hope] which she cannot have received. One was by the *Blue Grant* last year that did not go to the Cape. Lord Hanford's letter was to mention General St John to you at his particular request and to express a wish *for Trichinopoly.* She says little more except that my Brother was not well. It is dated in March. We have letters from him of a later date and I know William Keene tells her what he thinks which is not on the most favourable side.

It is provoking that you cannot get timber. I cannot imagine how you are to dispose of us at the Ameer Bagh. We are pretty well. Charlotte's spirits are not up yet as usual . . . We are on the bank of the Coleroon in a pretty place and have passed through a very rich country this morning but very deep roads over paddy fields. *Adieu.* Many loves to you I will *if I can* bring many beans in my *palanquin* from Tanjore. The box of millinery, which Thomas Harris received, is not what I want. It is another, perhaps gone to Bengal.

Adieu.
Ever my dear Lord,
Yours very affectionately
H. A. C.

September 17th, Henrietta's journal

This morning General Bridges and those who had attended me to Thanjavar returned to Trichinopoly. The road was filled with water and was much through paddy ground, which added to the rain the night before made it almost a river the whole way. Much of it was by the side of the Coleroon and in one part a fine avenue of Banyan trees on each side. The country is entirely fertile and covered with paddy and topes. I have not seen any so pleasant or so fruitful. It was a long journey, but the place was very pretty where we were encamped near the large Annicut or dam, which turns the Cauvery towards the Tanjore country and gives it all its fertility. In the evening there was a most violent storm of rain, thunder and lightning which seems the usual consequence of the hot day in this moist country.

On September 18th Charly noted: 'It rained very hard in the night, and the noise the frogs made was beyond conception. We went to see an old pagoda full of bats.'

September 18th, Henrietta's journal

Came through a most delightful wood to Coilady. The village is small and there is an old *pagoda*. It is one of the places mentioned in Orme's *History*. There was a *pandal* created and the tank was near it. In the evening I took a walk and afterwards there was a tremendous storm, which obliged us to go in *palanquins* to the tank. There were many very large trees by the roadside this morning, particularly some bamboos of a very great size. One teak tree I saw, but a small one. The vegetation is extremely great and the journey which was only four miles and a half was really delightful.

September 19th Came to Trivady. The country is still more cultivated than yesterday with large trees in different parts of the field – some that reminded me of English trees. There was much rice and the road runs by the side of the river in many places. There are a great number of villages near it. In short it was a most continual chain of inhabitants (the men, chiefly Brahmin) bringing cocoanuts, limes and flowers and the women singing and joining in a chorus of screaming which was the same as at Caroor. While they scream they move their tongue which makes that yell they think musical and is used at all ceremonies (marriages and funerals) and is likewise a great mark of joy and respect. The first time I heard it, the *havildar* thought it was meant to affront me and rode up to the women in a great rage but it was explained to be a civility. At this place is a very pretty pandal erected by the Collector, Mr Harris, in a choultry by the side of the river.

As there is no good place for the tents this evening I shall continue my road to Tanjore where I expect to be before 7 o'clock. The village is very large and rich. It is belonging to *Brahmins* who pay no taxes or rent to the *Rajah* but the whole is as almshouses in England endowed for the maintenance of the *Brahmins*. There is a large *pagoda* lately finished with a considerable tank. The view from the *choultry* where we dined was delightful. The river is very broad and its banks covered with trees and cultivation. The *Rajah*'s relations, two old women, wives to his adopted father and real uncle, live here. They have palaces on the riverside and very large gardens. I went into one of them where there is a very large tree unknown in this country supposed to have been brought by some pilgrim. I think it is like the *arbor vitae* from China.

The rivers we crossed were four in number and almost equally broad and the country between the two first beautiful beyond description. It was quite dark before I arrived at the last river. The *Rajah*'s Minister met me there with his troops, elephants, *sepoys* and a variety of noises, which attended me to Mr Torin's house. The road seemed to be lined with people and to be so almost the whole way. Mr Torin's house is excellent, but it was hot and in the night a great deal of rain fell.

Tanjore: September 20th–22nd

'... the Rajah sent his cattle to visit me ... [he] desired I would take as many as I pleased as he had many of them. They are so beautiful that Mr Torin [the Collector at Tanjore] chose a large gentleman and two ladies of the first size and age and a second set of ladies about half grown. Besides the Rajah desired to send some of the small ones to the girls in his own name. They are little beauties and have just passed by on their road to Madras.'

September 20th, Tanjore, Henrietta to Lord Clive

We are delighted with the country. Charlotte is reviving. Her spirits are getting up again. The evening and morning are cool and pleasant though the middle of the day is hot. We have had violent rain and thunder and lightning every evening. Yesterday we had a long march through a most glorious country from Koilady to Trivady. It is completely cultivated with rice and there are large trees like a park in England and very much inhabited. There were almost all the way villages to the left and the Cauvery almost always to our right. The *brown* men came out and uttered such strange noises to show civility that it was more like savages than people in a rational country. Mr Torin came to us at Koilady and advised me not to go to Nijapatam. But to go by the side of the Coleroon which has been confirmed by Mr and Mrs Campbell this morning by their having met with a vast deal of water and mud. As the place where we were encamped yesterday was in the village and very close, we came here in the evening. But unfortunately, as we had four rivers to cross, it was dark before we arrived. It was a pity as we did not see all that we might have done. The *Rajah* sent troops and ministers, elephants and flowers. Tomorrow he comes here and the next day we go to him. He speaks English, which will be an advantage to us. This minister has just been here and the sketch will be made for you of the *Rajah* tomorrow.

This place is delightful. We are in an excellent house surrounded by grass and trees. I cannot say enough of the beauty of the country and the rivers. I mean to remain here til Sunday evening on account of my visit. I have to present shawls and a dress, which Mrs Torin says is *unavoidable.* I have desired that he (Mr Torin) wills what is to be done and to keep clear of jewels which were to be offered . . .

We shall go by Tiverum and see the best part of the country throughout to Tranquebar. *Adieu.* Many loves to you and many respects are from Mr Torin. William Hawkins came here with us. He puts me in mind of Mr Keene very often and is much older than Admiral Whits in his appearance. Mr Torin says he has no timber for you. They say that at Zappadin there are a great many excellent houses which are sold for materials and that there is a great deal of very good teak timber in them, that many people buy them on purpose for it and the town is much decayed that it costs very little I believe.

I have this minute received the *Rajah* and his minister's picture sent by him to me. They say very like him . . . It really is very well done for that sort of thing. They are at full length about six inches high. Signora A is to take a sketch while he makes his visit tomorrow, which is the only time in which it can be done. This was settled by his Minister this morning who said he had a picture of him which he should send her to assist her afterwards which is what I have just mentioned.

Adieu, my dear Lord.
Ever yours,
very affectionately
H. A. C.

September 20th, Tanjore, Henrietta's journal

I walked out this morning in the garden. It is very pleasant. There is a degree of vegetation here I have never before seen in India. Mr Torin has several antelopes in a very well constructed building of bamboos in which they have a considerable range. He gave one of them to Harriet. Dr John from Tranquebar and two other missionaries came after breakfast to visit me. I am sorry to find that the Danish settlement is to be removed and that the formerly remarkable collection of dried insects and birds are almost dispersed . . .

In the evening I went to the former residence of the commanding officer and resident. It has a charming garden and is near a large tank much more pleasantly situated than where Mr Torin lives at present. They both belong to the *Rajah*. An officer sometime ago refused to let the late *Rajah*'s people take flowers for the ceremonies of the *pagoda*. The moment he quitted the house, it was pulled down.

September 21st I drove out in the morning . . . The view of the country is very extensive and fine and likewise that of the fort and *pagodas*.

At eleven o'clock the *Rajah* came to make me a visit, in great state with all his troops, elephants, camels, men in armour and colours. He rode a horse covered with cows' tails on each side. I think there were four or five. His bridle had an ornament of diamonds and emeralds. He had a broad band of vellum stones set loose across his head. The *Rajah* is large but a very fine looking person and really handsome. He was magnificently dressed in a full petticoat, with a sort of jacket of *kincob* and a large red turban covered with pearls and had a prodigious fine emerald hung from his neck. He had scores of pearls, some very fine and of a good colour and one emerald ring that seemed to be very perfect. He speaks English tolerably well. He learnt it from the Danish missionary, Mr Schwartz* for whose memory he has the greatest respect and regard.

I delivered a message from Lord Clive, which I believe was particularly agreeable to him as he had some fears he was under the displeasure of the Government. His countenance brightened directly, as well as his Minister, who has served him faithfully . . . He attended him everywhere and was of course with him at Madras and slept at his door as his servant. After he had been half an hour and had asked many questions concerning the girls, he asked if he might see Major Hill's boys do their exercise. As I had before mentioned it, all was ready, as well as the bodyguard. He seemed much pleased when we came into the

* C. F. Schwartz, who founded a mission in Tanjore, educated *Rajah* Sarboji and helped him regain his throne.

veranda and saw them drawn up. They did this exercise on foot in great perfection but the space was too small for the horses to be managed or performed with much sweep. Afterwards the boys performed more manoeuvres and he was most continually pleased and seemed to understand the sword though it was so much more rapidly executed than two of his own people whom he ordered to come out and perform. His horses were all brought before me very magnificently dressed. After the usual presents of shawls to him and his Minister, he went away. The visit lasted nearly two hours and his suite was very entertaining. The figures were unlike any I had seen.

In the evening I drove out to the fort and saw the *pagoda* of the famous bull. It is thirteen feet high and carved in granite. We were not permitted to go into the court. There is a fine tank in which there are seven wells that supply it with water by a miracle as the *Brahmins* say. But Mr Torin discovered that the sources of their wells are from the river, which communicates with them and therefore fills the tank without any miracle though every person uses that water. There is also a chapel built by Mr Schwartz, and an inner fort where the *Rajah* lives. The streets are tolerably wide but dirty yet from the appearance of activity in the *Rajah* and his great desire for the good of his people I have no doubt he will soon improve it extremely.

September 22nd As I was to go this morning to return the *Rajah*'s visit I did not go out except to walk in the garden and see some new birds, the small ducks which are to be sent to me. At nine o'clock I set out in great form to the fort in my *palanquin*. The first of the palaces is of an immense size and there was a building begun by the late *Rajah* the model of which I have seen and it is much like the palace at Bangalore. There were many lackies under the arch of the gateways and some who were obliged to give an account of every person who goes in or comes out of the palace in the course of the day which is also done by peons at the gates of the fort.

After going through their courts I came to the *Durbar* which is under pillars and is long and narrow where the *Rajah* was sitting not so magnificently dressed as the day before on a throne of a large cushion placed in a chair without much support behind. He came to meet me . . .

After sometime he asked if I would go to his ladies which I accepted with great pleasure and he conducted me through a large verandah upstairs into a large room where his two young wives were . . . His adopted Father's [Swartz] widow was on the floor with another old woman who takes care of his child and his sister, who was as beautiful as any fairy-tale princess, were all near a bed at one part of the room. The ladies did not *salaam* but got up and seemed much distressed at the sight of strangers. When he had anything to say a little boy was called who conveyed the message to the eldest wife. He sent for his little girl of whom he seems extremely fond. At first when she came near me she screamed and seemed much afraid but in a short time she sat quietly on my knee. It was really pleasant to hear him talk about this little thing, saying how she played and seeming quite happy when she was lively.

He sent, too, for patterns of the different manufactories [silk] which he showed me. Some of them were very pretty. He is anxious to employ his people and to get every sort of pattern of European or other things to occupy them and is persuaded they can make anything that is shown to them. The ladies gave me and Harriet each a dress and put some flowers over our heads which gave me an opportunity to see their faces under the gold trimmed red veils that covered them. The eldest is I think the least handsome and seems deformed. The second was a very pretty girl . . . I did not hear them say a word and after these ceremonies I went away. They had a great many ornaments, particularly a large one that covered the back part of their hands and many rings amongst them: one of a small looking glass set in gold. They had bracelets and anklets with so many ornaments on their toes that they moved with difficulty. Their complexion was very light. After I came down stairs again I received shawls etc. from the *Rajah*, the same as I had given the day before . . .

In one of the courts there was a large royal tyger and a hunting *chita* in the first court. I returned home in the *Rajah*'s chaise. It had been sent from England some years ago. He now never uses it since he came to the throne.

After my return home, the cattle of the *Rajah* came to be seen. He desired Mr Torin to say that if I wished to have any they were much at my service and desired to give some of the small ones to my girls. Mr Torin chose some that were very large and beautiful and these for the girls were equally handsome and under three feet high. In the evening I went round where there were many rivers. The same I had crossed in going to Tanjore, which occasioned some delay. It was quite dark when we approached the landing place. Upon their calling for light, a blue light was brought by a *Brahmin* that illuminated the whole river and *choultry* completely. It was the same sort as those used to discover the enemy at a siege. There was a very good parade ready for me and as we were encamped on the side of the Cauvery, it was very cool and pleasant.

September 22nd, Tanjore, Henrietta to Lord Clive

Though I have one eye a little sick I must write and tell you all that has passed these two days. Yesterday morning the *Rajah* came here. He had asked Mr Torin if he should come in his country manner with attendants in the Mahrattan* dress, which he told the *Rajah* he was sure, would be extremely agreeable. Therefore he was with all his troops, horse and foot, with some in ancient armour and in short with more appearance of Eastern magnificence than anything I have seen. He rode a prancing horse dressed up very much. He speaks a good deal of English and we are all charmed with his countenance and his manners . . .

I copied your message which Captain McAllum the Mahratta interpreter told him. His countenance brightened extremely and I find from Mr Torin that he has been in some anxiety about you and that this message made him quite happy. He has a very fine sensible countenance with much animation and good manners.

Signora Anna was to draw him during this visit which lasted altogether near two hours, but she tried and said she could not succeed.† Today I have been to return his visit and to his ladies. He was not so fine as yesterday in jewels: some of which were magnificent, the emeralds and some pearls. After sometime I went with all my belongings to the

* Great warrior

† Anna Tonelli later completed her portrait of the *Rajah* of Tanjore, *Rajah* Sarbhoji, and after her return to England in 1801, sent it to Lord Clive at Madras.

ladies. They are very young and handsome as far as we saw but they were wrapt up very much and did not speak. When he wanted to say anything it was as a third person to them. He has a nice little girl, of whom he seems very fond. She screamed terribly at me at first but afterwards sat upon my knee. He showed me the great Durbar . . . a magnificent old place. After walking about it he left us . . .

It was not very hot and we are all much pleased with all we have seen here. All his cattle are this moment come to visit me and I must end my letter. This evening we go to Inirare and as there is no *tappal* on that road perhaps I may not be able to write for a few days. Mr Harris was here yesterday. He is a quiet sensible looking man in great grief for the loss of his wife – *Adieu*. We are all well. Charlotte is quite alive again.

Ever, my dear Lord,
yours very affectionately
H. A. C.

September 23rd, Combaconum, Henrietta to Lord Clive

Here we arrived this morning through the most glorious country I ever saw. We left Tanjore in the evening and found *pandals* erected by Mr Harris ready for us. Yesterday we had one that was beautiful and today I am writing in a house of cocoanut leaves where there is a gallery, which beats the great room at the Garden House. All is Colonel Gent's ingenuity. It is impossible to describe the luxuriance of the trees and the cultivation. It is really beyond everything I recollect in England. We are still by the riverside, which supplies all this immense vegetation without any tanks except for the *pagodas.* In short it is perfection. Mr Harris received us here. We halt tomorrow and are to see the village, which is the largest in the country. The girls are well and in good spirits. Charlotte is herself again. I shall be anxious for her about the time we are at Pondicherry. Whenever it *is necessary* we must remain quiet. She is the only person that is likely to retard our journey, but it is unavoidable.

We shall be at Tranquebar the 29th September. Dr John was at Tanjore. I made acquaintance with him. I am afraid things are decaying there. A good deal I have promised you. Send him some seeds of the cinnamon or a cutting or two. He has left all his treasures for me to see but was ill the last day. Therefore I could not see him before I set out. He is gone to Trichinopoly. *Adieu.* Many loves to you I wish I could bring the Florentine [Charly] as well as she is now –

Ever, my dear Lord, yours very affectionately
H. A. C.

September 23rd, Henrietta's journal

We came through a delightful country today to Combaconum where there was a magnificent *pandal* and a room built for me hung with a variety of garlands and ornaments. After breakfast the head of the country, formerly a very troublesome man,* came to make his *salaam.* I never saw a more horrible countenance or expression than in this man's face. A person came with a very pretty little fountain, which he wished to give me but I declined having it. It was a large copper *chatty* from which a fountain rose through a small tube to a considerable height and supported what appeared to be a guava in the air for some time. Afterwards it was explained that the fruit was only a piece of wood in that shape. In the evening I walked to a *choultry* raised upon the bank of the river and just built and afterwards, a mile from the town. The thermometer was at 87 at the highest.

The night was moonlit and they returned by boat to the pandal which had been illuminated for them.

September 24th Came through the most beautiful and rich country I ever saw by the side of the Cauvery . . . The multitude of villages and inhabitants was quite extraordinary being nearly lined with people. We scarcely lost sight of one set when another appeared. In short, it is impossible to inquire the population. The country is covered with rice and even the banks of the fields are sown with dry grain in certain distances are double sluices from the Cauvery to distribute the water and everything has such an appearance of being fertile that it is impossible to express the pleasure it gave me. The

* Tondiman, the head of the *polygar* chiefs, wished to give a present of jewels to Henrietta, but she had him informed that neither members of the Government, nor their families, could accept such offerings.

cocoanut topes with banyan and other trees are dispersed about and the whole has the appearance of a garden.

At this place Mr Harris the Collector met me. He had prepared a real house for me consisting of a fine gallery and two good bedchambers and, of course, nut leaves and thatched. The inside was ornamented with cloth of different colours beautifully arranged by a black man. Ten days before it was an uncultivated jungle. It was on the bank of the river and was really delightful. In the evening I went across to see the village. It is the largest in the Tanjore country and was once the residence of the *Rajahs*. There are some fine *pagodas*, one lately repaired and painted with a variety of colours, but the sculpture was such that I was told it would not do to be seen. I went to a large tank round which there are many small *choultries* illuminated at night which mixed with the cocoanut trees etc. had a very pretty effect. One curiosity I met with there, a cocoanut tree with two heads which is very uncommon. After passing through the town I went down the river about a mile in a boat to Mr Harris's house. The night was moonlit and we returned by boat to our *pandal*. This place once was extremely rich till it was plundered by Haidar. He committed many depredations upon the *Brahmin*'s to force them to give up their treasure. He even killed some of their holy cows and placed them under their bleeding bodies that the blood might drop into the eyes and mouths of the *Brahmins* till they discovered all their treasure. It is now recovering fast and will soon recover its former splendour.

At the end of the evening under a full moon the travellers glided down the river looking at an illuminated riverbank where, according to Charly, there were six pagodas whose lights 'floating at their base had a brilliant effect'. Their *pandal* had been illuminated as well.

September 24th, Henrietta's journal
The news of Dhoondiah's death and Colonel Wellesley's victory came to us.
September 25th This morning I went to the different silk weavers and saw some very pretty silk cloths, some of which I intend to have made for

myself. There are several very different from what I had seen at Bangalore. One particular of brown muslin with a very handsome gold border which is the same as the *Rajah*'s wives wore. The houses are larger and much cleaner. It was hot early, more so than yesterday. The therm was at 86.

In the evening I drove off for an hour and returned to see some very beautiful fireworks. The country is everywhere delightful. This day before dinner the chief attendant on the deposed *Rajah*, whose name is Ameer Sing, came with fruit and flowers and a very civil message. I never saw fireworks better accented or better dancing girls. They were magnificently dressed and the four first performers from Tanjore were really very graceful in their manner not withstanding their strange dances. Mr Harris has prevailed on them to leave off their tomtoms and to dance to a country pipe which with a jew's harp and a guitar composed the band. The second set of dancers were more violent, particularly one who appeared as if she could have knocked down the whole company.

September 26th, Combaconum, Henrietta to Lord Clive

I quite forgot to tell you that when the *Rajah* sent his cattle to visit me Mr Torin told that if you wished to have any of them the *Rajah* desires I would take as many as I pleased as he had many of them. They are so beautiful that I answered for you that you would be much pleased with them and Mr Torin chose a large gentleman and two ladies of the first size and age and a second set of ladies about half grown. Besides those, the Rajah desired to send some of the small ones to the girls in his own name. They are little beauties and have just passed by on their road to Madras . . . The *Rajah*'s answer to Mr Blackburn's message from you I have got but by a mistake they have carried away my writing box. I thought it as well Mr Blackburn should write down what he said as I might make some jumble.

Mr Harris has taken great pains to make us comfortable and to answer us. We had last night the best fireworks and dancing girls I have ever seen. The night before we floated down the Cauvery from the town by moonlight and tonight we go the whole stage instead of having done it in the morning in a boat with an awning and though it is sure the water is nothing: up to a man's chin in the deepest place or you may suppose I should not have hazarded by boats upon the water. Charlotte is perfectly well and in excellent spirits. I wish I could keep her just so till you see her. Harriet is in perfect health. I have a little fear of Charlotte about the 7th of next month. We shall then be at Cuddalore as it is our halting day there. We hear flying reports that you are coming but I do not hear it yet from you. I should like much to see you again I assure you.

The day before yesterday we had the account of Colonel Wellesley's victory over Dhoondiah from Trichinopoly. The particulars are not yet arrived.

Adieu. This is a charming place.
Ever, my dear Lord,
yours very affectionately
H. A. C.

On September 26th the entertainment continued; the hosts carefully adhered to that which they deemed to be appropriate for British females. After an early dinner, the travellers went down the Cauvery in a boat, covered with a pretty *pandal.* It was pleasant and cool. When they passed by the village, the water was so shallow, that the villagers brought them fruit and flowers as they drifted along. Afterwards they got into their *palanquins,* and went on to Cadra Munglum, where they found their tents pitched, and a very nice *choultry.* It rained hard during the night.

September 26th, Henrietta's journal

As this was our idle morning I did not go out till just before breakfast when some very good tumblers, belonging to the *Rajah,* made their appearance. They did several very extraordinary things, which appeared almost incredible. One set raised a pillar like the mast of a ship and after many turnings and strange postures threw himself from the top of this mast (forty-two and one half feet high) to the ground which was made soft by being dried up a good deal. Another fastened himself upon his stomach to the top of a pole almost as high as the other and turned round with the greatest velocity, contracting his legs and arms for a long time. A woman did the same to my great astonishment.

This evening I quitted Combaconum and intended going by water all the way to Cadra Munglum. A small squall came on soon after we set out which deranged us a good deal and made us wet. The awning was obliged to be taken down. The boat was large and with a deck on which we sat in great comfort from a little after four till past seven when the shoals of sand increased a good deal and the length of the voyage being too much I left the boat and proceeded in my *palanquin*. As the road by land, so was that by water. Dined with people who brought fruit and flowers. Amongst the rest, the chief man from Ameer Sing, with a variety of both. Another excellent *pandal* was ready here where I slept, but unfortunately a violent storm of rain came on and a good deal of it came through the walls into my room.

September 27th The road was very indifferent at first owing to its being new and the storm has made it very wet and deep. I was obliged to leave the *bandy* and go in the *palanquin* to Col Dyrie's encampment where I breakfasted. The line was drawn all when I passed consisting of some detachments of *sepoys* and 2 companies of the 19th Foot. Came to Mayaveram. The Cauvery runs through the town, and it is fordable everywhere. The tope was so close that we quitted it and went into a large *choultry* once the palace of the *Rajahs.*

It was very hot and a violent storm of rain did not cool it much but laid the dust in the evening. I went to see the town and, as it was the great *dussera* feast, there was a *palanquin* as the god goes a hunting. He came opposite to the *choultry* with a great many lights, dancing girls etc and stopped there for some time for us to see him. We saw them taking three gods out on horseback. The crowd and the reflection of the lights in the river were very pretty.

September 28th Came through a more wild road and country but still very pretty. The trees scattered at times like a park. Came to Annacampettah where there was a good veranda much before the *choultry.* It was very hot in the tents and the thermometer was at 91 in them and at 87 under the *pandal.* After dinner I went to see a cart that had been purposely put in the mud that the elephants might pull them out with their trunks. They followed the cart and at first pulled it, but on being spoken to by the drivers they pushed the wheel with their trunks and lifted the cart entirely out of the mud. Afterwards I went to one of the largest spreading banyan trees I have ever seen. The diameter was forty paces. At night there was an immense scorpion found near the veranda.

September 28th, near Tranquebar, Henrietta to Lord Clive

We are within five miles of Tranquebar and shall go there tomorrow. Charlotte is not quite so well as for several days past. It seems like a little bile which Hausman thinks a little rhubarb will remove and which she will take presently. It is hot but we have a sea breeze and it is very comfortable. Yesterday we were at Myaveram in a large *choultry* and tolerably cool there. I have great hopes the sea will do us all good, particularly Charlotte. It is a most charming country. We breakfasted yesterday with Col Dyrie at his camp on our road to Myaveram.

Have you received any lemons from Mr Hurdis, which he sent about the 12th to you? Do you like the trees he sent? I have just heard that he has sent some more down of which he has sent me the list. He believes them to be of good sorts and wishes them to be tried. Pray let great care be taken of the Malabar names (*tied to them*) when they are planted. I have specimens of some of them, which I shall show to Dr Rotthem. Captain Brown is just gone to Tranquebar and returns tonight to settle all about us as there is a dislike we hear to any troops going into the fort in which case if he offers his house Brown thinks we had better remain in our tents as we do not choose to be without my friends the bodyguard.

I shall write to you from Tranquebar. I enclose you what the *Rajah* said which I desired Mr Blackburn to write down as he gave it in Mahratra to your message, which I had sent on with the baggage by mistake.

Adieu. Charlotte desires her love to you and says she shall write soon to you which I think if it is not very soon will not be in time at least I hope so –

Adieu,
my dear Lord.
Ever your very affectionate
H. A. C.

Tranquebar: September 29th to October 1st

'In the evening I went round the ramparts. They are very near the sea, which gains every year ground from the town.'

On September 29th General Anker's two aides-de-camp came to meet the travellers. Together they crossed the river, and went to Tranquebar, the Danish settlement, and breakfasted with General Anker, a most gentleman-like and pleasing person who received them most kindly at his country house. They went into the town afterwards and were received with great form, a salute being fired from the batteries. After dinner they went round the fort and the town's handsome principal street. September 30th: In the evening they went to a ball given by Colonel Meldorf and found him, according to Charly, 'a perfect specimen of old fashioned civility'. Being Commander of the Fort, his dress was military, and Charly delighted in the fact that he had 'immense red rosettes upon his shoes'. Some of the Danish missionaries came to see them whom Charly described as 'excellent people, but do little in the way of conversation, though their piety, humility, and charity, make them universally respected'.

September 29th, Henrietta's journal

Came to General Anker's Garden House, then from the fort he came to meet me at the ford and carried us in his boat to his garden. It is a very pretty place on the bank of the river with walls and a great many of the large lilies growing high upon their stems. After breakfast I went to the fort passing by a good many well looking houses and almost through an avenue the whole way. I was received in great form with cannon which diverted me much. The general's house is very pleasant and he gave up the greatest part of it to me . . . and he has covered the sides and had an artificial portico of leaves which had a very pretty effect and took off the great glare of light. The house is painted green and is very comfortable. In my room where I sat, there is a picture of the late Queen of Denmark and her two children. She is very like the King. In the evening I went round the ramparts. They are very near the sea, which gains every year ground from the town. I went up to the top of the house where we sat in a pleasant evening air till driven down by a storm. The General gave me such an account of Norway that I almost long to go there.

September 30th, Tranquebar, Henrietta to Lord Clive

General Anker . . . is quite like an Englishman and very pleasant. The place is much diminished in its curiosities, however. I have passed three hours with Dr Rotthem seeing shrubs, fishes and dried plants all in great order. Tomorrow we see the birds, beetle and butterflies and set out in the evening again a little stage of eight miles.

Charlotte took physic today. The little dose the day before yesterday was not quite enough but it is difficult to persuade Dr Hausman how little she requires. Therefore she is rather tired with it today, but will, I have no doubt, brighten up after dinner. If she is not strong tomorrow we will stay another day. The house is very tolerably cool though we had no sea breeze yesterday and we have good rooms. The General is most extremely civil. He reviewed the bodyguard this morning, having never seen the sword exercises which indeed they did in great perfection.

I am anxious to keep Charlotte well and stout and to strengthen her before the next time but some medicine was really necessary. Her spirits were excellent before this little bilious attack and are tolerable now, though not at their highest pitch. I shall be very glad to get her to you again. I feel so much anxiety in the change of this little soul. We hear everywhere that you are coming to meet us. At Tanjore they said you were to come there. But I do not yet hear it from you. I have seen some plants of wood here from Sumatra, the most beautiful that can be found. I sent you a very amusing letter from Captain Malcolm, which is just arrived. Charly is sitting with me and desires her love to you. I have a bad cold.

Good morning to you, my dear Lord.
Ever your very affectionate
H. A. C.

September 30th, Henrietta's journal

General Anker having expressed a wish to see the Second at ten o'clock we went out to see the bodyguard perform it on foot and on horseback which they did with very great precision. After breakfast I saw an old French officer from Pondicherry and went to see Dr John's collection of shells, fishes and a very handsome Mackaw. He showed me several books of shells, fishes and animals, the titles of which he is to give me, and some of his drawings of new fishes. I have many more shells than he has and duplicates of his most valuable ones. Afterwards I went to Dr Rotthem to see his herbarium, which contains 4,000 specimens of plants. Tomorrow I am to see birds, butterflies at Dr John's and in the evening I went to Dr Rotthem's garden where there are many curious plants and trees, but they are dispersed under the cocoanut trees and it was so late that it was scarcely possible to see them.

Afterwards I went to a ball given by Colonel Fiel's officers where I saw all the principal ladies of the place. There were very few that were well looking. Those were French from Pondicherry and they were all very ill dressed. Harriet danced and was much pleased with it. Charlotte not having been well stayed a very short time. I stayed till eleven o'clock. The heat of the night and mosquitoes were intolerable.

October 1st I went to see Dr John's collection of butterflies, which are very beautiful. Some of them, which I had never seen, had wings of the brightest purple. His insects are also very good. Some from the Isle de France are very rare. Dr Klien's birds are not so curious as I expected nor dried in a most complete manner than those hastily done by Dr Hyzer and sent to Ryacottha, except one, a white and black with a long tail which I remember to have seen in Edward's book of birds. Dr Rotthem thinks the plants of cinnamon &c. that I brought from the Daraporam country will not be of any use either there or in the Carnatic. He disliked most of those I brought from the Annamallee Woods. I have desired him to get for me a collection of insects, butterflies and birds packed properly to be sent to England.

Coromandel Coast to Madras: October 2nd–14th

'In the river we passed there are many alligators that continually swallow or draw down small horses, bullocks and sometimes men in crossing it.'

October 2nd, Sheally, Henrietta to Lord Clive

The mosquitoes were so great the night before that we agreed the sooner we all left Tranquebar, the better. General Anker was most extremely civil and attentive. He came with us across the river where he received us and means to come here today and to dine here and has offered me a house at Porto Novo . . .

I saw Dr John's beetles and butterflies yesterday, Dr Rhine's birds and Dr Rotthem, who I like much. Dr John is very loud and worrying we all thought.

I am anxious to hear from you and if you are likely to come and meet us I shall be very happy to see you and Dr Thomas. Dr Hausman is perfectly attentive and certainly understands the climate extremely well, but I do not think he has been much used to females, at least not in the way of Thomas and I am particularly anxious about Charlotte if this time does or does not come on again, as it ought to do. I do not mean anything more than that. I should like to talk her over with Thomas if he should come with you or come before you though that may be difficult to do (as H: is rather a *touchy person*, though not so to me, and they did not like one another very much of the journey). Without offending Dr H: I tell you things as they come into my mind. Charlotte has not recovered her spirits since her physic and I am particularly anxious to strengthen her again and proposed halting here tomorrow, but as it is rather a damp place, Dr H advises going on to one more dry which will be either at Chillumbarum or Porto Novo. Harriet is perfectly well and in excellent spirits. I have a cold and entirely lost my voice yesterday. We are now within one hundred fifty miles of Madras and I trust you will send away the ships and meet us soon. I shall be too happy to see you once again.

Adieu, my dear Lord.
Ever yours very affectionately
H. A. C.

On October 2nd the travellers went through fine country to Shealty, once a very populous village, but no longer. They crossed five rivers: two in boats; the rest in *palanquins*. The *pandal* was at a distance from the tents, which at first was thought an inconvenience, but it did not prove so. In it they were much cooler. The thermometer was not above 83. General Anker and his staff came to dine and after walking round the village returned home.

October 3rd, Henrietta's journal

This morning Mr Torin, Lieutenant Hawkins and Hunter, who came with us from Trichinopoly, left us and returned to Tanjore. Part of the road this morning was bad though very pretty and there were many hillocks rather deep to pass before we came to the river, which we crossed in boats, not very pleasantly. The flat-bottomed boats of the country are much more pleasant. I could soon have been sick from the motion on crossing the second. I again entered the *Nawab*'s territories where his *havildar* and his troops met me with great civility. The roads were extremely well mended, particularly the banks of the river on each side which was raised to the height of the top of the boat and of course very easy for removing the *palanquins*. The *pandal* was placed in the front of a large *choultry* facing the river at Chillambrum and I found it very comfortable all day and remained in it in preference to the tents. About the middle of the day there was a storm, which cooled the air completely.

After dinner I went to see the famous *pagoda*, which is by far the most lavish and handsome of any I have seen. The *choultry* round it contains one thousand pillars of granite of one block and coarse sculptured. At the end of it there are some steps leading to the roof where I went to see the whole below. There are four *pagodas* within the walls: two large and two smaller . . . There is a very large and handsome tank with steps to the water and many small *choultries*. This is within the second wall. There are still two more, which we were not permitted to enter. In the *pagoda* at one side is a *fakeer*, who *they say* has lived there ten years without eating, drinking, sleeping or speaking. He is a sort of prophet and foretells everything that is to happen in the village. I could not go and see him as he is entirely without clothes, but I requested Captain Brown and Hansan to go which they did. I am not at all disposed to believe the story. He had the appearance of perfect health and strength and so far from being starved was fat. They conversed with him, but his answers were in acting. He threw a handful of sand upon the stones and wrote with great facility. I regretted I could not see him. This *pagoda* is . . . dedicated to a goddess who they say was in one of his transformations and came down to the spot where she is worshipped.

October 3rd, Chillumbarum, Henrietta to Lord Clive

I think you will be glad to have a few words to hear how we go on. Charlotte is better today and was in better spirits yesterday evening. This morning she complained of a little pain in her back, but it is gone again and a little in her head. Dr H: thinks there is more bile but I am rather afraid of much medicine just now. I have this minute had a letter from Dr Thomas by which I hope you will set out when the ships are gone on the 6th and 7th. We shall be at Cuddalore. We have several things to see there (and if Charlotte has any occasion for a farther halt it is the best place as Mr Rinehart's house is, they say, cool and pleasant) which brings us to Pondicherry. The 8th, 9th, 10th I do not know the name of the stages. 11th at Madras.

The *Nawab*'s people have made us an excellent road. We crossed the Coleroon in an awkward boat this morning and are in a very good *choultry* and *pandal* near the tents. I have one of my vile coughs. All the rest well. I think when I see you again it will be one of my most happy days. Charlotte is much pleased that you are making a place for her antelope. She has a great favourite here, besides. And I have some beautiful doves for which I beg you will prepare a habitation. C will write to you today.

I believe ever, my dear Lord,
yours very affectionately,
H. A. C.

October 4th. Porto Novo was formerly a Portuguese settlement and many of the houses had a European appearance. The travellers preferred their tents. As a great compliment the inhabitants spread yards of cloth for some distance. Unfortunately for Charly, one of her *palanquin* boys slipped and fell down; no one was hurt. An odd circumstance happened while they were walking out in the evening. They observed a vessel coasting along the shore that afterwards lay to. Captain Brown thought it prudent to take some precaution, so ordered the bodyguard to sleep on their arms, as well as the *sepoys*. The vessel disappeared before morning. Afterwards they heard that a privateer had been seen on the coast, and was believed to be a Frenchman. Much later on when Captain Brown was returning from India, he was taken prisoner into Mauritius, and there heard that a privateer (at the time of their being at Porto Novo) had been almost tempted to make a descent for plunder, but was induced to give up the plan on seeing an encampment in the neighbourhood.

October 4th, Henrietta's journal

Left Chillumbarum came to Porto Novo. The road was extremely beautiful and much better than yesterday. We came to a very small point of the company's country and again to the *Nawab*'s. General Anker had offered me a house belonging to the Danish factory, which was prepared, but the tents being pitched near the sea in an open green spot I preferred them to the town. It is very pleasant. I hear the waves with pleasure and there is a freshness in the air which I have not felt for sometime in the evening. I went to the seaside and sat there till a storm came on. It was remarkably pleasant.

October 5th Left the encampment very early and came by the sands to Mr Rinehart's houses at Cuddalore. The morning was delightful. Though we set out very early, the drive made ample amends for being disturbed. The sea was particularly calm and agreeable. We crossed two rivers. At the bank of the last was a large boat ready to receive me and with Colonel Dupard, the Commanding Officer. We passed the old town and fort, the house being in the new town . . . In the river we passed there are many alligators that continually swallow or draw down small horses, bullocks and sometimes men in crossing it. We crossed another in the *palanquins* between the fort and the new town. Mr H's house is very pleasantly situated and was built ninety years ago by Governor Pitt and was lived in by the late Lord Clive. There is a large garden and a broad gravel walk round a lawn shaded completely by trees. We had no sea breeze today. In the evening I went towards the river for a little walk.

Cuddalore formerly had been a large town, but the sea had swept entirely over it, reconfiguring it so that only when the tide was low could the brass tops of the *pagodas* be distinguished. The travellers visited one pagoda which had escaped destruction, but was unused and in a ruinous condition. They could gain no information as to the history of this submerged town that had vanished beneath the water.

October 5th, Cuddalore, Henrietta to Lord Clive

We came here this morning from Porto Novo and had a very pleasant journey by the sea side though we set out terribly early. We were rewarded by air and freshness of the beach. Charly is much better today, in good spirits though looking a little delicate. Dr H still thinks she has some bile but is afraid of medicine. The air last night was so good and it is so here that I have great hopes of its doing great good . . .

As I find the post is to go early tomorrow I must write though I am very sleepy. I intend to bring you a muster of table linen and any other thing I can meet with.

I hear of alligators of a great size in the river. Luckily all our horses have escaped them. I have seen little of this place, but it seems very pleasant and Mr R says it is never hot as at Madras. He thinks there is some timber to be had for you here. I shall know tomorrow. *Adieu*. The girls are asleep or they would send their loves to you.

Ever, my dear Lord,
yours very affectionately
H. A. C.

October 7th, Henrietta's journal

I went this morning to see the ruins of Fort St David. It is in complete desolation. The fort is small but of the immense heaps of masonry. It appears to have been very strong. We breakfasted in a very pleasant bungalow on one part of it looking over the river and the sea. Mr R told me that after I was gone away he saw a very large alligator. I am sorry I'd not seen it. In the evening I went to Mrs Fraser's. The river which was not more than knee deep at one o'clock was become very high and the *palanquins* were obliged to be put on the shoulders of the bearers. The place is indeed very pretty and upon a little hill looking over paddy fields on one side and a fine lake on the other with a distant view of the sea. The centre of the house is a bomb proof where Lord Clive and the family used to go for a day or two from Fort St David's to give balls sometimes or for change of air. There is now a veranda built round it and some other additions by Mrs Fraser. It was a complete jungle when she first chose it or I believe it was her son that lived on it for her by taking up the trees. There is a pretty lawn with gravel walks down to the lake and in different directions, which with the cattle and sheep gave it the appearance of an English place. The river was still rising at our return and in the dark it was not very pleasant passing it. There was much rain in the night.

October, no date, first part 10 o'clock, Henrietta to Lord Clive

I was very sorry to find by a letter of Thomas's to Captain Brown that you have a boil. I hope it is not so troublesome but you will be able to meet us somewhere on the road yet. I am not quite sure if we go from hence tomorrow or not. There is not appearance of any reason in Charlotte except bile which Dr H is quite convinced she has still. She does not eat as she should and has a pain in her head and a little sickness after eating. He does not of course choose my medicine, yet wishes a very slight emetic. I am also afraid of it yet it seems less violent than medicine and she has appearance of bile on her tongue and a little yellowness in the eyes. We shall see this evening if it is to be taken. She cannot travel tomorrow morning and the road will not now admit of going in the evening, as there are four rivers and one bad road. Before I send this letter I shall know more. Her spirits are better but still she is not herself yet and has caught a little cold and cough, but it is now gone. I have it still.

This is a delightful place. We breakfasted this morning at Fort St David's which is a terrible heap of ruins. Everything is green and we have had a good deal of rain every night.

Half past 6 o'clock, Wednesday morning, Henrietta to Lord Clive, continued

Dr Hausman was so decided about the emetic that it has been given. She bore it very well and is now asleep. Her stomach had a great deal of phlegm. I trust she will not be relieved for a long time. If this letter does not go too early I will add a word in the morning. We shall not go tomorrow from hence.

Charlotte has slept well, has not headache and is as she says much better. Her cold is much the same. In short I am pleased with her appearance today.

Adieu. Many loves to you.
Ever, my dear Lord,
yours very affectionately
H. A. C.

On October 9th the travellers found Pondicherry, formerly the capital of the French possessions, to be a rather shabby but still a handsome-looking place. The fortifications had been destroyed; the inhabitants were mostly impoverished French. Some specimens of petrified tamarind trees in large heavy, hard pieces of a dark colour mixed with red were given to Henrietta; she was told only that in a large space near the town many such trees had been found.

October 9th, Henrietta's journal

I left Cuddalore and came to Pondicherry. I passed two rivers in boats. The second was with an awning and very pleasant and brought me to where Col Campbell met me. I was disappointed in the appearance of the place. There is not a vestige of the fort remaining. The street is hard and planted on each side with trees. Near the Governor's house are some large pillars of granite carved which were to have been sent as ballast in ships to build a *choultry* at Versailles and there are some new houses built. One in particular by a man upon speculation in case the French ever return. The government house is very handsome. Much more magnificent than any I have seen though it is not above half the size it was intended to have been. In the evening I went round the principal streets. They are handsome and contain many large houses all still. There is an appearance of desolation. It had rained much today and did so again in the evening.

October 9th, Pondicherry, Henrietta to Lord Clive

We came here this morning pretty well. Charlotte has a bad cold and cough but considering that is much better. Her emetic has certainly relieved her. The pain in her head is gone and her spirits are much better when her cough does not torment her. In short I am much satisfied with her today. This is an excellent house and Colonel Campbell has made it very comfortable to us. We go on tomorrow to a *choultry* but I do not know its name and on the 13th shall breakfast at Madras if nothing impedes us. We have nothing to see here. Mr Rinehart told me there was not any large timber at Cuddalore. Pray frank the enclosed letters to Mrs Rothman for us. Love to you from the girls.

Ever, my dear Lord,
yours very affectionately
H. A. C.

October 10th, Henrietta's journal

I left Pondicherry and came through a sandy and pleasant road to the encampment near the Conalty Choultry. I saw some pretty plants on the road, particularly the red seeded creeper. In the evening we picked up many pretty shells and sat till it was late near the seaside. We had occasional showers but it was not very hot.

October 10th, Henrietta to Lord Clive

We are now near to Conalty Choultry fifteen miles from Pondicherry. Charlotte has a bad cold but otherwise is well in spite of a cough and its being much in her head and eyes. The appearance of the weather is so much like an approaching monsoon that I shall be glad to get on as soon as I can. We had much rain in the middle of the day yesterday and a little this morning. The road is good though sandy and it is not very hot. The temperature at 83 degrees at 3 o'clock. I hear the ships are to sail today which I hope is true and that I shall now hear something from you. It is just a month since you wrote last. The girls desire their love to you. Harriet is quite well. *Adieu* my dear Lord. I trust I shall not have many more letters to write to you.

Ever your very affectionate
H. A. C.

October 11th, Henrietta's journal

Came partly by the road and partly by the beach to Allamparva. We passed a very fine lake which is in the shortest road but the inconvenience of travelling two miles in water in and out of the *palanquin* made me determine to go round a mile or two to avoid it. The old fort is a mile from the place where we are encamped across the river. It is of a singular appearance, all the bastions being pointed in the middle. [Here Henrietta's journal ends abruptly.]

Undated, no place indicated, Henrietta's last letter of the journey

My dear Lord Clive – You must not, my Dear Lord, be offended at my writing to you. I feel so much on the subject that it is too painful to me to begin in conversation though I am anxious to do so when you have read my letter. I am so seriously alarmed at the alteration in those dear girls that I think it a duty to you, to them and to myself to tell you what is my opinion, though I am afraid it has not always great weight in your mind. Dr Hausman's opinion was (as I told you) that if Charlotte remained six months longer in this country, she would be especially injured by it. When I talked them over at Sadap with Dr Thomas his opinion expressed the same apprehension and he told me several probable symptoms that with great concern I see gradually coming on more and more everyday. Her weakness at her menses is perfectly unlike girls at her age in England. From myself at the same age and from everybody I have seen and it has so apparently increased since we were at Trichinopoly that within these few days I am alarmed more than I can express and I entreat you if what I believe is the case that you have not perfect faith in Thomas's opinion which I have for the experience of their constitutions during these years and his competent knowledge of female constitution in general that to quiet my anxiety if it is unfounded and for my sake you will oblige me by consulting some medical person in whom you can trust and be guided by him.

Having come here by my own choice, how much I may dislike the country, I could remain here as I have done as patiently as I could the time you wish to remain and I must say what I have often expressed to my Brother, that you have in many ways made the place as comfortable as it could be, but it appears to me now that it would be at the real and serious risk of the health of both, if not the life of one, of the girls. The idea is so much on my mind that I can scarcely bear it. (Or did anything happen to that child equally dear to us both as we were happy or contented in our minds.) Though you have appeared so determined to stay a long time here, I hope you will not really do so and it is that which makes me feel it incumbent on myself to say so much to you. You have seen fatal instances, weak nerves and constitution in your own family. I am well aware of all the miseries and inconveniences of being absent from you and feel them most sensibly, yet under such circumstances it appears to me really indispensable that you may not imagine it is a wish for England added to the dislike of this country. I have not the least desire to be in London, but to remain at *Walcot* only . . . Let me entreat you to consider what I have said and not to be displeased with me. My mind is in a state of the greatest anxiety and I shall be glad to talk to you on the subject whenever you please.

Ever, my dear Lord,
your very affectionate
H. A. C.

Charly provided some information during the final days of the journey when the travellers continued on their way through a flat, low country with the sea on one side and, on the other side, scattered villages and temples.

October 14th, The Seven Pagodas, Charly's journal

The rocks had been carved with figures of all kinds; some of them were so much buried in sand that it was not possible to dig round them . . . A short distance away we found an elephant, partly buried, but wonderfully well carved so far as we could see; the work must have been laborious for the stone is so hard. The natives no longer had instruments for such an undertaking, nor could they give any history of their origin. They [the rock carvings] occupied a large space of ground . . . Papa, having met us before we came here, was so pleased with the carvings, he wished to purchase one, of two monkeys very well executed, but the natives would not part with them.

It rained very much during their journey to Covelong, and the travellers were glad to find themselves housed in an old ruined Roman Catholic church. They dined at one end of it, and had their beds put at the other. The evening was fair, and they took a walk by the seaside. Some dancing girls performed before them until they went to supper. On October 17th the party had a wet morning to go to Madras. They breakfasted at a pretty village, and then proceeded to the Garden House.

The entire distance that Henrietta, Harry, Charly and Anna had travelled in their journey was one thousand and fifty-three and a half miles.

Soon after their return to Madras, they moved to the Ameer Bagh while great improvements were made to the Garden House. There was no apartment for great receptions and they were obliged to go into the Government House in the fort when such things were to be given, or have a temporary erection in the garden. They remained at the Bagh until they left for England in March 1801, some five months later.

December 30th, Fort St George, Lord Clive to the Earl of Powis

The last letter received from your lordship is of the 9th May brought by . . . the *Rottingham*. Your account of the boys therein contained is most satisfactory. As this letter mentions not your own health we should have concluded it to have been according to our wishes had not one in June from Wm Strachey informed us of the serious indisposition you had been afflicted with. The same dispatch however brought the consolatory intelligence of you having quickly and lively recovered confirmed by a few lines of the 3rd July from Wilding at Brighton. You having been able to resume the exercises of driving and riding and return of your gaiety and spirits notwithstanding so favourable a result of an unpleasant attack, we looked with no common anxiety for the confirmed account of your health by the *Georgiana* or by land dispatch.

From the time of the reception of these accounts Lady Clive's thoughts have been anxiously turned toward England and other reasons have since contributed to induce me to give the fullest consideration to her opinion and wishes upon the important subject of her return to Europe. Notwithstanding what I must feel upon such an occasion and that I regard the separation from my family more particularly the female part of it as a real misfortune. The result has been the adoption of the measure for a conviction upon my mind of its wisdom and propriety. My daughters are now in great health and spirits and I think Lady C is well though she has fear about herself. The girls however arrived at a period of life when every attention should be directed to the confirming of . . . the constitution and there is no doubt that during last hot season and even since the commence of what we call the cool season they have at times manifested such a degree of languor and debility and such an incapacity to support fatigue as to excite serious alarm in Lady C and myself and to determine our opinion of the inexpedience of exposing their health to the effect of this climate during another year.

Upon the very day of the morning of which I had fully discussed this plan with Lady C, Harriet had an attack of a very unpleasant appearance, which though such a complaint is not peculiar to this climate would have determined my opinion of the propriety of the voyage to Europe had that not been before decided. She fell back during the time of dinner. Mr Thomas and I carried her in to an adjoining room. This attack had the appearance of being slightly epileptic though it had not the stronger character of that disorder which I have unfortunately known too much of not to have had my attention forcibly directed having circumstances that happened. There has not been any distress nor any symptoms indicative thereof. I hope what happened may be ascribed to temporary debility and not having a permanent course and have expectation of great advantage to the whole party from the voyage and sea air. Mr Thomas is to attend them. Excepting to your lordship I shall not mention this unpleasant occurrence to any not even my most intimate confidential friends in England. I have not as yet been able to engage a passage but have written to Bengal and am in constant expectation of ships from England.

My own health is good, better in my opinion than it would have been at home. Grievous as this separation will be, anxious as I am about my friend's health, I am still satisfied he will approve of my steadfast adherence to determined plans both on public and private grounds . . .

Our love to the boys. Your nieces look to share your protection with them. However amicable the boys, I venture to say the girls will not have less claim to your regards if Lady C: does not spoil them upon the passage.

Affectionately yours,
Clive

1801

Aboard the *Castle Eden*

'The mystery of love, hid behind the veil; search
For it amidst the intoxicated drinkers of Wine
For such things belong not to religious men of eminent degree.'

Hafiz, translated from Persian by Lady Henrietta Clive

On Saturday March 21st, Henrietta, Charly, Harry and Anna Tonelli boarded the *Castle Eden*, an Indiaman commanded by Captain Cummings. At 12 o'clock the ship weighed anchor and was out of sight of land within two or three hours. Along with two other ships, the *Sir Edward Hughes* (Captain Urmston, the Commodore, a naval officer, in this case a Captain holding the rank temporarily) and the *Prince William Henry* (Captain Basket), the *Castle Eden* proceeded to Vizagapatam to take in goods for trade with England. On March 23rd they arrived off Masulipattam and took in some of the ship's cargo. Charly found it 'amusing to see the English sailors on one side of the ship taking in the bales, and the *lascars* on the other, striving to see which could do most'.

Charly to Lord Clive

My dear Papa – I hope you did not feel the worse for crossing the surf at that time of day in which you left us. Mrs Baker told me she watched you safe on shore. I hope your leg is not the worse for your excursion. I thought it very much swelled when you were on board the *Castle Eden*. Captain Urmston spoke to us and asked after Mamma yesterday morning. The first day I did not feel at all well at times; I had such a bad headache that yesterday I took a little walk with Signora Anna on the deck which did us a great deal of good. Her fever still plagues her at night. We have none been really seasick except poor Mrs Hart who suffers a great deal. Mrs Baker is uncommonly well. Cockatoo and the rest of the beasts are very well, but the ship has the same effect on them as on Mamma for they sleep more than they are awake. I hope the cow, bull and my poor beasts are very well. Instead of feeding them in the morning and evening, I feed my birds which makes up a little, for I miss them very much.

Adieu, my dear Papa.
I am your dutiful and affectionate
Charlotte Florentia Clive

Pray excuse this writing for I can hardly see and the ship is very much on one side. Signora Anna begs I will present her kindest wishes to you and hopes you are quite well.

Monday morning, March 23rd, Henrietta to Lord Clive

I must write a few lines to you, my dear Lord, tho it is all I can do. Everybody is well, in general no sickness, except Harry once. She is now well and looks so, but cannot yet move much about. I have never left the couch nor have been able to sit up at all. Signora A is quite well except a little fever as she had at Madras. The weather has been very quiet and calm and we are near Masulipattam where we are to be in two hours. The Captain is extremely civil and sends newspapers without end and, indeed, we are as comfortable as we can be. Mrs Baker dined with us yesterday, sitting by my couch. Mrs Hart is the worst, not getting up from her cabin. Charlotte is quite well and feeding the birds finds complete occupation . . . The ship is very quiet and there the people disposed to be civil, in short, I believe all will do well but they are not in such complete order as might be. We lost sight of Madras about 3 o'clock on Saturday and Ennore about 5 and I only wish the time was come for your doing the same. I think of you very, very often.

God bless you, my dear Lord.
Ever your very affectionate
H. A. C.

We shall be glad of the telescope and Mr Cartwright says that you did not speak to him about the papers concerning Lt George Stuart. Therefore you will find them in the desk near your door of which Captain Wills has the key. Perhaps you will have time to send them by Mr Woodcock, who I understand is to follow in a packet to Vizagapatam, *Adieu.*

Monday morning 9 o'clock.

March 23rd, Henrietta to Lord Clive

We are all anxious to hear that your leg was not the worse for the ship. The girls both write to you which is a proof they are well . . .

at 10 minutes before 11

Since I wrote this morning we have heard from the *Sir Edward Hughes.* Mr Dick says we shall sail *tonight* and be at Narsapore *tomorrow* morning, if it is so we shall be many days sooner at Vizagapatam than was expected and we shall leave it on the 1st April which I thought was as well to tell you that your letters might be in time there. Pray remember to send those I copied to Probert and Hardman. We have more motion and less wind than yesterday as we are at anchor.

God bless you.
Ever your very affectionate
H. A. C.
1/2 past 1, Monday March 23

March 24th, Charly's journal

About the middle of the day we set sail from Masulipatam, and at five o'clock anchored off Narsapoor, five miles from the shore. March 25th The surf was so high, they were afraid of sending the bales of cloth, for fear they should be damaged.

March 25th, Henrietta to Lord Clive

We left Masulipatam yesterday at 11 o'clock and arrived here at five after a great deal of motion which has deranged us a little. The swell is still very troublesome but we are in hopes to get away today to Coringa where there is a better situation. The boats are sometimes apart right before they can pass the surf but there is a report that they are coming. I saw Captain Urmston yesterday. He does not think we shall clear the coast before the 4th or 5th. Mr Dick cannot make them do what is impossible. We are pretty well. I am always upon the couch except now while I write. Harry is uncomfortable sometimes. Charlotte eats a great deal and is in high spirits. Mrs Baker dines with us every day. Mrs Hart I have not yet seen. Everybody else visits her by the little staircase. General de Meuron is in high spirits. The only grievance I have heard was that the first day no chair could be found that would contain him. We are comfortable. I heard the calking is very bad, but likely to mend and want of management.

Everybody's love to you, God bless you.
I cannot write any more my head is so strange.
God bless you, my dear Lord.
Ever your very affectionate
H. A. C.

March 28th, off Coringa Bay, Henrietta to Lord Clive

We passed thru very uncomfortable days and nights off Narsapoor with a great deal of swells some wind at anchor. I did not leave my bed for two days. Harriet was sick yesterday. In the middle of the day we sailed and all revived directly. I have been once on deck last night for half an hour, but was weak and poor Charlotte is not quite well today but for that there is *another* cause besides a little sickness.

This morning we are now near Coringa and the boats are coming with the bales. It is a vile beginning perpetually. Anchors and sallies make us very uncomfortable.

Yesterday there was a signal for a passenger dead on board the *Sir Edward Hughes*, but we do not know yet who it is. In general we are pretty well arranged. The Captain very civil, but his servants without method and not good; however, it is all mending.

Mrs Baker is very well. We open our doors all day and air all together with her. Mrs Hart I have not yet met but I believe she will come up today. General de Meuron has great spirits. Tho we have been so near shore all Thursday we have not profited not having had anything from Narasapoor. There are very pretty fields in sight from Coringa. We expect to remain here today and tomorrow till evening and perhaps get to Vizgapatam on Monday morning. We are all in great joy at the thoughts of dry land.

Already I have a hope to meet with a letter from you. I am anxious to hear of your leg.

I have been obliged to bring Sally to sleep in the stern gallery. Her cabin is very close with a heap of things of her companion who is not very amiable and the child very noisy. This is our coast history.

Charlotte has been till today in great spirits and very comfortable. Harry quiet and taking care of us. Signora A, still with a little fever. I will endeavour to tell you anything more than I can before these are sent away. The girls desire their loves to you. They are very glad to find that none of the feathered tribe are sick. Cockatoo bears his fate very well. The grey mare is in perfect health and the other mare never leaves her habitation. Mr Read sent me the handle of a country plough which was very lavish and as I was too rushed to unpack it I sent it to you. If it is worth it, send it at some time to me, but I had scruples about room. He likewise sent some very fine feathers and a beautiful stuffed bird.

God bless you, my dear Lord.
Ever your very affectionate
H. A. C.

Vizagapatam, India

'My elephant spread great horror in the fleet.'

March 30th, Charly's journal

At four in the morning we set sail from Coringa, and saw the land all the way to Vizagapatam, where we arrived at 9 o'clock. We also saw the Ouxa hills. Vizagapatam appeared very pretty by moonlight. We saw Captain Blackmore's house on the Dolphin's nose, a high rock overlooking the sea.

March 31st, Vizagapatam, Henrietta to Lord Clive

We anchored here last night at half past ten o'clock and are now at Mr Malcolm's. Very happy to be on shore and all well. It is a very excellent home and we are much at our ease. I write only a few words that you may have news we are so far safe. There is not a letter yet from you. I am very anxious to hear of you. We shall probably stay till Sunday at the latest. I have received a pair of Swiss horses from Captain Evans as a present to me. They are famous having been given by the Emperor of Delhi to Lord Cornwallis and as he could not receive them they are come to me. Mr Webbe's elephant is here I have now seen him. You see our animals do not diminish. The girls are well: Charlotte a little delicate and Harry quite well on land. I have my time to say God bless you as Mr Dick is going to take this with him to the Fort, which is 4 miles distance.

Ever, my dear Lord,
your very affectionate,
H. A. C.

April 1st, Vizagapatam, Henrietta to Lord Clive

Just after I had sent away my letter yesterday yours arrived to Mr Cartwright and another this morning. Tho' none is yet arrived to myself, I rejoice at your being well. There is a vessel in sight, which is supposed to be Mr Woodcock and the packet, and that he may bring more news. We are very comfortable again: and in a very airy house, which we have to ourselves. They say it is never warmer than at present, which is perfectly to be endured 83½ where I am writing. The girls are well. Signora A has her fever increased, I think, by Thomas giving her too small a quantity of bark to be of the least service to her and she alarmed about herself extremely. We are to remain here till Sunday or Monday. I hear that Captain Urmston has a mind to go into the Cape for which I am very sorry. It will prolong our voyage and send us into the worst weather. I am afraid it is for the abominable market. One of the Frenchmen, that Major Waring said he should have thought ought to be hanged, got away last night with the long boat undiscovered. I am glad of it: he had a vile countenance.

Mr Malcolm has prepared oranges, yams and tamarinds in profusion for us, which will be a great relief. He is extremely civil. Mr Webbe's elephant made us a visit today. I am afraid he cannot go with us as he drinks 14 gallons of water a day. I shall write again before we go tomorrow we are to go to the top of the Dolphin nose to breakfast at sunrise. There is not much to see as sights, but the country is a good deal like Simmons Bay and very pretty as new plants, shrubs or stones except some wild myrtle of which I shall desire you, my love, some seed. Did I tell you that Mr Corbet's Charly Bird is so coarse and ugly I will not attempt to smuggle it. I shall show it to Mr Dick for his opinion. *Adieu.* The girls are in good spirits. The Bay horse is better and the Sultana perfectly so. The former has got a cold. I shall send you my pure horses. I should like them above all things in England. I know you will be impertinent about their shape and my own. They are not thin and I am sure would be very strong and useful in our roads. I should like them much if there was the means of conveying them, which we have not. God bless you, my dear Lord. I rejoice to hear your leg is better I assure you if you find the home *quiet* without us we miss you as much. The more I think of all we are to do the more I wish you were with us.

Adieu.
Ever your very affectionate,
H. A. C.

April 2nd, Vizagapatam, Henrietta to Lord Clive

This morning as we came down from the Dolphin's nose, I had the great pleasure of receiving your letter. Tho we have a little rarity of scene to relieve us which you do not, yet we think and speak of you continually and of your being separated from us and those are not the most cheerful times of the day. I gave your love to the dear girls who received the message with great pleasure. They are well and charmed with this place, which we are to leave on Sunday. I am very happy to find your leg is so much better. I was not a little anxious about it and very glad Mr Webbe is to be with you.The more people you have with you the better and of course all affairs must go on with expedition and ease when they and you can meet . . . whenever you please in a moment. I have received this morning a very gracious letter from Lord Wellesley enclosing one for his spouse by express which shall acknowledge tomorrow which I suppose it is right to do. I am very glad that all is going on so well . . . I shall be always glad to hear a little what is going on in this country, which I can only do from you. The news is not likely to travel to me in England from anybody there.

We went this morning to Captain Blackmore's. He is a fine old man and says that he had very bad health till he lived upon the Dolphin's Nose and that here it is perfect. I am sure you would like it much. The view is not over a rich country but so pleasant that one forgets the want of trees. He has a good garden in that the soil has travelled up the hill, which was the most barren of places naturally and rather difficult of access. I really think it the most refreshing place I have seen next to Bangalore and we wished you to see it whenever you come to England. Mr Malcolm was much pleased by your response to him. He is very much like his Brother and very attentive to us.

The French man is taken, for which I am sorry. I am afraid he will be kept in irons and I dislike his countenance so much that I had much rather he had gone entirely away. I find that everybody thinks we shall go into the Cape. Captain Urmston is believed to intend it and to say that his numbers of passengers are so great, that he will be obliged to go there tho there are now 200 ships ready for anybody here besides all other things. Mr Dick will tell you what he will say to him on the subject. Mr

Woocock is not yet arrived. I removed the telescope and did not bring the drawings . . . because I thought they were to be copied for you first before they were to come to me . . .

Signora Anna is a great deal better from bark and port wine. I have not got your picture yet. Mrs Gordon's is to be done first. Mr Cartwright I do not think is much obliged to Strachey and you for sending him letters to copy that to Mr Scott he says he copied at Madras but is doing it again. You have not sent me the Duplicate to Mr Strachey and Rodson, which I copied. God bless you, my dear Lord. The girls send so many loves to you and everybody else requests many respects and compliments.

Adieu. Ever your very affectionate,
H. A. C.

April 3rd, Charly's journal

Went up to the Dolphin's nose, breakfasted with Captain Blackmore, and returned to Mr Malcolm's house. One of the principal natives in this district sent Mamma a beautiful little sucking elephant as a present. We longed to keep it, it was so young and small, and covered with a handsome cloth and long tassels, but it was thought it would require so much water to drink, it would not be right to take it.

April 3rd, Henrietta to Lord Clive

I shall just tell you that we are all well because we are so vain as to think that you will like to hear it and we three have agreed today that it is right for you to hear every day while we are here. There are letters begun to you, which I believe, are to go tomorrow. Signora A is much better. I begin to think I am as good a physician as Dr Thomas. I insisted upon bark and port and from that time she recovered fast and has had a very slight return of her fever. I have seen Capt Urmston today who protests that he has no intention of going into the Cape unless from any unavoidable necessity if the sailors should have the scurvy or the animals want water but that in any case he should not stay more than forty-eight hours and promises still that we shall be in England in the course of August . . . but I rather doubt.

My elephant spread great horror in the fleet. Everybody was afraid he was to be sent to their ship. I send you the letter about him and will you be so good as to say to Mr Alesana who has charge of him what is to be done with him.

The *Rajah* of Vizagapatam sent me all sorts of sweets with a message by Mr Webbe, the resident or collector, with an Essence bottle and *betel* box which I did not accept, except the eatables. I have given up all thoughts of Samachilum. The thermometer there is at 102 and the dear girls are so well that I wish to keep them so without running any risk. I believe we are to embark on Sunday morning. Col Torin is so ill that I believe he is to remain being worse since he went on board. Col Strange is going I hear but he has been invisible they say because he is not quite sober nor has not been so these two days. *Adieu.* God bless you my dear Lord. The girls send many loves to you.

Ever your very affectionate

H. A. C.

No news of Woodcock yet.

April 4th, Vizagapatam, Charly to Lord Clive

My dear Papa – I was very glad to hear through Mamma you were so much better and I hope by this time you are able to walk in the garden. I am afraid it is not so cool at Madras as it is here. The Thermometer is at 84 but the breeze is so strong we are as cool as possible. It seems as if every place almost is cooler than Madras, which is very unfortunate as the Government, and most of the inhabitants are there. I suppose you have not been to the Red Hills yet; as the weather is not growing much hotter I think you will find the Island the coolest place although there is no garden there. I daresay you will like it.

We landed here on the 31st of March at a little before 6 o'clock in the morning. There was no surf in the little river where we came on shore, which is a very pleasant thing, and I hope we shall have none going on board again. The *Castle Eden* is very far from the shore as Capt Cumming is the youngest Captain in the Fleet and is therefore obliged to keep on the Commodore's left hand and the *Prince William Henry* is on the right.

I began this letter yesterday and since that have received yours which I am very much obliged to you for it. It was a pleasure I did not expect . . .

Signora Anna was very ill with her ague two days after we arrived here but is now better but does not seem to have any wish to return to Madras. I am very glad to hear you are able to stir out again but should be still more so if I heard you were quite recovered. The Turcomans [horses, presumably from Turkmenistan] have indeed very short legs and I think they are the *largest little beasts.*

Fevorsan, Mamma's little elephant, is a very nice little beast but as they say he drinks 15 gallons of water a day he would not be a good person to have in a ship; he came the other day into the house to pay us a visit and seemed very tame.

We have not found any pebbles here and only some wild myrtle and carpet grasses on the rocks. I never saw any place so barren as this. The Cape was not very well cultivated but I think it more so than this. The appearance of the land from Coringa to this place is very like it. I am very happy to tell you the Sultana is in perfect health as well as the cows and bulls. The horse on board the *Sir Edward Hughes* has had a very bad cold but is now much better. Likewise the Tanjore people are very well and the Mango Tree. Captain Brown says the Pineapples are shooting out and he thinks they will produce fruit, which will be very pleasant. Pray give my compliments to Tipu. The Tipu that is on board the ship is in very good health and spirits.

Adieu, my dear Papa,
I am ever your dutiful and affectionate daughter
Charlotte Florentia Clive.

Signora Anna presents her best respects to you and says she thinks she will be prey for fish of the sea if her fever is so naughty again.

April 4th, Vizagapatam, Harry to Lord Clive

My dear Papa – I was glad to hear in your letter to Charlotte (which she received this morning) that your leg was very near well, and that you intended taking again your usual walk round the garden . . . as well as looking at the new building. I am afraid the heat is growing more oppressive everyday at Madras. It is tolerably cool here, but we found it very hot in the ship, particularly when we were at anchor. We went up the

Dolphin's nose to Captain Blackmore's House, the other day, and took a walk round the top of the hill, it is a very pretty place, I hope that when you come to England (which I sincerely hope you will soon do) you will come by this place, for I am sure you would like it very much. There is a little garden near it in which Captain Blackmore says everything thrives very much. All the soil is brought up from below. We did not see it. He caught seventeen cheetas in one year with traps. I do not think he has caught any lately. It is a very rocky hill and was at first covered with them and jungle. He told us he made a road three miles long but it was too expensive to continue it.

We have seen the people inlaying the ivory. It appears very simple. They draw the pattern they intend with a pencil and then cut it out slightly with a small piece of iron. They afterwards put hot lac upon it and when it is dry scrape it off and polish it. The lac remains in the marks made with the piece of iron.

We usually sit upon deck in the evening, as we used to do in the *Dover Castle*. When we first left Madras, we had fine moonlight nights but unfortunately they are now all past. We dine and breakfast in the stern gallery which is very pleasant but there is more motion there than in our cabins which makes it disagreeable in rolling weather. When we were at anchor off Narsapoor (where we had no great deal of motion) we could not sit there. Coringa was much more pleasant. There was scarcely any at all, as the ship was in a kind of bay, but it was very hot then.

We expect to sail from hence on Monday, but are not quite sure. Mr Dick says he does not think we shall be later. The *Prince William Henry* is not ready, she lost an anchor off Coringa, and Captain Basket says it may detain us a day longer. Cockatoo is in perfect health, I hear (we left him in the ship) and is grown much more reconciled to his cage, but he does not much approve of having a cloth pined round it to prevent the sea spray from touching him. All the birds and beasts are very well not excepting Dhoondi, who is very frisky and a little fatter than he was at Madras.

Believe me, ever, dear Papa,
your dutiful and affectionate daughter,
H. C.

April 4th, Henrietta to Lord Clive

As you have two letters today I shall keep mine till tomorrow. We were all much pleased with yours this morning. I long to take my Turcomans but Mr Dick looked *so wise* about hay and water that I did not dare. The governor may do as he pleases and I should like much if they were to follow me. They seem just the sort of things to bear a great deal of work and a road not quite so smooth as that to the Mount and Bandstand. They are very long lived. God bless you.

You must excuse mistakes. We do not make foul copies of letters now and it is done by themselves.

April 5th, Vizagapatam, Henrietta to Lord Clive

We are still here and likely to remain till Sunday. Captain Basket lost an anchor off Coringa and was obliged to change his latter and do a great deal which prevented him from taking in the everlasting bales. He has sent word that he cannot be ready till Tuesday. Mr Woodcock arrived at 4 o'clock yesterday after a bad passage. We are all very well. Signora A, a great deal better. It is impossible to look better than the girls do. We have a sort of land wind that is far from pleasant and I feel it a good deal. Col Torin was supposed to be almost dying but he is revived and may possibly go on to England. One of General de Meuron's boys has the liver complaint. They are very good-humoured souls and I am sorry they are ill. Captain Urmston promises that we are to cross the line in three weeks and be in England in August, but I do not quite believe him. I will take care of your letter to Mr Ashton and am much-obliged to you for those to Hadean and Mr Strachey.

I wish I could wake and find myself within sight of England. It is a horrible voyage and I cannot help thinking of the Cape and the Britannia which we saw coming in there . . . The Thermometer is at 85 and indeed our climate is not now better than yours.

We hear sad accounts from Ganjam.* All the villages burning and the people flying in every direction and the Bengal *sepoys* not yet arrived but I believe are within six days march.

* Once a chief port and town in the district

Mrs Baker is a very comfortable person to us . . . The girls send their best love to you. Charlotte is singing, not like a nightingale and old Harry taking a little care of herself just now but I have no fears for her from her healthy countenance. I am not at all sure if there had been new habitation upon the Dolphin's Nose if we might not have remained another year. The air seems really perfect.

Your letter delighted Charlotte very much. I hope the next will be to old Harry who looked a little disappointed I thought.

God bless you.
Ever, my dear Lord,
your very affectionate
H. A. C.

April 6th, Monday morning, Henrietta to Lord Clive

Mr Dick has hurried us on board and we are once more in the *Castle Eden*, tho the *Prince William Henry* will as everybody says not be ready to sail till tomorrow to which Mr Dick had agreed. I am on the couch and very uncomfortable. Since I began to write we have had a violent storm of rain, which has cooled us and done us good. I believe they are afraid of squalls from the Northwest.

All the animals are well but a few of the plants dead for which I am very sorry. Harry is extremely well and Charlotte in good spirits. I shall take all-possible care of them but I confess I am very anxious for the rest of my time. I feel how much I have to take care of continually and the more I think of it the more uncomfortable I am at our separation. We have been so much more comfortable for these last years than we have ever been that I cannot help having much anxiety for the future. The common habits of life are so different in the different countries and all is so changed that it is all uncomfortable. I shall endeavour to do as well as I can and as nearly as I think you would. I beg you will write a great deal by every opportunity and a word by the overland dispatches. It will be a great pleasure and relief to me and I will write to you, you may be afraid. If any letter comes, which of course there will by the ships, pray open those from our own family but return them to me as I like, even tho' I shall be at home to know who wrote and what they said. And all those from my own friends which can have nothing that can interest you, I hope to have unopened. I have desired Captain Brown to take care of any packets and to dispose of them. We have thunder and a great deal of swell and I wish we were off.

Everybody's love to you.
God bless you, my dear Lord,
and send you soon to us in England.
Ever your affectionate,
H. A. C.

Charly's journal of April 7th provided details about their fellow passengers and their living arrangements aboard ship. 'Our party consisted of twelve persons: Mamma, Signora Anna, my sister and myself, in the round-house; Mrs Baker, in a small cabin next to us; Mrs Hart, half the great saloon; General de Meuron, the commanding officer of the Swiss Regiment, in the Company's service, the other half, Mr Torin, Colonel Doveton, Mr Cartwright, and Mr Thomas, (surgeon) cabins on the gun-deck.'

On April 9th the *Castle Eden* set sail. Captain Brown returned to Madras.

April 9th, on board the Castle Eden, Henrietta to Lord Clive

There is a small vessel in sight, which we hope may be something going to Madras. Therefore I shall prepare letters with a chance of its arriving with you. We are all pretty well, Harry and Charlotte extremely so. Harry begins to look healthy, at least I think more so than she did. Charlotte in great spirits. I am unable to sit up yet. Tho' I am not sick, I am unable to move. Signora A is well again and everybody satisfied. We are all now in the Latitude of Madras. Godbless you. They will not let me write any more.

Ever your
very affectionate,
H. A. C.

Charly's journal provided a running account of their voyage: '*April 10th.* We spoke to a Company's ship going to Madras, and Mamma and Mrs Baker, sent letters by her.' '*April 12th.* Sufficiently calm, for Mr Thomas to read prayers on deck. The calm prevented our making progress till the 17th and then a little breeze sprang up, and we made a degree a day.' '*April 19th.* We had a hard gale, as Captain Cummings called it, and three of our sails were split, but though we had to alter our course, no other harm was done. The weather tolerably favourable til the 23rd when we crossed the line.' '*April 27th.* A violent squall. Mrs Baker much frightened. Signora Anna lost her pillow to our great diversion, and every article, not lashed, fell down to the ground. Our swinging table was most useful.' '*April 29th.* A hard squall in the night, and the ship pitched so, that I struck my head against the bed. The wind died away towards morning, and on May 1st we found ourselves six miles nearer Madras than the day before.' '*May 4th.* The sea like a looking glass. Captain Cummings and Mr Torin went on board the *Prince William Henry*. The ship's company had some grog, as it was the anniversary of the taking of Seringapatam.' '*May 5th.* A little breeze, and then we saw a very large shark, but could not catch it. We also saw three pilot fish.' '*May 6th.* We caught a very large shark.' '*May 9th.* Continued squalls. The ship laid over very much. Captain Cummings said he was sure we had got the East trade winds.' '*May 11th.* So hard a squall that the mainsail split. The *Prince William Henry* made a signal that they saw a large ship sailing to the northward. A signal was made to chase her, but as she appeared to get away fast from us, we resumed our course.' '*May 14th.* In the afternoon, the *Prince William Henry* made a signal to speak to us, and Captain Basket desired Mr Torin would come and see Col Torin as soon as the sea would permit, he being seriously ill.' '*May 15th.* Spotted the *Prince William Henry*; the sea so high no boat could go on board.' '*May 16th.* A signal to change our course, and steer South-west by west.' '*May 17th.* In consequence of a signal from the *Prince William Henry*, we lay to, for Mr Torin and Mr Thomas to go on board her, on account of the illness of Colonel Torin. Mr Thomas returned, leaving Mr Torin behind. We killed a bullock, and sent part of it to the Commodore.' '*May 20th.* The *Prince William Henry* signalled a death. It was Col Torin.

About 2 o'clock a poor man fell overboard. He was tying up the highest sail, when the rope under his feet slipped. He fell first on the anchor, and then into the sea, and must have been dead before he reached the water. A boat was lowered, but they did not find the body.' '*May 30th.* Toward evening Captain Urmston, Mr Grant and Mr Hardgrave came on board. The wind more favourable.' '*June 2nd.* A fairer wind in the morning and about the middle of the day the Commodore made a signal to steer west. In the evening, but little wind. Until June 14th no event, except slight changes of wind, but on that day, we had a shower of hail. Captain Cummings said some of the stones, were the size of a large nut. The wind foul, but suddenly changed and the sea came in so much through the stern windows, that all Mrs Hart's things were wetted. The deadlights were put in, but the motion of the ship was so great, that we could not dine in the cuddy.'

June 6th, Latitude 27°21′, Longitude 43°21′, Henrietta to Lord Clive

I am not sure, my dear Lord, if this letter will reach you but as there is a possibility of Captain Cummings going into the Cape, I shall tell you how we are. The voyage has hitherto been very favourable and good and we are all well. Scarcely any sickness and the girls improved already in looks, health, and spirits. Harriet has been well except once about ten days ago, I believe, owing to the cold and going out before breakfast. But I can scarcely call it an indisposition. She only complained of a pain in her head and as soon as she lay down and took some castor it was over. She is really stout and well. Charlotte is perfectly so and has been the same. I suffer as usual a great deal from the motion, but no sickness. Instead of that my stomach is much affected. Signora Anna quite well. The Captain perfectly attentive and our situation much better than in either of the other ships. We have every reason to be satisfied. Various are the suspicions going to the Cape since Captain Urmston spoke to the other Captains who refused to go there. Whenever the wind has been good he has constantly tacked or done something to obstruct our going on. We are now tossed a great deal in consequence of it. I am very anxious to get on and am afraid there is now no chance till the end of September.

I wrote to you on April 10 by a Mosslman's vessel. We have only seen one vessel besides supposed to be an Armenian, but it did not stay to speak to us. Col Torin died about a fortnight ago, which was expected when we left Vizagapatam. The old General is quite alive playing with Harry. In short we are as well off as we could be and much more so than our neighbours. I shall write from St Helena and send this to Captain Urmston's ship the first opportunity. The plants are well. The Sultana in great health and all the other horses and cows and birds likewise.

I wish you could feel the cold wind that is now blowing upon me. The Therm was this morning at 68. I shall keep this open till late as I can that you may have a little more. We think and talk of you very often and sincerely wish you were with us and that we were all at the end of our voyage. Mrs Baker has been unwell but is now revived and quite alive. She is a most pleasant person to us all. Mrs Hart often ill but much improved. *Adieu* for the present.

June 7th, Henrietta to Lord Clive, continued

We have a fine day and very fair wind and are therefore in good spirits as to the passage if it continues. I wish you could see the two dear faces I do at this minute. They desire a great many loves to you and would have written but I have not given them time and there was a great deal of motion yesterday. I have no doubt of being able to send you good accounts of them after we are once settled in England.

God bless you my dear Lord.
I hope you will write by every opportunity
to your very affectionate
H. A. C.

On June 15th Charly's journal spoke for the travellers: '*June 15th.* The same hard gale, the waves rose mountains high, and the ship rolled and pitched dreadfully, a wave taking us up, when we could see the other ships plainly, and then dashing us down again, so that we could not even see their masts.' '*June 16th.* The wind as foul as ever, and perfectly against us.' '*June 18th.* The wind not quite so high. Three strange sail in sight, supposed to be the Ceylon fleet. The Commodore (who is on the *Sir*

Edward Hughes) made a signal to bear down, but afterwards we resumed our course.' '*June 21st.* Fresh gales and, later in the day, cloudy.' '*June 24th.* More moderate.' '*June 27th, 28th, 29th, and 30th.* The weather still bad, but occasional moderate winds.' '*July 1st.* The Commodore fired 3 guns. We lost sight of the other ships, and put up blue lights. Captain Cummings thought there must have been some mistake in the signal. He tacked again and spoke to the Commodore. It blew rather hard, and contrary to our expectations the current had carried us 70 miles to the west. We were on the bank in the evening, and when they heaved the lead it was 12 fathoms. At 10 o'clock it was again heaved, and was 33 fathoms. We had been quite under the influence of a gale, such as the Cape of Good Hope generally produces, and this very severe one lasted the whole of the moon. All the portholes being closed made the cabins very dark.' '*July 3rd.* Early in the morning a fair wind sprung up, and at 12 o'clock two ships were in sight, supposed to be the Commodore, and the *Prince William Henry.* At the same time land was sighted, which was thought to be Cape L Agulhas and later in the day we saw it plainly from the quarter-deck. At 12 o'clock at night the wind changed, and in the morning, we were off the bank.' '*July 4th.* We saw an American ship, and had a shower of hail.' '*July 5th.* Still stormy. It was settled that we should go into the Cape. The ship rolled more than ever. We saw Cape L Agulhas.' '*July 6, 7, and 8th.* Hard winds.' '*July 11th.* Landed at Simon's Bay, Cape of Good Hope. Signora Tonelli painted a watercolour.'

Simon's Bay:
The Cape of Good Hope, South Africa

'The most melancholy news.'

July 11th, Simon's Bay, Henrietta to Lord Clive

We are now in the act of anchoring where you will be surprised to hear of us in Simon's Bay after a most tedious passage of fourteen weeks from Vizagapatam and the last four in almost a continual gale. We are all well now and rejoicing at the prospect of land tho' we have suffered a great deal and have not slept quietly or well above four nights for this last month by which as you may suppose we are much affected. I shall give you as the most interesting the history of our healths and then with our adventures. Harriet has had a complaint once in her bowels from the motion of the ship and some alarm at the weather and was much reduced and nervous but nothing alarming but is now reviving. You will receive the first part of our voyage in a separate letter which will bring you to June 6 as the ship by which it was sent is not yet come in here.

Charlotte has been well in great spirits except for what I am now going to tell you. Signora A has had her ague a little which it now appears was owing in great reason to her having starved herself ever since we came down the country for an eruption unknown to Dr Thomas and which has ended in a violent not *Scotch* but *Malabar Gaul** which Charlotte has

* The Malabar itch is a common and painful skin condition found in tropical countries. The eruptions can cover most of the body, but may commonly be seen between the fingers and on the front of the wrist. Usually it is accompanied by fever and alimentary complaints. It is said to be a form of ringworm and is extremely contagious through personal skin contact or through clothing and bedding. Lard and sulphur were used in treatment, as well as baths in diluted nitric acid.

caught and from which she is now recovering though her hands are not pretty. I have lived in some alarm of its spreading as there was difficulty in explaining the disorder. I have in general been much better than I expected but from the want of rest and much anxiety am as nervous as possible and weak. However, I trust a few days on land will revive us. Mrs Baker has been ill, not alarmingly so but suffering a great deal. She is now better and tho' this has been the case, Thomas says, and I am persuaded of it too, that her indisposition is likely to be the means of producing good health hereafter and of being essential to her. Mrs Hart suffers a great deal and has now been a month with the ports shut and dead lights with the water continually passing through the cabin in damp and darkness. So much for the females.

Our voyage was prosperous as far as the end of Masulipattam. And as it is the opinion of all in this ship and I believe all in the *Prince William* that Captain Urmston was determined to come in here and certainly as they declare shortened sail when he ought to have gone on and done several things that appear either to have been done from ignorance or design. The former is not likely. In short he is in great disfavour with everybody.

On the 14 June we had the most violent storm of lightning I ever saw. The whole night there was a complete illumination with terrible thunder and hailstones of an immense size from the time till today we have had continual gales, some tremendous. In one on 4 July, we were separated from the other ships owing to the mistake we suppose of a signal at 12 at night and we are now anchored and find them now coming into the Bay. Everybody is tired to death of it and upon our being alone and with a fair wind for a few hours Captain Cummings determined to go on to St Helena, but in less than twenty-four hours a gale came on and after three or four days we were obliged to come in here. We have great reason to be satisfied with the Captain. Tho the table was very bad at first it became after Vizagapatam very tolerable and by far the best of the three. Captain Urmston's the worst and, by all we have heard, we were lucky in not coming in his ship. Captain Cummings is indefatigable in his attention to his ship and never quits the deck day or night if there is anything to be done. He is perfectly disposed to be obliging and that we should all have every thing that the ship can produce or that can be contrived for us.

July 13th, Henrietta to Lord Clive, continued

Mrs Cartwright came back with the sad account that there were neither lodgings, fruit, milk, butter or bread to be had. A most dismal prospect. We had Mr Goodwin, who you remember of the *Tremendous*, who came on board with news, which astonished us of the changes in the administration. All we could do yesterday morning was to go on shore [and find] all to be had, which by the greatest civility of the Admiral and the storekeeper I have got two excellent rooms sufficient for the necessary servants. Mrs Baker and Signora Anna are to establish themselves there today or tomorrow. This suits both of us. Mrs Baker is unable to bear much moving. Indeed has not left her great chair except to come to us. But perhaps it is as well not to say so to Mrs Baker. And Signora Anna's state requires a warm bath and various other things, which could not be so well done in the ship, and she was very anxious to be on shore and wished not to go to Cape Town.

I have had a great deal to do to arrange myself. Everybody is civil and attentive. General Dundas, *the Governor*, wrote to me directly to offer carriages for my removal, which I have accepted, and we go tomorrow to Chussenburgh, where the girls, myself, Sally, Mr Cartwright, and Dr Thomas will remain tomorrow night and perhaps the next day as we feel. (Dr Thomas going backwards and forwards to the sick) I am really so weak and shaken by the long voyage and bad weather that I can scarcely walk. At least I could not without great trembling and I feel it all over me. Harry, too, will not bear much therefore we shall go as quietly as we can.

I wrote to Lady Anne Barnard when I came and she has sent me an invitation to her house which I have accepted as it is both economical and convenient. As we are few in number cannot be a great inconvenience to her. Thomas Harris refused positively to go on shore without his wife. His first message to me was improper *at least*. The Lady said he should not go without her after all he spoke to me and as she is *in a way*, he says he is afraid of her killing herself if he left her. I will not be troubled with her as we are enough for one carriage and she must have another and her child. She does *nothing* for the girls, is very dirty and impertinent so I go with my two gentlemen and no servant. I believe she thought by keeping Thomas to force me to take her too. But my Welsh spirit would not do it. If I write a little irregularly you must excuse it and take things as they come into my head.

The night before last the other ships came in and were surprised to find us here. Captain Urmston having sent a note early to the Admiral to say that he had parted company with us and that we should probably be soon here when lo! We were here before him. I have seen him and Col Blaquiere. Your horse is well and the little cattle, the mango tree very sick, and I am sorry to say that tho the Sultana is in perfect health, she has not produced nor does not *intend* it, being pronounced not in a way. I am afraid we shall be much puzzled to get hay or oats for her. The account of the want of provisions . . . is terrible and Captain Urmston is abused most heartily by all his passengers and all agree that a considerable private investment for this place and while he was swearing to Mr Dick he had no thoughts of coming to the Cape he was buying cotton at Vizagapatam for this place. They have had no mutton or wine for six weeks only half a pint of water and had candles from this ship. We are to have the *Star* bring our old acquaintance to St Helena and England which gives great joy to the fleet as it will lead and end all our troubles sooner than they would otherwise be accomplished.

You will have a chart of our voyage if possible by this ship. Cockatoo has picked one to pieces that was to have been prepared for you. We must get one at the Cape. This letter will be given to the charge of Captain Richardson who married one of Mrs Harris's nieces at Madras. I saw last night a Dr Moffat who says he saw a Mr Clive in London. I was obliged to describe complexions to know which and found it to be your Uncle William in perfect health in February.

The token of Hapsburg* will, I am afraid, be a sad affair to us and our

* Treaty of Luneville, 1801, in which Austria was forced out of the French Revolutionary Wars

overland dispatches and make me fear that none of ours are safely arrived concerning my return.

Your plants in this ship are poorly from the bad weather, but I hope many will survive. I shall try to get some seeds and bulbs here. I hear Sir George Younger went away at twenty-four hours notice in some disgrace. I expect to hear a great deal from Lady Anne. I shall finish this letter when I leave the ship and go on writing and sending them till the *True Britain* sails which some say is to be in two days.

Our society is very pleasant. The General, I like extremely and pick up a great deal of information from him. Mr Sorin is a little pompous. Col Doveton talks about Persian to me and Mr Woodcock is the only person we all dislike. He is most terribly noisy and forward. Mr Cartwright does all he can but seems terribly puzzled about enjoying houses or carriages or any household affairs but always in good humour. Dr Thomas quite alive and well, giving one a little bark another a little camphor, another a little brimstone in short having a great many falls during the bad weather and a variety of little messes to mix which you know makes him quite happy. The 86th Regiment is here and very sickly. The Commanding Officer here is a Major Stuart, brother to one in Ceylon and tho' not of *the most favourable* appearance has been so civil to me and so ready to do anything to assist in procuring lodgings that if the Regiment goes to Madras which they expect, pray say something civil to him. General Dundas has sent an *aide de camp* to me. Captain Mores, a complete Scotchman in dialect. He is to go with us tomorrow and the General Camaige is to meet me at Kalk's Bay.

I shall continue to write as long as the ships remain and I hope with a little less confusion. For at present, I am really in a sort of fidget having so much to arrange that I am quite worried about it. Have met with some old newspapers but cannot see anything of the Shropshire or my brother which I was in hopes would have been the case. You would be glad to feel cold as we do now. We have suffered a great deal from it since the bad weather began. The therm has been at 54 and a half. I still defy flannel but condescend to wear a shawl sometimes. *Adieu* my dear Lord. We hear here that Ld Glenberrie and Glouster Douglas is coming here. I could not help thinking if these changes would affect you and send you to us once more.

Adieu.

I am very anxious to hear of you again.

Ever yours, very affectionately,

H. A. C.

The girls are to write to you from Cape Town and give you the particulars of the stones.

July 16th, Cape Town, Henrietta to Lord Clive

I am writing to you my dear Lord from the Cape Town where I am established with Lady Anne Barnard. Everybody is most extremely civil indeed . . . We went as usual on Tuesday Morning in Captain Holtam's boat to Kalk's Bay where as before we had a fine shower of rain. There the General's chariot and curricle [a two wheeled chaise drawn by two horses] met us and we went with great ease and comfort and without fatigue to a house at Wynberg which belonged to a person who General de Meuron knew where we stayed that night very comfortably tho' it was not an inn. After walking about in search of plants, Dr Thomas and Mr Cartwright were with us. Here we arrived yesterday and are as comfortable as possible.

Lady Anne is in great health and spirits and good humour. We are anxious to have a convoy from hence as we are certainly too late for that at St Helena and to have a *head*, which we may follow, as Urmston is in much disgrace with everybody and it will be safe, too. I understand that the disputes here between Sir G: G and Gov: S were very great. That when the order came for his being dethroned it was put in execution in *three hours* and he remained a month here before he could sail and went off quickly saying he was going to sea when the vessel would be ready to sail but that he never came on shore again. The complaints against him are giving an order that all business must come to him three times a week thru the hands of his private secretary Mr Blake who it is very strongly believed had something for his trouble in proportion to the affair and a great deal of money spent in sad ways. Ships pretending to have taken prizes and slaves and goods paid for by Government which had only been bought at Mozambique, a strong suspicion of some trading with the Spaniards, in short a variety of things not of a good sort.

I have not seen General Dundas or his spouse yet but expect them this morning. I have seen a son of Dr Roxburgh's who is to let me have a great many seeds and some bulbs. He is in hopes to go to Madras as he says. But you had not heard of him I believe when I had left you. He is a little dark and, not unlike some of my most bovine friends, a little of a quiz.

4 o'clock: When I wrote the above this morning I did not expect the most melancholy news that Lady Anne Barnard has since told me. I cannot express what I feel for the loss of that dear brother for which I was quite unprepared by the last accounts. However, I will do all I can to support myself at this time and take care of my dear children. We shall be now indeed forlorn and I feel what I hope you will that your return to your family is indispensable. Mr Cartwright has behaved with the greatest good sense and kindness to me and so has Lord A. My poor girls were writing letters of nonsense to you. This has overthrown us all and you must accept their excuse they are much affected tho they do not yet know the whole, which I was afraid, would be too much. Thomas has not left us today. We have every attention from all here but I feel I shall not have that meaning or pleasure I had expected to when I land in England. Thank God the boys were well in March. This letter must go the day after tomorrow. I will write again.

God bless and preserve you, my dear Lord,
and send you to your family.
Ever your very affectionate,
H. A. C.

July 16th, Mr Thomas to Lord Clive

My Lord – Your Lordship has been informed by Captain Brown of the journey which took place after our departure from Madras until we reached Vizagapatam and her Ladyship and the Young Ladies will give your Lordship a minute detail of what has befallen us from that time until our reaching this place, a period in which we suffered much bad weather and obliged us to come in here. Not withstanding all these trials of patience and courage, I am happy to inform your Lordship they are in good health and certainly improved much in their looks. Miss Clive seems to be regaining her health and strength daily and very few symptoms which could be supposed in any way similar to what was observed at Madras have occurred then very slight, and immediately went off... she is in every respect stronger and better, and will no doubt derive all the advantages which the passage to England was supposed likely to produce. Miss Charlotte is extremely well is grown very stout and her looks show that neither hard living nor hard gales can affect her. The improving health of the young ladies was certainly very satisfactory to her Ladyship which has enabled her to endure with the most exemplary fortitude this tedious and barbarous passage and as necessity has sent us to this place, much pleasure was hoped from the surprise it would give and the probable benefits which exercise would produce, and it is with much sorrow I find their progress in some degree obstructed by news from England of a most unpleasant nature. I cannot hear of any misfortune on your Lordship's family without sincerely sympathising with you and I do particularly now, from the situation her Ladyship is in, it being distant from you – it will be great consolation to your Lordship to hear she is with Lady Ann Barnard, whose care and attention will I hope... very much alleviate her distress...

It will probably be ten days yet before we embark again, during which time I hope though her ladyship cannot take the exercise she hoped for... will get frequent airings and the hospitable and friendly treatment received here, will enable her to endure the remainder of the passage without any material inconvenience... By these ships from England now laying here and by which we learnt the death of Lord Powis, we likewise learnt that the two young gentlemen were in perfect health and the rest of your Lordship's family...

July 19th, Cape Town, Henrietta to Lord Clive

I am sure you will be glad to hear of us again and as the ships wait for a wind it is likely that this letter may yet be in time. We are pretty well. I see the dear girls' spirits are much dependent on my own and have endeavoured to keep up my own as much as I can after such a heavy misfortune which I did not expect though last accounts, before we left you, being good, yet you knew I have had much alarm at different times in my mind. We know as yet very few particulars but from what has been known, Thomas thinks it must have been the gout. Thank God, the dear boys are well or at least were so in March. My anxiety will be great till I hear of them. My proposed happiness in landing in England most fatally diminished. Lady Anne has behaved with the greatest kindness and attention. She could not have been more to a sister and I have done what I like. The girls are well and very much what you would like in regard to me. They have a terrace on the top of the house where they walk, which has been of great service to health and spirits.

I have been able to provide what clothes were necessary for us on this sad occasion here, which is a satisfaction to me. I cannot express what I feel at the thought of what is here lost nor how much I shall feel it on every occasion. The girls desire their loves to you. I did not tell them I was going to write to you.

God bless you,
my dearest Lord.
Take care of your health for our sakes
and return as soon as possible to your very affectionate,
H. A. C.

Charly chronicled the next few days of their stay in Cape Town: '*July 20th.* We went to walk in the Governor's garden, which is not kept in very good order, though it has good plants in it.' '*July 25th.* We left Cape Town, to return to the ship. Mamma and my sister went in General Dundas's carriage, and Sally, and Signora Anna and I, in Mr Barnard's. After we had got two miles from the town, we met two of the largest pigs I ever saw and they frightened the horses so much that they ran into a ditch. Luckily the pole broke, or we must have been overturned. We walked up to Mamma's carriage. Some of the gentlemen overtook us, and we got safe to Wynberg.' '*July 26th.* We proceeded to Simon's Bay in

General Dundas's carriage. Having made friends with the owner of the house at Wynberg, who was a Government contractor, we got a good supply of bread, in spite of the scarcity, and the strict orders for parsimony in the distribution of it. We went on board in the evening.'

July 28th, Simon's Bay, Henrietta to Lord Clive

As there is not the opportunity of your hearing from me before we leave the Cape, I will not let it pass. The Dorchester came in the day before yesterday and is going on directly to Madras. This letter will be carried by a Miss Hardgrave of whom I will tell you more by & bye. We are all pretty well and returned yesterday, Saturday the 26th to the ship. Tho Captain Urmston hurried me away we are not likely to sail I find till Wednesday or Thursday and I am here before his own passengers. Harriet has had a stiff neck with a great deal of pain and is just able to move her head today but intends writing to you if possible. Charlotte is well and there have been some circumstances respecting her increase of strength that give me great hopes that with a little care she will be very stout in England. I am better for having been obliged to exert myself which I found necessary for the girls and everyone. I have had such great attention and kindness from Lady Anne and Mr Barnard that I shall ever feel myself obliged to them. If Col Crawford who married Miss Barnard and is in the 9th ever comes to Madras which he hopes to do pray be civil to him for this reason. I was much affected last night by receiving a letter from Miss Hardman who is sister to the Captain of the *LaForte* enclosing one from my poor brother which contains such strong recommendation of her that I have desired Mr Cartwright will be so good as to copy it and I enclose it to you as I would not part with the original. Mr Cartwright went with her this morning and explained my situation and declined receiving her which she had proposed, that I promised to send a letter by her to you as you will see that any civility to her will be pleasant.

In his [Henrietta's brother, the Earl of Powis] letter are some attended to that must have arrived since I left Madras which I hope you have sent to me painful as it may be to me I wish to have them. It seems, too, as if he had been ill at Weymouth and afterwards, tho Mr Strachey said otherwise in November. It is a most terrible stroke to me, but I will bear up as well as I can.

General and Mrs Dundas have been very attentive to me and sent me their carriage to Kalks Bay with a very careful *Dragoon* to take care of us from thence. We came in a very tolerable wagon that Mr Barnard had provided which I preferred on account of the cold and Harry's stiff shoulder and neck. I called once on Mrs Dundas but of course did not dine there as I did not feel equal to it but they did once with Lady Anne while I was there. I have had some seeds from Mr Roxburgh. He seems an intelligent man drawing flowers very accurately and well and understands a great deal of botany. I hear Mr Basser has written to you about him. The Bassers leave the Cape at the first opportunity which they expect to be in three months and he will send news on by them. At St Helena there will not be anything as there is a problem more decidedly than at the Cape from having fewer resources.

Governor Brooke is gone to England. There is a report from Maderia . . . of Abercrombie having landed near Alexandria. The first day was reported with some loss on both sides. The second day a general engagement took place in which we had 500 men killed, the French more, and the loss was to be besieged directly with great hopes of success. You know probably better than we do, yet I thought it as well to mention it. I shall finish this after dinner, therefore *adieu.*

Signora Anna and Mrs Baker came on board this morning. She is well and in good spirits. Mr Torin came to me a few days ago to enquire if I had any objection to a new passenger. His name is Crusoe. I believe he has been many years at Poonah and Hyderbad as a surgeon and Mr Torin said he was recommended to him by his brother and that he would answer for him. This I thought I could not object to but I desired Mr Cartright to inquire and see about it and I believe he is on board. I must again say how attentive Cartright has been though I believe he has been very much tormented not being used to the charge of a family and my not having any servant but Sally we are much at a loss. As we were in want of a variety of things from the unusual length of the passage, we had some difficulty in getting them. But Mr Thomas wrote to Thomas

Harris advising him to come to me at Cape Town which he did for two nights.

It is extremely cold in the ship and we are starved to death but the change will soon be felt when we have once passed the Cape. The wind is now contrary therefore there is little chance of our sailing till it is nearly over that we may not yet again to the Southward. I am not able to attend a great deal to anything just at present, but when I am at sea and the worry is a little over, I shall be much better.

Tuesday Morning The signal is made to unmoor, yet we doubt when we shall go. Unless the wind changes we can only go to lie to on the outside of the bay as it is northwest and we have had experience of that already. I am afraid we shall not have an opportunity of writing to you again til we are in England which we shall not be certainly til the end of October or beginning of November.

I dread the fog of the channel and all the cold we are to endure before we get once again to Walcot. We shall just land at the worst time . . . The *Star* Brig is to convoy us, but as there are two ships added to us and they are not quite ready, it is uncertain if we are to wait for them or not.

Harry's neck and shoulders are much better today and I hope she will be able to write a little to you. Their attention and behaviour to me and their feelings for their poor uncle has been just what you would wish and they have been a great comfort to me indeed. Colonel Maxwell of the 19th saw Mrs Baker and told her that he had seen both the boys well in April, but I cannot imagine where it was and unfortunately missed seeing him at the Cape as he went there the day I left it. *Adieu* my dear Lord. I shall seal this up the last moment that you may know all you can of our sailing.

The wind is now fair and we are likely to sail in an hour, therefore I shall close my letter. God bless you my dear Lord. I hope to find letters from you in England. I almost now dread hearing more ill news of our remaining family and friends.

Adieu.

Ever your very affectionate,

H. A. C.

1801 – Simon's Bay: The Cape of Good Hope, South Africa

July 28th, Charly to Lord Clive

My dear Papa – I had begun a letter to you as soon as we arrived at the Cape but the melancholy news which we heard the day afterwards obliged us to give up sending by the *True Briton* what we had written. I am sure you will be very glad to hear that we are all well and I believe my Sister and myself are much grown; fatter I am sure we are and have something like Europe complexions. I shall keep all the news of the voyage till I can write from England or St Helena as I have a great deal to tell you and we have but a short time to write as we expect to sail in a few hours. I hope it will not be long before we hear from you and that the hot weather has been very mild and has not in the least injured your health. Signora Anna begs I will present her best respects to you. Pray give our best compliments to your Aides-de-camp and Secretaries.

Adieu, my dear Papa.
I am ever your affectionate and dutiful daughter,
C. F. Clive

From July 28th to the end of the journey on November 1st, a despondent Henrietta apparently wrote neither letters nor journal entries. Charly, however, continued throughout the duration of the voyage to record a cursory record of their experiences: '*July 28th.* We weighed anchor, and set sail.' '*July 29th.* We lost sight of the ships, but by crowding all sail, rejoined them in the afternoon.' '*July 30th.* A dead calm, but in the evening a hard gale.' '*July 31st.* A hard gale, and the sea so high, I think I never saw it worse; it was tremendous to see the waves, whenever the ship rolled, wash over the rigging and deck. The storm increased through the day, and we were confined to the cabins, the sea having rushed in before the ports were closed, and wetted everything in them. Mamma and Harriet kept their beds. I wedged myself into a corner and sat up all day with Mrs Baker, in her cabin, where I dined, and received a portion of Irish stew, with pleasure, our appetites not failing us. But alas! The fire in the kitchen had been three times extinguished, and we found that what appeared to be pepper, in the stew, was particles of charcoal. During the dinner, which the gentlemen were enjoying in the cuddy, we heard an exclamation, an uncommon uproar, and our merry old General calling out, "Miss Charlotte, Miss Charlotte, *venez me voir couronne de mouton*." The sheep for our consumption had been secured on the poop and their pen giving way, it broke through the skylight, and the sheep came tumbling upon the guests and dinner table. I, of course, went to the door to see the confusion, glasses and plates were scattered and such a smell of sheep! Happily no other harm was done and the accident proved a source of amusement. In the evening, the wind lulled.' '*August 1st.* We were again able to walk the deck.' '*August 2nd.* We had a current of 34 miles in our favour and found we were 20 miles more to the south, than yesterday. It came on so hazy in the afternoon, that we lost sight of the Commodore, and put up 3 blue-lights successively.' '*August 3rd.* A fine breeze, as fair, as it could blow.' '*August 4th.* The Commodore made a signal to steer more to the westward. The weather continued very calm till the 7th when a fine breeze sprung up and we spoke to the Commodore, who told us, the strange sail in sight, might be the *Hornet* from Bengal.' '*August 8th.* We were now in a fine pleasant trade wind, which continued.' '*August 13th.* The Commodore made a signal to know our longitude. We differed much; he made it 3.D 19m. The *Prince William Henry* made it 1.D 5m. and we made it 4.D 5m.' '*August 14th.* The Commodore made a signal for land. We saw it from the quarterdeck, and it proved by observation by sun and moon that our log was right.' '*August 15th.* When we arose in the morning, we were very near the island of St Helena, an immense rock rising out of the sea. Its appearance was most barren, but within an hour or two, we rounded the point. We came upon a beautiful valley where St James's town is situated. Col Doveton went on shore to find a house in which to receive us. Anna Tonelli painted the S. E. view of St Helena, Sandy Bay, Diana's Peak, Longwood, Barn Point.'

St Helena, British Colony

'An immense rock rising out of the sea.'

Charly continued her journal while on St Helena. '*August 16th.* We landed and went to the house, which Mr Doveton, the deputy-governor, lent us. He is cousin to Colonel Doveton. The town is a very small one, but the principal street is very handsome and the houses are very pretty. The Governor, Mrs Robson, and Mrs Doveton called on Mamma.' '*August 17th.* We walked about the town, and went into a very pretty garden belonging to the Free Mason's Lodge.' '*August 18th.* After breakfast, we went up a hill on the left-hand side, by a very steep path, to see Mason's fortification; so called, from having been taken by a captain of that name.' '*August 19th.* After breakfast, we went to the Briars (a small house with a garden belonging to it). It is a mile-and-a-half up the valley. It rained very hard all the time and we were up to our knees in mud. The house belonged to a Mr Dun, and has a very pretty garden, full of all sorts of flowers – roses, camellias, quantities of blackberries growing wild all round the place, and mignonette in great quantities, which flower, we had not seen for a long time. Colonel Doveton had ordered cold refreshments for us that we were too happy to eat. We crossed a brook on our way home, or rather, we waded through it. There never was a more merry, or more dirty party, I believe, at St Helena.' '*August 20th.* We went to the Plantation-house, where the Governor lives. I rode with Captain Hodson and Mr Blake. Mamma, Mrs Robson, and Signora Anna, and my sister came in a sort of sociable, drawn by six bullocks. Mrs Baker came in a sedan-chair and Mrs Hart in a tonjon.' '*August 21st.* My sister and I rode with Colonel Doveton part of the way to Longwood and back.' '*August 23rd.* We went to Church, but I was not well enough to go with Mamma and my sister to see Colonel Robson's collection of curiosities.' '*August 25th.* We went to Sandy Bay near Mount Pleasant, the only landing place on the island, except the anchorage at the port.' '*August 28th.* We went to a ball at the Governor's.' '*August 30th.* My sister and I, and the rest of the party, went to Longwood. Signora Tonelli painted a watercolour of Longwood Ridge. It is a beautiful situation, much more so than the Plantation-House, placed on a hill, between two valleys. There is a road, which conducts from the house to the end of a hill, from whence you may see every ship that comes in. It is a small, but very pretty house, occupied by Major and Mrs Cox, who received us most kindly. Amongst other beautiful flowers, geraniums abound.' '*August 31st.* We returned to the town. The *Endymion*, commanded by Captain Durham, had arrived to convoy the fleet home.' '*September 2nd.* We went to Sandy Bay, and to see Mrs Doveton's pretty house at the foot of a green hill, called Mount Pleasant.' '*September 3rd.* We re-embarked on board the *Castle Eden* and weighted anchor. Our fleet consisted of 23 ships and each vessel had its appointed station. The setting sun had a beautiful effect as we left the island, showing its singular and abrupt form. The Church and other buildings, interspersed with trees, completing the view.

In Charly's journal a pen-and-ink drawing of a fleet of ships, each numbered, gave the fleet and the order of sailing from St Helena.

1. *Endymion*, King's ship. The Commodore.
2. *Star*, King's ship. A brig, sailed about with orders.
3. *Sir Edward Hughes*, East Indiaman.
4. *Prince William Henry*, East Indiaman.
5. *Castle Eden*, East Indiaman.
6. *Earl Spencer*, Indiaman.
7. *Tellicherry*, Indiaman.
8. *City of London*, Indiaman.
9. *Walsingham*, Indiaman.
10. *Hawke*, Extra ship.
11. *Harriet*, Extra ship.
12. *Hope*, Extra ship.
13. *Lucy Maria*, Trader.
14. *Anna*, Trader.

15. *Thetis*, Trader.
16. *Surat Castle*, Trader.
17. *Marianne*, Trader.
18. *Herculaneum*, Trader.
19. *Denmark*, Trader.
20. *Swede*, Trader.
21. *Cornwallis*, Whaler.
22. *Queen*, Whaler.
23. *Salamander*, Whaler.

The *Castle Eden* was on the port side of the line of three ships; the *Edward Hughes* and *Prince William Henry* immediately after the lead ship, the *Endymion*, the King's ship. The lines of ships alternated with three or four per line.

On September 5th Charly resumed her journal: 'My sister's birthday: General de Meuron gave her a fete in his cabin and surprised us all with the sweetmeats and cakes his servant Francois produced. I believe the General himself did not know he possessed such a store.' '*September 8th.* The weather became much hotter. Some of the fleet saw the Island of Ascension.' '*September 11th.* We went on favourably till this day, when a gale arose, and the *Endymion* lost her bow-sprit and top-gallant-mast.' '*September 12th.* My birthday: Mr Torin presented me with a copy of verses. Captain Durham, Mr King, and Mr Shipley Conway dined with us.' '*September 13th.* Mr Thomas as usual read the prayers. We crossed the line with a fine breeze and the weather continued fine and favourable.' '*September 18th.* We went on board the *Endymion*, a beautiful frigate in the highest order.' '*September 21st.* A strange sail in sight. Captain Durham spoke to her and came to tell us that she brought good news.' '*September 22nd.* Quite a dead calm. The Commodore sent us some Newspapers. This weather continued.' '*September 24th.* A poor man in a fit of delirium jumped overboard. Happily one of the sailors saw him, as quickly followed, and saved him.' '*September 25th.* A fine breeze decided to be the North-east-trade wind.' '*September 26th.* The *Walsingham* so far to seaward, we were obliged to bear down to her. She informed us a strange sail had been hovering near her, three nights running. She suspected her to be an enemy and had pursued her, as we had discovered. The Commodore desires, if she appeared again, that she should be attacked.' '*September 27th.* Captain Durham came on board; he had seen a strange ship in the night and supposed her to be a homeward-bound. The weather calm till September 30, when we had a fine breeze, but we were often delayed by the bad sailing of the ships.' '*October 1st.* A rough night.' '*October 2nd.* The *Endymion* again took the *Thetis* in tow. The *Harriet* sprung her topmast, and was nearly out of sight. Mr Thomas read the service.' '*October 5th.* We crossed the tropical line.' '*October 7th.* The Commodore let the *Thetis* go in the evening.' '*October 8th.* A very fine breeze.' '*October 10th.* The Commodore made a signal in the evening for the *Hawke* to take the *Thetis* in tow, and then the *City of London.*' '*October 11th.* Captain Durham and Mr Shipley Conway came on board. A breeze got up, but it did not prevent Mr Thomas reading prayers.' '*October 12th.* We went on delightfully till the *Walsingham* lost her fore-top and make a signal of distress. The Commodore then bore down to her. The weather squally at night and a great deal of swell and unpleasant tossing.' '*October 14th.* Rain all night.' '*October 15th.* A stormy night and the ship rolled amazingly. The Commodore made a signal to lie to (as there were only 17 ships in company), to wait for the others. The water came in at all the ports, and we were obliged to put in our dead-lights. We were all wet through. At one o'clock a signal was made to make sail again. As the Commodore passed us, he just said "How do you do." At 5 o'clock a signal to lie to again, and in an hour, we again went on.' '*October 16th.* The sea and wind as high as the day before. Signal to wait. All the ships in company but one.' '*October 17th.* A good deal of swell in the morning, less in the evening; variable winds, or rather Zephyrs. The Commodore sent a boat on board.' '*October 18th.* Quite calm. Captain Durham and Mr Shipley Conway dined here. A fine moonlight night.' '*October 19th.* We had to form the ships, and then went on again.' '*October 20th.* Missed two ships, but as the wind was fair, soon overtook them.' '*October 21st.* A strange sail, which proved to be an American from Philadelphia; she told us the French had evacuated Egypt. We spoke to the Commodore, the *Prince William Henry*, and the *Dane.* The wind was not very fair.' '*October 23rd.* A strange sail to leeward. Captain Durham dined with us and told us it was the *Ploughboy*, an American ship. Her news was that the people of Liverpool had made peace with the French, which we thought was a fable.' '*October 25th.* The *Herculaneum* was in company.' '*October 26th.* The Commodore spoke to a ship from Cape Clear, who on October 9 had spoken with the *Sir Edward Hughes* and the *Earl Spencer.*' '*October 28th.* Spoke to the Commodore. He had seen a ship from Lisbon who had heard nothing of the peace.* A rainy and foggy day. Spoke to the Commodore twice in the course of the day. At night one of the ships fired three or four guns. Some put up blue lights. We had to light twelve of them. It cleared up and we heaved the lead in 82 fathoms of water.' '*October 29th.* Two strange sails: one, a ship from Hamburg. The Commodore went to look out for land.' '*October 30th.* The Commodore at 12 signalled, "Land in sight".'

* Peace of Amiens, not signed until 1802. This peace treaty signed by France, Spain and the Batavian Republic, on the one hand, and Great Britain on the other. England was to give up most conquests made in the French Revolutionary Wars and France was to evacuate Naples and restore Egypt to the Ottoman Empire. The peace lasted barely a year.

England

'Happily on shore at Deal.'

Charly persevered with her journal: '*October 31st.* We saw land very plainly. At 3, we were off Dover and saw the Castle quite distinctly. At 4, we cast anchor off Deal. Mrs Baker went on shore with our fellow passengers in the evening. Mamma had promised Papa she would not be too impatient to land. We therefore remained on board that night.' '*November 1st.* A stormy night. Landing today by no means safe and we sadly feared we could not have a boat to take us on shore. Towards the middle of the day, the wind somewhat abated and a pilot came on board and said that if we could be ready in 20 minutes, he would undertake to land us. We lost no time in preparation and were soon happily on shore at Deal, and delighted to find ourselves at length in old England. We thought the inn, a palace. Our voyage had been an unusually long one: seven months and ten days.' '*November 2nd.* Some perplexity this morning to know what was to be done. The landing at the Cape and St Helena had exhausted our funds. Mr Cartwright, who was the manager of our affairs, was puzzled. After breakfast, the discussion was interrupted by the Banker of the place, who came to offer his services, thinking we might require them; they were gratefully accepted and by the middle of the day, we were able to proceed to Canterbury, where we slept, feeling very odd in Hack chaises after our long abode in the ship.' '*November 3rd.* Reached London, having on the road met Lord Cornwallis's suite, who were going to Paris to negotiate the peace.'*

* Treaty of Amiens

Coming Home

By a knight of ghosts and shadows
I summoned am to a tourney
Ten leagues beyond the wide world's end:
Methinks it is no journey.

'Tom O'Bedlam', *Popular Ballads, c.*1620

On March 21st 1801, Lord Clive saw his family and Anna Tonelli aboard the East Indiaman, the *Castle Eden* that lay at anchor in the roads off Madras. Henrietta's varied cargo included plants and a menagerie of birds and animals, among which was Tipu Sultan's mare, a gift from Lord Clive to his brother-in-law, the Earl of Powis. Indeed, there were a number of objects that had belonged to Tipu Sultan including his red-velvet-lined Mughal-style slippers encrusted with gold and silver wire, spangles and coloured glass beads with a long strip of leather that curled toward the toes. Tipu's travelling sandalwood bed, a dais-throne, complete with a quilt and carpet and his elegant floral-patterned state tent, made of chintz were also stashed away. Later, much to Henrietta's dismay, the gift of a young elephant, presented to her by the Maharajah of Ganjam, had to be left behind at Vizagapatam because he drank fourteen gallons of water a day: 'Everybody was afraid he was to be sent to their ship.'

From the *Castle Eden*'s deck Henrietta gazed for a last time at Madras, a pretty sight with Fort St George and the town's white polished *chunam*-covered buildings glistening against the cloudless blue sky in the heat of the Indian sun. Watching the disappearing palm-fringed Coromandel Coast, which like her beloved South India itself was receding in the distance and her past, Henrietta was beset by apprehensions of the extremely hazardous voyage ahead. She found leaving India a wrenching experience. The cultural sea-change that she must undergo between the time of her last glimpse of India and her sighting of land in England was just getting under way.

Throughout an exceptionally tedious journey to the Cape of Good Hope, Henrietta was buoyed up by her hope of receiving news of 'my dearest brother'. She was devastated, however, when on arriving in South Africa, she was informed that the Earl of Powis had died in the preceding January at the age of forty-five. Her frequently reiterated fears fuelled by the 'chasms in one's correspondence', had become reality. Throughout her India sojourn, Henrietta's thoughts had been continuously with her beloved confidant, likening their separation to 'banishment'.

The remaining months of travelling at sea were Proustian, allowing Henrietta a period of withdrawal wherein she could let the fragments of her feelings and memories take form. As hard gales monotonously and repetitiously pounded the *Castle Eden*, a grief-stricken Henrietta struggled with her sense of loss, adjusting as best she could. Dispirited, she wrote neither letters nor journal. It was left to Charly to record the quotidian events and to convey the sway and pitch of the *Castle Eden* as gigantic waves washed over the rigging and the decks. A call into the remote island of St Helena refreshed Henrietta somewhat, but she remained heavy-hearted. In early September the *Castle Eden* joined a large convoy at St Helena and proceeded to England. In the latter stages of the voyage, the *Castle Eden* endured 'a great deal of swell and unpleasant tossing', and became 'extremely cold'. 'Strange sails' stalked the waters; danger hovered about.

The *Castle Eden* landed in heavy fog at Deal on November 1, 1801. Henrietta's voyage had taken seven months and ten days. After nearly four years out of England, no one was there to meet her. On her way to London, dressed in proper black mourning acquired at the Cape, Henrietta, Charly, Harry and Anna Tonelli passed the carriage of Lord Cornwallis as he was en route to sign the Treaty of Amiens.

In the ensuing winter days, and indeed in the years to come, Henrietta would continue to watch carefully over her brother's financial affairs to ensure that the debts attached to the Powis estate would be greatly reduced by the selling of outlying lands. Lord Powis's astronomical debts of £177,000 made it impossible for her to realise his bequest of £500 to be paid to her in quarterly instalments as long as her husband was still alive. Were Lord Clive to die before Henrietta, her brother had designated that she would receive an annual sum of £1,000. Further, the terms of the will stipulated that Henrietta's son Edward was to be heir to Powis Castle on the condition that he would assume the name and arms of Herbert in lieu of Clive. He did so by royal licence in 1807, thereby continuing the name that had been associated with the castle since 1587. Powis Castle and gardens would be refurbished with Clive money.

Soon after her return to London, Henrietta wrote letters to the Dowager Lady Clive attempting to keep her tone cheerful for her mother-in-law: 'Tomorrow a cow and calf from India set out to Walcot. I shall order them to call upon you on their way; they are from Tanjore and are very beautiful and different from what you see in this country.' Playfully, she inserted herself into her letter, adding: 'You will be surprised though not very sorry to see a face you have seen before at Oakly Park some of these next days and perhaps to have a fish caught for your dinner.'

With Lady Douglas, Henrietta was more candid, indicating that her sorrow for 'my dearest brother' had not abated. 'I am living in his poor house, sitting in his little room, and though I am as well as possible outwardly, it is really almost beyond me to keep myself up. I feel every hour more and more his great loss. I write not a word more on this sad subject.' From this trusted friend she did not attempt to hide her melancholy: 'Suddenly it appears to me that people are grown very old and not handsome since I went away. I suppose I am the same to them, but really it is sad . . . The Queen [Charlotte] is I think much altered but He [King George III] is not the least changed except being much quieter. Their great attention to my poor brother at Weymouth and in London made me uncomfortable and a civility of Princess Elizabeth was almost too much for me in such a place.'

A reclusive Henrietta remained subdued: 'Of the world as yet I know nothing as I have not put my foot out in an evening,' then with a touch of her resolute self, she quickly added 'but I will do it.' Another time she commented 'I have scarcely seen anybody since I came to town'. She fretted about her upcoming court appearance: 'The extreme kindness of the King and Queen and I may almost say the friendship the former most particularly showed to my poor brother and since to us, will make that an uncomfortable day to me. My nerves are much affected with India and other things and it will require all the courage I can collect to go through that day.'

Lord Clive also continued a variety of building projects, which he had begun in 1800 while Henrietta was travelling. Using the mathematician/astronomer Goldingham as architect, he had first remodelled the Clive family residence, the Garden House at Triplicane. Pleased with Goldingham's ability to adapt his constructions to the climate by using deep shady verandas and allowing the breezes of the Coromandel Coast to enter freely, Lord Clive commissioned him in 1801 to build a Government House comprised of a complex of Georgian buildings and a spacious banqueting hall that commemorated the Siege of Seringapatam as well as the Battle of Plassey. The Board of Directors of the East India Company became incensed at these expenditures, deeming them to be far too extravagant, and recalled Lord Clive in August 1803.

Relieved that the East India Company had 'made it proper for him to return', Henrietta confided to Lady Douglas that 'Lord Clive has taken it just as I wished and returns home directly, which pleases me on all accounts'. When her husband was finally on the seas she wrote, 'In every account his family requires a head . . . though I have every reason to rejoice in the good disposition of my boys, as well as my girls, yet I am sure a young man ought to have a father near him.' On his return to England, Lord Clive wrote to his mother to say 'that your ladyship is about to be relieved from the necessity of having the title of Dowager prefixed to your name, at least till the period of Edward's marriage, by my promotion to the Earldom of Powis with the title of Viscount Clive of Ludlow for this second title'. On November 21st 1804 he was created Earl of Powis and Henrietta was henceforth known as the Countess of Powis.

In 1822, Henrietta, once again moved by her strong awareness of 'so much uncertainty in human life', wrote to her son Edward to ask that he would act as her executor. 'Despite the fact that I know that as a married woman I have not any legal right to dispose of whatever I leave behind,' she wanted him 'to see my wishes performed as you would do in any more momentous affair of the same kind.' It was her desire to be buried 'in the Parish church at Welshpool in the family vault and as near the remains of my poor brother as circumstances will allow. I say decently buried because I think the showy funerals of my poor father and brother were much more to gratify the vanity of the living than to show regard to the dead.'

Henrietta's request was not honoured. On June 3rd 1830, she died at the age of seventy-two at Walcot and was buried at Bromfield, County Salop. Her husband, who continued in his later years to work frequently in his Walcot garden, died at eighty-five at his London house, 45 Berkeley Square, on May 16th 1839. He was buried next to Henrietta at Bromfield.

* * *

I had first seen Henrietta's notebooks and letters in 1989. For a number of years, other endeavours held precedence in my life. Not until a trip to South India in November 1992 did I visit in a piecemeal fashion some of the destinations of Henrietta's 1800 travels: some were already familiar to me from earlier visits to India, making them seem a dual adventure. However, neither elephants nor *palanquins* figured in my journey; instead I travelled in a clunky old, made-in-India, white, Hindustan Ambassador car. Henrietta's extreme luxury – of travelling with her bedding, her tents, and her things – was denied to me. Nor did I have an accompanying cook. Instead I feasted on South Indian vegetarian *thalis* served on banana leaves in simple restaurants or on metal plates in fancier ones. Delicious vegetable curries and *sambar* (a lentil soup) of the day were piled on top of rice; mango pickles and yoghurt were added. There were, as well, *iddlis* (steamed rice cakes) and *dosas* (rice pancakes) plain or filled, served with *sambar* and coconut *chutney*. Fiery dishes complemented bland ones; dry tastes offset wet ones.

Fully aware that historical moments are indeed always on the verge of vanishing from sight and smell and sound, I retraced some of Henrietta's and my earlier steps. In Madras (Chennai), despite decay and encroaching modernity, I could still see an entrance-way tall enough for an elephant to have delivered an eighteenth-century passenger. Strolling through Pondicherry, I found elegant, albeit faded, French-style houses and squares, that maintained a vague essence of a former eighteenth-century self. In cosmopolitan Bangalore, now a centre of technological and medical research activities, I sought my favourite bookstore, Premier Books, where the owner had continued to set aside a stack of books he knew I'd like, believing in my eventual return even after some time had elapsed. The remains of Tipu's abandoned palace had fared rather badly: the elegant colours so admired by Henrietta were greatly diminished. The botanically lush gardens of the Lalbagh still gave an indication as to how profuse it once had been with its magnificent flowering trees, including flaming red gulmohur and deep blue jacaranda, enhanced by flowing cascades of cerise bougainvillea. The scent of roses enveloped me. In Seringapatam, Tipu's monuments were thronged by tourists who quenched their thirsts with tender coconuts even as I was doing and Henrietta must have done. The hill fort Nandidrug persisted in its isolation and enveloping fog; in a courtyard red chili peppers were spread to dry whenever the sun made its appearance. Despite traffic congestion, Mysore, with Chamundi Hill hovering behind various domes, spires and palaces, continued to exude charm. There in R. K. Narayan's fictional world, Malgudi, I easily acknowledged Gayatri, the goddess whose five heads are depicted in as many vivid colours and whose bounty assures ordinary people that their enterprises will be successful. Both Henrietta and I had our own surprising encounters with multi-headed goddesses.

Ooty (Ootacamund) still offered the respite and the quiet beauty of what was once a heavily forested, mountainous India with many tigers and no roads. Even today spirit dancers wearing tiger masks and costumes still honour tiger spirits (Pilichamundi) in Kerala and South Kanara, at festivals permeated with the smell of night-blooming jasmine. In this instance, a rainy night was enlivened by the appearance of a nest of rats when I turned back the covers on my bed. Rats remain ubiquitous in India. At Ryacottah, Henrietta's 'rock' retreat, the silence was broken not by a scolding displeased goddess, such as had threatened Henrietta, but by a band of menacing monkeys – Charly's friends – who also accompanied me as I hiked to a long-deserted bungalow. It was there that once the 'discordant sounds' of harp and pianoforte had prevailed as Charly and Harry practised their musical instruments under Signora Tonelli's supervision.

Still following in Henrietta's footsteps, in Trichy (Tiruchirapalli) I, too, found the streets awash with sheets of rain sweeping inland from a violent coastal storm. Never could anyone have imagined such rain. Below the fort, water ran thigh high in the passageways. Water was everywhere. 'Nothing happened,' the driver greeted me cheerfully the next morning as he summed up our previous day's journey by saying, 'When we drive on banks of river, there is no railing. No nothing. It is a bad road.' He took, however, the precaution of gracing the car's dashboard with an offering of fresh jasmine and incense sticks whose scent accompanied us. Where the road is (or is not) proved to be difficult to decide as we continued to Tanjore (Thanjavur) making our way amidst swimming snakes, fallen trees and paddy fields become ponds. I looked, but saw no 'gentlemen cows or their ladies'. Unlike Henrietta I did not get to travel by boat.

Nobody, including the driver, seemed to know how to reach Tranquebar (in Tamil, Taramgambadi: 'village by the sound of the wave'). Indeed Tranquebar, built by the Danish East India Company in 1620, nestles right on the edge of the sea. On our arrival roaring waves relentlessly lashed a variety of churches, tidy rows of red-tile-roofed houses, and the impressive fort: a pinkish-yellow ochre edifice that gleamed despite the steady heavy rain. As the driver and I struggled to gain access to the ramparts of the fort and shelter within, waves began to sweep over the parapet.

'Never will I forget Tranquebar,' said the driver, well pleased with our having survived. Neither will I forget. Nor, I feel certain, did Henrietta, who would have delighted in my having come on board to experience this battering of wind, rain and waves. Her journal entries in Tranquebar recorded the presence of enormous mosquitoes; of the encroachment of the sea; of Danish naturalists who discussed their marvellous collections (butterflies, shells, plants) and Danish missionaries, 'who do little in the way of conversation'; and a wonderful Commander of the fort who dignified her visit with a salute fired from the battlements and who wore immense red rosettes upon his shoes at the ball given in her honour.

* * *

Henrietta's writings from India save from extinction fragments of a time long removed from our present. Her words, certainly not written with today's reader in mind, nonetheless maintain the ability to evoke with fresh immediacy what it was like for her to be in South India in the years 1798–1801 as she followed the changing contours of military maps made for military campaigns. As a traveller she had an overwhelming desire to experience the here and now intensely – 'as long as I can, as I am here'. She had the gift of embracing each moment. Frequently, the Indian realities she encountered were disappointing: the dirty and dark *zenanas* were decidedly not the *seraglios* of *The Arabian Nights*; the women who inhabited them were, for the most part, not beautiful and not bejewelled. The splendour of the East was less opulent than she had wished: the shabby *Nawab* of the Carnatic 'had neither pearls as large as pigeons' eggs nor diamonds'. Nonetheless, she persevered despite having found 'nothing like Haroun Alraschid or the Viccer Giafor' (*The Arabian Nights*).

Henrietta, a dynamic traveller, acknowledged the poetry of place as she came to know India first-hand, holding firmly to her belief that 'a little change is necessary to keep on being alive'. She found vestiges of Oriental splendour: Tipu's shower room at his abandoned Bangalore palace and the ruins of his *zenanas* in the gardens overgrown with white rose trees. She visited ancient bazaars aglow with colour and vibrant with scent; she participated with multitudes of Muslims at a Hussein Hassan festival; she received wet garlands of flowers from priests at Hindu temples. Monsoon storms and relentless heat became part of her life. Alligators threatened her river crossings; 'tygers' stalked her party in mountain passes. She called on the heir to the Mysore throne, the six-year-old *Rajah*, ensconced on red velvet cushions given to Tipu Sultan by the King of France. She visited the *Ranee*, the *Rajah*'s extremely fat grandmother. Although the very sounds of South Indian place names – Madras, Arcot, Trichinopoly, Tranquebar, and Seringapatam – continued to allure and nurture her fantasies, Henrietta partook fully of the realities she found before they were to vanish. Following in her footsteps, I savoured the duality of her moments flowing within mine in that instant before they disappeared.

Just as Great Britain was about to become the dominant world power, Henrietta in India came to know first-hand three of the players who assumed significant roles in altering the course of history for the next century. Two of these were the Irish Wellesley brothers. Lord Mornington, the Governor General of India (later created Marquis Wellesley) had empowered the British Empire by orchestrating the defeat of Tipu Sultan. Although Mornington ran afoul of the East India Company for extravagant expenditures at Calcutta and his reception in England was less gratifying than his expectations, he was ultimately acknowledged for his India services and awarded £20,000. Colonel Arthur Wellesley, later the Duke of Wellington, whose military skills were honed by his battle tactics in his various India campaigns, went on to lead England in its defeat of Napoleon at Waterloo in 1815. And third, Henrietta's emphasis on 'learning with all our might', as she described her pursuits in India and those of her daughters, would serve Charly well when, as the Duchess of Northumberland, she was appointed governess for those impressionable years age eleven to eighteen (1830–1837) of Princess Alexandrina Victoria, the future Queen of England and Empress of India.

Although Henrietta had pursued drawing with a passion during her earlier travels in Italy, she later wrote dismissively of her abilities saying simply, 'I used to draw.' During her India journey, she refrained from sketching and chose to rely on Anna Tonelli for pictorial details of the scenes and people along the way. Some years later, Charly's India journal with the unwieldy title, *Journal of a Voyage to the East Indies*, and during a residence there, *A Tour Through the Mysore and Tanjore Countries &c, & and the Return Voyage to England* by C. F. Clive was copied by calligrapher W. H. Ramsey on paper watermarked 1857 in a handsome crimson leather-bound edition with metal clasps. In it Charly included copies of Signora Tonelli's India watercolours, excerpts from Henrietta's journal, military maps of South India used on their trek, and the architectural plans for Lord Clive's government house in Madras. Together the trio – Henrietta, Charly and Anna Tonelli – achieved a pen and brush account of their journey.

Through her India letters and notebook entries Henrietta provided a select circle of friends and family with vivid descriptions of her unique travel experiences. Likewise readers today can sample her eighteenth-century interests, tastes and feelings. Whether or not Henrietta fully comprehended the Sufi mysticism of Hafiz's ephemeral ambiguities, she resonated to his imagery. The emptiness she experienced on her return to an England devoid of the one person with whom she shared the greatest affinity might well have caused her to recall a Hafiz line which she had translated, 'For here there is nothing caught in the snare but wind.' Despite her sorrow, she rallied, applying her energies to sorting out her brother's legacy to her son Edward, who on assuming the name Herbert assured the continuation of Powis Castle within the Herbert dynasty.

Among Henrietta's Indian treasures, that she unpacked in 1802 when she was home again in Wales, was a bejewelled gold tiger-head finial salvaged from the destruction of Tipu Sultan's golden throne and given to her by Lord Mornington. Shortly after the celebration in Madras following the fall of Seringapatam, Lord Mornington had commented to Henrietta 'that it seemed appropriate there should not be a great victory in this country without a Clive being concerned with it'. Be that as it may, Henrietta, steadfast in her attempt to come to know as much as she could about the oriental culture of her dream of the East, had not sought the crass bounty of thoughtless and rapacious colonists. In Wales, as she ruefully examined her specimens of Indian flora and fauna, she noted of Dr Heyne that 'he mineralises better than he packs up'. While arranging it all she described herself in a typically Henrietta way as feeling 'as great as any Eastern Princess in the midst of her treasure'. Included among those treasures were a stuffed tiger, tiger claws and a bunch of tiger whiskers on red velvet. In her will she would bequeath all her 'Stuffed Birds and beasts with the Cabinets of Minerals' to her eldest son, Edward, 'hoping he will in time increase the Collection, as well as ensuring fires to be kept to preserve them from damp'. Apparently he did not; her collection of birds at Powis looked to be a bit bedraggled with the passage of time.

The records of Henrietta's experience – her notebooks and letters – speak to those ephemeral moments of her travel to, within and from India and as such provide gifts of appreciation for the India of that day. Henrietta's words allow other travellers in heart and in mind to walk in her footsteps and thereby experience the vibrancy of her independent 'Welsh spirit' as she actively quested for and partook of the East: 'I believe I am thought a strange restless animal,' Henrietta wrote in 1800 as she crossed through the Guzelhutty Pass into Coimbatoor Country. 'A black woman never moves and the white ones in this country are not much more active. Besides I descend from my dignity and walk upon my own feet at every place where I take up my abode.' What she found when she walked upon her own feet rarely matched the Orient of her imagination, but she had that rare capacity to embrace each moment wholeheartedly. The real 'treasures' that Henrietta took home with her were not in trunks and boxes, but in her mind.

A Brief Bibliography

Manuscripts

Clive, Lady Henrietta, India journals and India letters 1797–1801 (Powis MSS, National Library of Wales, Aberystwyth)

Clive, Charlotte, India journal 1798–1801 (Oriental and India Office collections, British Library, London)

Sydenham, Thomas, Captain, Letter to Charlotte Clive and Military Descriptions of South India, included in Charlotte Clive's Journal (Oriental and India Office collections, British Library, London)

Selected Works

Archer, Mildred, *Company Drawings in the India Office Library* (London, 1972)

Archer, Mildred, *Tippoo's Tiger* (1959)

Archer, Mildred, *Early Views of India: the Picturesque Journeys of Thomas and William Daniels 1786–1794* (London, 1980)

Avijit, Anshul, 'The Artist's Eye: India 1770–1835', *India Today,* (Kolkata, 9 March 2001)

Barnard, Anne (ed. A. M. Lewin Robinson), *The Cape Journals of Lady Anne Barnard 1797–98* (Cape Town, 1994)

Barnard, Anne (ed. A. M. Lewin Robinson), *The Letters of Lady Anne Barnard to Henry Dundas from the Cape and Elsewhere 1793–1803* (Cape Town, 1973)

Beatson, Lieutenant-Colonel Alexander, *Geographical Observations in Mysore & the Barramaul with an Examination of the* Passes *of . . . Ryacota & Anchitty* (Madras, 1792)

Becker, Carl L., *The Heavenly City of the Eighteenth-Century Philosophers* (New Haven, 1932, pbk, 1959)

Buddle, Anne, *Tigers round the Throne: The Court of Tipu Sultan 1750–1799* (London, 1990)

Cokayne, *The Complete Peerage*, Vol III, p. 324

Dalrymple, William, *White Mughals: Love and Betrayal in Eighteenth-Century India* (London, 2002)

Davies, Philip, *Splendours of the Raj: British Architecture in India 1660–1947* (London, 1985)

Fay, Eliza, *Original Letters from India* (1817)

Forrest, Denys, *Tiger of Mysore: the Life and Death of Tipu Sultan* (London, 1970)

Gardner, B., *The East India Company* (London, 1971)

Graham, Maria, *Journal of a Residence in India 1809–1811* (London, 1813)

Gentleman, David, *David Gentleman's India* (London, 1994)

A Handbook for Travellers in India, Pakistan, Nepal, Bangladesh & Sri Lanka edited by Professor L. F. Rushbrook Williams (London, 1978)

Impey, O. and Macgregor, A., *The Origins of Museums: the Cabinet of Curiosities in the Sixteenth and Seventeenth Centuries in Europe* (Oxford, 1985)

Keay, John, *The Honourable Company: A History of the English East India Company* (London, 1991)

Kindersley, Mrs Jemima, *Letters from the East Indies* (London, 1777)

Lord Macaulay's essay on Robert Clive, *Edinburgh Review* (Edinburgh, January 1840)

Madras Tercentenary Commemoration Volume (London, 1939)

Moon, Sir Pendral, *The British Conquest and Dominion of India* (Duckworth, 1989)

Morris, Jan, *Stones of Empire: The Buildings of the Raj* (Oxford, 1983)

Narayan, R. K., *The Emerald Route* with sketches by R. K. Laxman (Bangalore, 1977)

Orme, Robert, *A History of the Military Transactions of the British Nation in Hindustan*, 2 volumes, 1780

Parkes, Fanny, *Wanderings of a Pilgrim in Search of the Picturesque* (London, 1850)

Powis Castle (The National Trust, 1989)

Rowell, Christopher, 'Clive of India and His Family: The Formation of the Collection', *Treasures from India: The Clive Collection* (Powis Castle, The Herbert Press in association with The National Trust, 1987) pp. 17–30

Sévigné, Madame de (Marie de Rabutin Chantal, Marquise de Sévigné), *The Letters*, Vols 1–8 (Philadelphia, 1927)

Small, Lisa, *Napoleon on the Nile: Soldiers, Artists and the Rediscovery of Egypt* (New York, 2006)

Spear, Percival, *The Nabobs* (Cambridge, 1963)

Stuart, Louisa, *Memoire of Frances, Lady Douglas*, ed. Jill Rubenstein (Edinburgh, Scottish Academic Press, 1985)

Teachings of Hafiz, trans. Gertrude Bell, intro. Idries Shah (London, 1979)

Treasures from India: The Clive Collection at Powis Castle, edited Jonathan Marsden and Julia Mackenzie (London, 1987)

Weller, Jac, *Wellington in India* (London, 1993)

Duke of Wellington, *Supplementary Despatches* (1858) I, 87

Yule, Henry and Burnell, A. C. , *Hobson-Jobson: the Anglo-Indian Dictionary* (London, 1886)

Index

4th Regiment of Cavalry 203
5th Regiment 203
6th Black Regiment of Cavalry 112
10th Foot 83
19th Dragoons 112
19th Regiment 156
25th Regiment of Cavalry 69, 112, 113
33rd Regiment 69
51st Foot 83
74th Regiment 84

Abdul Khaliq 115, 116
Aboukir Bay, Battle of 18, 33, 72
Agra, Major 180
Alesana, Mr 269
Alexandria 69
Allamparva 39, 255
Allan, Major 173, 223
Allen, Major 71, 81, 83
Allen, Peter 54
alligators 113
Amber, Mrs 165
Amboor 122, 151
Ameer Bagh 150, 228, 257–8
Ameer Sing 240, 242
Amiens, Treaty of 297, 300
Amoor 208
Anker, General 244–7, 250
Annacampettah 242
Annamallee Woods 217, 246
Annamalleecottah 201, 204, 206, 208
antelopes 144
Apennines 121
Arabian Knights 41, 66, 90, 214, 306
Arcot 110–11, 113, 127 – *see also* Nawab of Arcot
Armenians 174
Ashton, Colonel Henry Harvey 63, 71, 135, 171, 272
Ashton, Mrs 167
Attapilly 138
Attour 106
Austen, Jane 28

Baillie, Colonel 181
Baker, Mrs: a comfortable person 273; frightened by storm 275; good health 261, 263; Henrietta writes to 169; sat up all day with 291; unwell 277, 280, 281
Ball, Mr 225
Bangalore: Captain Brown at 130–2, 138; Dhoondiah Waugh and 134, 135; fruit from 125; General Ross in 143; Henrietta pleased with 139; leaving for 137–8; palace described 139–40; pleasant weather 97–8; technological centre 304; Tipu Sultan dismantles 138–9; Tipu's palace 38, 306; a unique place in the East 214
banyan trees 105, 113
Barahmahal 136, 141
Barnard, Lady Anne 31, 228, 281, 284–8

Barnard, Lord 228
Basket, Captain 260, 271, 272, 275
Basser, Mr 289
Beedadee 177
Bengal 52, 93–4, 95
Benkipour 141
Bhavanee, River 198
Birsema, Major 219
Blackburn, Mr 240, 243
Blackmore, Captain 265, 267, 268
Blake, Mr 284
Blaquiere, Colonel de 69, 112, 282
Blue Grant 228
Bonansalie 80
Boodicoop 197, 198
Boosepoor 196
Bothwell 52, 89
Brahmins 189, 230, 234, 239
Brant, Joseph 92
Brathwith, General 152
Brave 55, 56
Brazil 44, 49
Bridges, General 222, 224, 228, 229
Brinjeveram 118
Bristol, Bishop of 42
Britannia 55
Brodie, Mr 95
Bromfield 303
Brooke, Governor 289
Brown, Captain: accompanies 98; Bangalore 130–2; council matters 62; daughters go riding with 60; Dhoondiah considers attack 170; dismisses Sergeant Smith 152; drilling 74; 1800 excursion 103; a horse for 64; Lord Edward's expenses 144; seriously ill 124–6, 129–30; taken prisoner to Mauritius 250; Wilding and 175
bubris 180
Buchanan, Francis 155
Bucherow: Captain Marriot 195; dull appearance 178; Henrietta requests pictures 181, 189; met by 190, 192, 195; part company with 196; seating arrangements 192
Bull's Mouth 137
Burrah Balapoor 169–70
Byron, Lord 28

Cadra Munglum 241, 242
Calcutta 72–3
Calicut 197
Call, William 86, 102, 145
Calumbankam 104
Campbell, Colonel 221, 231, 254
Campbell, Lady 61, 63
Campbell, Montgomery 63
Canatacadavoo 205
Canoor 220
Cape of Good Hope 31, 49–51, 56, 278, 300
Cape Town 38, 54, 284
Caragolly 171
Carangooly 106–7
Carnatic: cinnamon plant and 246; fog 214; Haidar Ali invades 119; hot weather 150; landscape 194; transplanting trees 148
Caroor 208, 219, 220
Cartwright, Mr 262, 265, 268, 285, 288–9
Cartwright, Mrs 281
cassowaries 58
Castle Eden 260, 269, 273, 285
Castles of Alnwich and Warkworth (Charlotte Clive) 16
Cauvery, River: beautiful country around 238; crossing 227; dam on 229; floating down 240–1; marching alongside 231; Mayaveram 242; sluices 238; timber floated down 208

cedars of Lebanon 223, 224
Ceylon 64
Chamundi Hill 304
Chantilly 181
chaplains 45
Charlotte, Queen 29
Cherut feast 157
Chillambrum 248
Chingleput 122
Chingleput, Rajah of 122
Chinnapatam 178
Chinnery, Mr 136
Chirbury 25
Chitteldroog 131, 147, 155, 156
Chitterbury 118
Chitty, Arnachellum 91
choultries 108–9, 228, 239
Christian, Admiral Sir Hugh 52–5
Christians 117, 122, 183
Chunda Sahib 117, 183
Clark, Mrs 187
Clive, Honourable Miss Charlotte Florentia (Charly): affected by heat 114, 149; bearing the climate 77; birth 30; boards *Dover Castle* 45; delicate and weak 224; elephant 91; gaining strength 286, 288; gazelle 210; governess to Victoria 307; Haidar and Tipu's wives 182; health issues 121, 126, 129, 137, 141, 171–2, 174, 245, 254; an Indian education 34; interest in plants 145; journal 46; *Lettres* bequeathed to 35; menstruation 256; mini-biography 15–16; mosquitoes 80; nose bleeding 121 122, 129, 130, 132, 220; portrait 14; Seringapatam 187; seven month Indian excursion with Henrietta 23; smallpox vaccination 31; Sydenham's advice on map-reading 123; on widows 177
Clive, Dowager Lady 18, 30, 60, 301
Clive, Lord Edward: attachment to India 86; boards *Dover Castle* 45; building projects 302; cabin on *Dover Castle* 46; concerned he had incurred the Government's displeasure 233; daughters' education 34; death 303; easy going nature 33; finances 173; in charge of whole judicial and civil adminstration of India 102; ivory miniature of 37; leaves for India 31; letters delayed 127; marriage discussed 28, 30; mini-biography 15; Mornington and 78, 82, 85, 98; overnight travel 108; Petrie's influence 62–4; popularity 79; Seringapatam 36; shares Henrietta's naturalist interests 39; 'Treasures from India' 24; Walcot 73; Wellesley's opinion 32
Clive, Edward (son of Lord Edward): amiability 172; bequests from Henrietta 309; birth 30; birthday 120; effects of Eton 88; guardianship 18, 31; heir to Powis Castle 301; news 212
Clive, Honourable Miss Harriet Antonia (Harry): bile 156, 157; birth 30; blooming 142, 155; boards *Dover Castle* 45; bowel disorders 75, 156, 279; embarks on *Dover Castle* 31; an epileptic attack? 259; harp playing 90; an Indian education 34; mini-biography 15; portrait 14; putting on weight 168, 202; seven month Indian excursion with Henrietta 23
Clive, Lady Henrietta Antonia: attitude to daughters 34, 39; boards *Dover Castle* 45; bird of passage 41;

cabin on *Dover Castle* 46; comfortable financial position 173; cough 126; death 303; death of brother 300; death of father 29; documents studied 25; early interest in India 28; the French 43–4; effects of climate 74; fortieth birthday 60; great concern expressed over daughters 255–7; Great Pagoda 109; Hussein Hassan feast 84; height of children 96; importance to of brother 18, 27–8, 29, 39–40; India of her imagination 100; interest in animals 145; learns Persian 34, 89; life in Madras 36–7; maid seduced 69; marriage negotiations 28, 30; mini-biography 15; narrative style 26–7; naturalist interests 38–9; notebooks 46; nursed by daughters 152; an open and interested mind 31–2; pet lion 37; poetry of place 306; relations with and opinions of other participants 18; reminded of Maidenhead 109; Reynolds's portrait 29; sets forth to Southern India 23; travel routine 37; 'unpleasantness of absence' 39

Clive, Henry 131

Clive, Lord Robert (Clive of India): Arcot 111; death 30; Fort St David 252; Lord Edward Clive and 15; Henrietta's mentor 28; marriage 60; mini-biography 18; Orme's account 35; *pandal* 227; 'Treasures from India' 24

Clive, Robert: accounts of 87, 88, 212; birth 31; a change of school 172; guardianship 18, 31;

Close, Lieutenant-Colonel Barry 133–5, 147–52; advises re presents 189; arranges Persian tutor 38, 137; Colonel Dallas's *havildar* 168; Doulat Baugh 181; sends supplies to army in Dhoondiah campaign 157; suggests route to Colar 162; tells of defeat by Dhoondiah 159, 160; tells of plots 154; thinks Henrietta's journeys will be safe despite Dhoondiah 158

Cochbasse, Mrs 107

Cockatoo 123, 125, 261, 264, 271, 282

Coilady 229

Coimbatoor: arrive at 200; Dindigal and 176; disappointed by 209; discovering new trees 215; Dr Hausman's interest in 150; leaving 205; met at 199; road to 196; route to be taken 171; safety aspects 158; setting out 194

Colar 130–1, 158, 162, 164–6, 168

Coleroon, River 227–9, 231, 249

Combaconum 238, 242

Conjeveram 109, 110, 136

Cook, Captain James 193, 209

Coomer ud Deen 81

Coorloor 200

Coote, Eyre 96

Copper, Major 143

Corbet, Mr 266

Coringa 262–5, 270–2

Cornwallis, Lord: Bangalore taken 214; Grant recommended by 63; hostage princes 115; portrait 96; Swiss horses as gift 265; Treaty of Amiens 300

Coromandel Coast 58, 299, 302

Cotton, Colonel 69

Coulasgurr 118

councils 62

Covelong 257

Cowes 46
Cox, Major 294
Cox, Mrs 294
Cragrie, Major 135
Craven, Lord 212
Crawford, Colonel 167, 288
Crusoe 289
Cummings, Captain 260, 269, 275–6, 278, 280
Cuppage, Colonel 169

Dache, Mrs 223
Dake, William 224
Dalkeith 89, 165
Dallas, Colonel 168
Danes 232–3, 244, 245, 250, 305–6
Daniells, Thomas 26
Daniells, William 26
Daniels, Lieutenant 104
Dannikencotah 196, 197
Darapooram 201, 208–9, 211, 217, 246
Daria Daulat palace 35–6, 119
Davies, William 151
Davis, Captain 119–23
Deal 298, 300
Dees, Captain 143
Deonelly 167
Devonshire, Duchess of 175
Dewan of Arcot 110, 111
Dhoondiah Waugh: anti-British uprising 133–5; 143; campaigns 170, 172, 186; death 239; defeats British army 159, 160; escapes 182; letters intercepted 169; mini-biography 19; 19th Regiment march against 156; Polygar of Verapachy and 210; prisoners taken 201; reports that he is beaten 148; reward offered for 171; travel arrangements threatened by 36; troops desert him 173, 179; Wellesley's victory 241
Dick, Mr 262–3, 266, 267, 271–3, 282
diets 104, 303
Dindigal 173, 176, 201, 210, 222
Diomed 71
Diwan (Khaja Shamsuddin Hafiz) 35
Doorten, Colonel 168
Douglas, Lady Frances: a delightful person to hear from 213; East India Company and Lord Clive 302; Henrietta on the death of her brother 301; mini biography 19; news of 165; personal references in letters 27; seeds sent to 223
Doulat Baugh 179–81, 189
Dover Castle: arrangements 46; description 45; gales 56; journeys back to England 95; memories 271; mutiny 53–4; the party embarks on 31
Doveton, Colonel 113–18, 283, 292, 293
Doveton, Mr 293
droogs 130
Duddoor 178
Dummul 179
Dundas, General 281, 283, 285, 289
Dundas, Mrs 289
Dupard, Colonel 251
Dupleen, Mrs 225
Durbar, The 234, 237
Durham, Captain 294
dussera 242
Dye, Mrs 224
Dyrie, Colonel 242, 243

East India Company: boundary of territory 122; Collector's house 37; Lord Clive's extravagances 302; Lord Clive's appointment 15, 41; Mornington 26; purchases William Place's house 107; weight of company ships 45; Wellesley 218

eclipse of the moon 50
Edmonston, William 161
Egypt 68
elephants: Charly rides 91; Fevorsan 270; gift turned down 299; permits for 152; prominence in narrative 38; a riotous beast 104; Josiah Webbe 163, 265, 266
Elizabeth, Princess 173, 301
Ennore 97
Errode 202
Exeter, Lady 167

fakeers 177, 213, 249
False Bay 51, 54
famine 73
Fay, Eliza 26
Fevorsan 270
Fiel, Colonel 246
Fisher, Charlotte 105
Flood, General 185
Floyd, Colonel 99
Floyd, Mrs 99, 224
Fort St David 252, 253
Fort St George 35, 60, 83–4, 97, 299
France: England at war with 43; Isle de France 52; Pondicherry 225, 246, 253; *Princess Charlotte* mutiny 54; privateers 250; Tipu's cushions 192
Franks, Mrs 168
Franks, William 223
Fraser, Mrs 252
French Corps 84
French Rocks 223
Friskey 58, 70, 80, 91, 93
fruit 58, 78
Fullarton, Colonel 204, 208, 219
Futteh Haidar 81, 115–18, 184

Galland, Antoine 66
gallopers 112
Ganjam 272, 299
Garden House 57, 103, 257–8, 302
Garland 56
gazelles 210
Gent, Colonel 237
George III, King 29, 301–2
Georgiana 258
ghauts 120, 126, 166, 196, 199
Giaffer, Mohammed 103, 108, 130, 177
Godavery, River 219
Golden Rock 223
Goldingham, John 302
Good Hope 51, 54
Goodwin, Mr 281
Gordon, Mrs 185–6, 194, 200, 203, 268
Gower, Colonel 186
Graham, Captain 122–3, 125, 138, 141
Graham, Maria 26
Grant, Captain (later Major) 62–4, 104, 112, 152, 188
Grey, Major de 69
Guntier 135
Guzelhutty Pass 188, 189, 197, 215, 309

Hadee, William 106
Hafiz, Khaja Shamsuddin 35, 38, 308
Haidar Ali: battery 121; burial place 166, 186; captured inhabitants 107; Doulat Baugh 181; Eliza Fay held captive 26; *fakeer's* tomb 177; house built for Tipu 185; mausoleum 180; mini-biography 119; palace intact 139; Tanjore palace plundered 239; wives 182–4, 185, 214
Hamilton, Count Anthony 42
Hamilton, Duchess of 166
Hanford, Lord 228
Hanuman 142, 203
Hardgrave, Miss 288
Hardman 262
Hardman, Miss 288

Harris, Lieutenant-General George: in command 57; fete for 93–4; a fever 55; a fool 80; homeward bound 101, 102; mini-biography 17; Ryacottah 123; Seringapatam plunder 82; Tipu's army surrenders to 81
Harris, Mrs 101
Harris, Thomas 164, 228, 237, 239–40, 281
Harrogate 212
Hart, Mrs 261, 263, 276–7, 280
Hartford, Lord 168, 171
Harun ar-Rashid 66
Hausman, Dr: advises on exercise 133, 153; advises that Charly should leave India 256; Bangalore 132, 139; bottled insects 160; Captain Brown's fever 124; Charly's cold 174; Charly's medicine for bile 245, 249, 251–3; Coimbatoor 150; order of *palanquins* 108; recommends rhubarb 243; Thomas and 153, 247; women and 247
havildars: Colonel Dallas's 168; hanged 167; Nawab of Arcot's 204, 248; raising troops for Dhoondiah 169; seeds obtained by 205, 208; stone table supported by elephants 164; surprised 226; village women screaming 230
Hazar Afsanah (A Thousand Tales) 66
Henry the Fourth (William Shakespeare) 80
Herbert, Lady Barbara 27, 29, 30
Herbert, George Edward Henry Arthur, 2nd Earl of Powis: death 300; importance of to Henrietta 18, 27–8, 29, 39–40; Probert's account 174
Herbert, George William, 7th Earl of Powis 25
Herbert, Lord Henry Arthur of Chirbury, first Earl of Powis 15, 27, 28, 29
Herbert family 211
Heyne, Dr Benjamin 38
Hickey, Thomas 96
Hill, Major 233
Hindus 109–10, 149, 178, 183, 306
History of the Military Transactions of the British Nation in Indostan from the year MDCCXLV, A (Robert Orme) 35
Hodgrove, Mr 110, 154
Holtam, Captain 284
Hornet 292
horses 64
howdahs 103, 113
Hudson, William 106–8
Hurdgul 170
Hurdis, William 207–11; advises on route 201, 202; Coimbatoor 199; leaves 221; lemons 218, 243; re natives 204; teak 219
Hussein Hassan feast 84, 145–6, 306
Hyderabad 84, 151, 200
Hyzer, Dr 153, 160, 163–4, 166, 246

Indiamen 45 – *see also* East India Company
Inirare 237
Ireland 43
Irum 97
Isle de France 52, 53
Italy 212

Jaffar 66
Japan 174
Jason, Colonel 182
John, Dr 232, 237, 246, 247
Johnston, Governor 167
Journal of a Visit to the East Indies (Charlotte Clive) 307

Journey from Madras through the Countries of Mysore, Canara and Malabar, A (Francis Buchanan) 155

Kalich, Abdul 188
Kalk's Bay 284, 289
Kaprone, River 193
Kattymungalum 138
Keene, William 228, 232
Kennedy, Major 154
Kerala 304
Kindersley, Mrs 101
Kistnagherry 118, 122–3, 125, 136, 175
Kistrah, River 219
Klien, Dr 246
knauts 105
Koilady 231
Koran 161

LaForte 288
Lal Baugh 180, 181, 186, 187, 304
lascars 157, 159, 164, 195
Lennon, Captain 126
Lettres (Madame de Sévigné) 35
Longwood 294
looties 173
Ludlow 85
Luneville, Treaty of 282

Macalister, Major (later Colonel) 158, 200–3, 205
Macartney, Lord 53
Macaulay, Thomas 35
Mackay, Colonel 124–6; accompanies to Bangalore 138; breakfast with 134; jungle birds 151; Malacca oil 129; red wood tree 144; tree seeds 141
Macleod Captain (later Major): accent 197, 199; Coimbatoor 194, 196; district boundary 204; gold mines 198; information of presence of 158; intelligence received 210; intelligence sent 201; leaves 202; meeting 190; Trichinopoly and other roads 174, 175
Madagascar 55
Madras: anchored 57; arrival in 32; bad news from 55; bodyguard superiority 104; comes into view 56; described 59; dullness 101; Edward Clive as Governor 15; heat 143, 147, 173; Henrietta en route 53; Henrietta in 28, 36–7; Henrietta's last look at 299; January rains 100; level of entertainment 59; Lottery 38, 147; Militia 83; Mornington in 17, 33, 72; Muslims 109; return to 257; in 2009 304; women of 89
Madura 199, 204
Mahrattas 141–2, 159, 236, 243
Maidenhead 109
Malabar 141, 142, 225, 243
Malabar itch 279
Malacca 129
Malcolm, Captain 34, 218, 245
Malcolm, Mr 265–8
Malpaddy 122
Malperba, River 175
Manar 204
Mandeville, Colonel 188
Manila 154
maps 20–1
Marrington Hall 25
Marriot, Captain Thomas 180, 181, 195
Maskelyn, Margaret – *see* Clive, Dowager Lady
Masulipattam 260–2, 280
Mauritius 54, 56, 250
Maxwell, Colonel 290
Mayaveram 242, 243
McAllum, Captain 236
Meadwitte, Colonel 186

Meer Allum 92–5
Meer Dowraun 93–5
Meldorf, Colonel 244
Meuron, General de 263, 272, 284, 295
Modeen Sahib 225, 227
Mohurrum ceremonies 84
Monson, Colonel 87
Moorhouse, Colonel 107
Morel, River 205
Mores, Captain 283
Mornington, Lady 67
Mornington, Lord Richard Colley: arrives in Madras 72; empowering the Empire 307; fearful for his health 82; fearful for his safety 79; fondness for show and parades 93; friendship with Lord Edward 78, 98; gold tiger-head finial 308; mini-biography 17; pandal built for 122, 124; pomposity 33, 73, 75; praised for Seringapatam 85; precipitate and rash 64; receives Star and Badge 99; Seringapatam 36; speech at Fort St George 84; Wellesley 26, 32, 65
Mornington 130, 135
Moudean 178
Mount Road 60
Mousa Uddeen 115, 117, 185
Moyen Uddeen 115
Mozambique 285
munshis 38, 137, 161
Muslims: Colonel Close 134; countenances 116; Hussein Hassan 306; jewels and husbands' deaths 184; Madras 109; Nawab of Arcot 111
mutinies 53–4
Mya, River 197–9
Mysore: antelopes 186, 188; Barony 17; finest part of 162; Haidar Ali 119; Harris enters 123; Harris's return 94; Henrietta collects 160; historical sketch of 136, 141; Krishna Wodeyar 19; *pettah* for 123; R. K. Narayan 24; Ranees 307; tax advantages 112; in 2009 304; to be destroyed 215

Nahirs 127
Napoleon Bonaparte: defeat at Aboukir Bay 72; desiring peace 43–4; mini-biography 18; Oriental interests 33; Tipu's disappointment 77; Waterloo 17, 307
Narayan, R. K. 24, 304
Narsapoor (near Colar) 166
Narsapoor (near Vizagapatam) 262–4, 271
Narsingrow 178
National Library of Wales, Aberystwyth 26
Nawab of Arcot 58–60, 110–12, 221–3; boundary of territory 122; description 66; *havildars* 204, 248; permit to travel through domain 151; relations 226; a shabby potentate 127
nayres 204
Nelson, Lord Horatio 18, 33, 69, 72
Newcastle, Duchess of 166
Nigar 176
Nijapatam 226, 231
Nizam of Hyderabad 84, 92, 135, 141
Nore 53
Norway 245
Nugent, Mrs 167
nullahs 223, 227
Nundydroog 162, 167, 170, 172, 304
Nunjengood 195

Oakly, Lady 115, 116
Oakly Park 28, 42, 101, 198, 207
Oliver, Colonel 211, 212
Ooscotah 149, 167, 168, 175

Ootacamund 304
Orme, Robert 35, 111, 227–9
Osterley 65
Oudmalcottah 209
Ouxa hills 265

Padinaig Durgan Pass 119–21, 151, 197
pagodas 108–10; the bull 234; granite features 115, 219; mentioned by Orme 229; Samiaveram 227; Soobrahmanya's 205, 211–13, 217; Tanjore 239
palanquins: on boats 227; order of proceeding 108; Nawab of Arcot's 60; servants for 64, 134; suit Henrietta 154
Palaur, River 118
Paligautherry 204, 207
pandals: attributed to Clive of India 227; Combaconum 238; erected for Mornington 122; Harris's 230, 237; Nawab has built 221
pariahs 158
Patterson, Major 156
Pendangdroog 226
Peomony 221
Petrie, Mr 48, 60, 61–4, 68
pettahs 123, 156, 189, 225
Picton, Major 71
pillow 118
pirates 48
Pitt, Governor 251
Place, William 107, 110
Plassey, Battle of 302
Pollachee 201, 205–6, 209, 226
Pollicondah 118, 119
Poligaunteherry 202
Pollilur, Battle of 17, 119
polygars: assisting Dhoondiah 172–3, 201, a horrible countenance 206; Hurdis and 219; Macalister's suspicions 205; Queen of Delhi 209–10; Tondiman 238
Pondicherry 253–5; Charly 237; French at 58, 225, 246; a touch shabby 253; transporting plants to 171; in 2009 304
Poonah 200
Porto Novo 247, 250, 251
Portuguese 250
Powis Castle 24, 69, 211, 301, 308–9
Premier Books, Bangalore 304
Prince William 54
Prince William Henry: high seas 275; longitude 292; loses anchor 271; not ready 273; position in water 269, 295
Princess Charlotte 53, 54
Princess of Wales 79
Probert: copies for 262; on George Herbert 174; letters to 29, 30, 98; not to be disclosed to 64; payment instructions 168; situation to despair of 87
Pulicat 97, 98–9
Purneah 147–50; family 184; identity 116; portrait 154–5, 163; sandalwood trees 194; son 178
Pylney 201, 205, 209, 211–13, 217

Queen 165, 171, 174, 175
Queen of Delhi 209–10

Rainier, Admiral 55
Raj Mahat 106
Rajah of Mysore 141, 184, 185 – *see also* Wodeyar, Krishna, Rajah of Mysore
Ram 203
Ramsey, W. H. 308
Ramswamy 80
Ranee of Mysore 189–95
Rangherry 177, 219
Rannee Bednore 157, 159

Rant, Major 103
rats 304–5
Read, Mr 264
Read, William 178
Red Hills 70, 136, 269
Reed, Colonel 122, 126
Reynolds, Sir Joshua 29
Rinehart, Mr 249, 251, 254
Rio de Janeiro 49, 61
Rock of Trichinopoly 223–4, 226
Ross, General 143, 145, 187, 188
Ross, William Andrew 175
Rothman, Mrs 167, 169, 175, 186, 194, 254
Rothman, William 95, 98
Rottingham 258
Rotthem, Dr 243, 245, 246
Roxburgh, Dr William 38–9, 155, 285
Roxburgh, Mr 289
Royal Academy of Arts, London 16
Rubbathan, Sally 102, 105, 130
Ryacottah: arrival 126; austerity 38; bird collection 246; climate 136; letter from 214; Lord Clive's health drunk 168; hill fort 123; plans for 102; rare plants 226; redwoods 152, 164, 218; road to 118, 124; Rock 137–8, 140; trees to be sent 144

Sackfield, William 172
Saltemungalum 198
Samiaveram 224–6, 228
Samin, Colonel 180
Sampson, Captain 48, 49, 50
Sanikulrogdroog 208
Sarabhoji, Maharajah of Tanjore 19, 230–6, 240–2
Sautghur 119
Saverdroog 144
Saxon, Colonel 185
sayres 201
Schwartz, C. F. 19, 233–5
Scotch Brigade 115
Scotland 89
Scott, Mr 268
sepoys 70
Seringapatam: Major Allen at 83; bare rocks 179; battle of 17, 18, 35–6; besieged 139, 302; Charly's final impression 187; Daria Daulat palace 119; fall of 16, 82, 92, 94, 275, 308; Futteh Haidar and 117; Haidar Ali buried 166; Harris's booty 101; Henrietta's burning desire to see 23; martial law 81; not much to see 163; Mornington praised 85; Ross at 143, 145; sandalwood from 218; Tipu's monuments 304; treaty 141
Shealty 248
Sheriff, Mrs 154
Sherzapoor 162
Shias 84
Shremoogur 198, 200
Shropshire Regiment 41, 74
Sibpu 38
Simons Bay 53, 279, 287
Sir Edward Hughes 260, 262, 263, 270, 295
smallpox 31
Smith, Sergeant 152
Soubrahmanya 205, 211–12, 213, 217
South Africa 31
South Kanara 24, 304
Spain 285
St Helena 282, 284, 289, 292, 300
St John, General 212, 228
St Leger, Colonel 112
St Mary's Church, Madras 60
St Thomas's Mount 69, 70, 103
Stevenson, Colonel 171, 186
Strachey, George 65

Strachey, Richard 50, 61, 68
Strachey, William 76, 87, 101, 223, 258, 272
Strange, Colonel 269
Stuart, Lt George 262
Stuart, Major 283
Stubbs, George 225
Sufism 308
Sunnis 84
Switzerland 106
Sydenham, Captain Thomas: a desolate place 122; itinerary for Charly 113, 136; map reading advice 123; most respectable 62; road to Ryacottah 118; verandah 57
Sydenham, Mrs 136

Table Mountain 51
Tales (Count Anthony Hamilton) 42
Tanjore: Cauvery river in 229; cows 163, 301; dancing girls 240; Harris's route 228; largest village 239; leaving 237; Rajah of 230–6; road to 230; Schwartz's mission 19
Taraka 205
Tecknelodroogham 206
Tellicherry 201
Thanjavar 229
Thetis 65
Thomas, Mr: a child for 102; an actor 86; acts as chaplain 45; Charly 256; Dr Hausman and 153, 247; Falstaff 80; Harriet's possible epileptic attack 259; prayers on deck 275; treating Signora Tonelli 266; various remedies 283
Thomas, William 129
tigers: antelopes hunted with 188–9; as decorative motif 35–6, 115; Henrietta's baggage taken by 215; in the hills 80, 107; spirits of 304
Tipu Sultan: Anna Tonelli's painting 16; Bangalore dismantled 138–9; bed made of sandalwood 197; blunderbuss 82; burial place 180, 181, 186; cushions 192; Daria Daulat 35–6; Dhoondiah Waugh and 19; daughters 117; a dream 187; gold tiger-head finial 308; Henrietta's approach 26; Henrietta's fascination 23; horse 151; keeping Lord Edward busy 76; killed 81, 90, 184; Lal Baugh 181; *looties* 75, 89; mini-biography 17–18; Mohurrum ceremonies 84; Mornington and 64, 307; Mysore to be destroyed 215; Napoleon and 33, 72, 77; neck 116; Pollilur, Battle of 119; preparations for war against 32, 71; Purneah and 149; Ranee of Mysore's suffering under 192, 194; ruined prison 130; shower room 306; sons 90, 113, 182; stories of 137, 141, 161; succession 117; treaty of Seringapatam 141; various items 299; a village destroyed 205; wives 115, 182–5, 214
Tiruchirapalli 305
Tiverum 232
Tondiman 225, 238
Tonelli, Signora Anna: few complaints 122; first Western woman artist in South India 27; Henrietta relies on for sketching 307; included in Charly's publications 308; mini-biography 16; paints *Dover Castle's* chief mate 48; Rajah of Mysore 194; Red Hills 70; scorpion 125; sketches local Madras scenes 60; portrait of Rajah of Tanjore 236; sleeping arrangements 105, 139, 150; St

Thomas's Mount watercolour 69; Tipu Sultan 16; a treasure 90; various pictures 192, 278, 292, 294
Torin, Colonel 269, 272, 277
Torin, Mr 226, 230–6, 275
Torin, Mrs 232
Tour Through the Mysore and Tanjore Countries etc, & the Return Voyage to England, A (Charlotte Clive) 308
trade winds 44
Tranquebar 244–7; en route to 243; Danish presence 23, 58; Henrietta's enthusiasm for 186; naturalists 38, 171; plans for journey 216, 226, 237; Tamil name of 305
'Treasures from India: the Clive Collection' 24
Trichinopoly: arrangements 171–2; Henrietta's enthusiasm for 163; 171–2, 174, 199; leaving 227; plain of 223; plans for journey 216, 222; roads to 174, 199; Rock 225, 226
Tripatore 99, 120, 122
Triplicane 70, 84, 302
Trivady 229, 231
True Briton 291
Tuluva 24
Tumallah 196
Turcoman horses 270, 272
Tyler, Mrs 166

Urmston, Captain 266–8, 272, 276, 280, 282, 288

Vale of Evesham 164
Vandalore 104, 178
Vaniambaddy 122
Vellore: army at 74, 77; leaving 118, 119; magnificent situation 113; nursery 107; Tipu's sons 90; Josiah Webbe at 132
Verapachy, Polygar of 210
Versailles 254
Victoria, Queen 307
Victorious 56
Vigée-Lebrun, Élizabeth 67
Vinkatagherry 121
Vishnu 80, 122
Vizagapatam 260, 262, 264–5, 269, 282

Walcot 61, 73, 256
Walpole, Elizabeth 165, 227
Walpole 48, 54
Walsingham 295
Waring, Major 266
Warren, Captain 157, 175
Waterloo, Battle of 17, 307
Webbe, Josiah 62, 79, 132–7, 147; dined with 140–1; elephant 163, 265, 266; malice about 151; Persia 153; sorrow at losing 160
Wellesley, Colonel Arthur (later Duke of Wellington): assesses Lord Edward Clive 32; Bangalore 38; bodyguard reviewed 104; cushions 192; Dhoondiah Waugh 19, 156, 170, 172, 175, 179, 239, 241; East India Company's payment 218; godfather 194; *havildar*'s men imprisoned 169; honing of military skills 307; imposes martial law at Seringapatam 81; mini-biography 16–17; Mornington and 32, 65; Mousa Uddeen 115; news of 146; Rannee Bednore 157; regiment 69; scholarly bent 33; Seringapatam 151; takes over Ashton's command 71
Welshpool 303
Wetheral, William 175
White, Mrs 85
Whits, Admiral 232
Wilding 172, 174, 175, 223, 258

Wilks, Captain 105
Williams Wyn, Sir Watkins 15
Wills, Captain 262
Wodeyar, Krishna, Rajah of Mysore 19, 141, 189–92, 194–5215, 307
Wodeyars 119
Woodcock, Mr 262, 265, 272, 283
Woodhouse, Mrs (later Mrs Rothman) 77, 93, 95
Wynach, Mrs 220
Wynberg 284, 287

Yella Wanka 170
Younger, Sir George 283

Zappadin 232
zemindars 201
zenanas 118, 140, 183–4, 200, 306
Zundredroog 157